Map of the
WESSEX
of the
Novels and Poems

Scale of Miles

Septentrio

Oriens

Occidens

Meridius

Christminster

Lumsdon

R Thames

NORTH

The Brown House
Alfredston
Cresscombe
Marygreen

River Thames

WESSEX

MID

Marlbury
Downs

Gaymead
Kennetbridge

Castle
Royal
Aldbrickham

WESSEX

The Great
Plain

Batton Castle

Inkpen Beacon

Quartershot

Stoke Barehills

Weydon
Priors

Icenway
House

Stonehenge

U P P E R

our Head

Melchester

Wingreen

Leddenton

The Chase

Shaston
Marlott
Trantridge Cross
Shourcastle
Shottsford
Forum
ore
ulbarrow
comb-Ash
Warborne

The Slopes
Chaseborough
Knollwood Hall
Lornton
Inn

Fernel Hall

Deansleigh
Park

Wintoncester

WESSEX

Southampton

Portsmouth

The Great
Bramshurst
Forest

ESSEX

Welland
Kingsbere
Chene
Manor
Havenpool
Anglebury
Nether Mynton
Corvsgate
Knollsea
Castle
ghtship

Heath

Sandbourne

Solentsea

The Channel

Emery Walker, sc.

Thomas Hardy

HIS LIFE AND WORK

F. E. HALLIDAY

Thomas Hardy

HIS LIFE AND WORK

Adams & Dart | Jupiter Books

To the memory of Cecil Day Lewis
lover of Hardy

© 1972 F. E. Halliday
First published 1972 by Adams & Dart, 1a Queen Square, Bath, Somerset
Second impression 1973
SBN 239 00080 3
Distributed by Jupiter Books Ltd, 167 Hermitage Road, Harringay, London N4
Text printed by Redwood Press Limited, Trowbridge, Wiltshire, halftone plates
printed by The Pitman Press, Bath, bound in Great Britain

Contents

List of Illustrations

Acknowledgements

I am grateful to the following for allowing me to make use of manuscript and copyright material:

Manuscripts: Lloyds Bank and the Trustees of the Hardy Estate; the Trustees of the Dorset County Museum and the Hardy Memorial Collection.

Copyright books: Macmillan London Ltd and the Trustees of the Hardy Estate for Hardy's published works and the Map of Wessex; Jonathan Cape Ltd and the Letters Trust for T. E. Lawrence for *The Letters of T. E. Lawrence*, edited by David Garnett; Gerald Duckworth & Co. Ltd for H. Vere Collins's *Talks with Thomas Hardy at Max Gate*; the Hogarth Press Ltd and the Author's Literary Estate for Virginia Woolf's *A Writer's Diary*.

Illustrations: the Dorset County Museum, and Council of the Dorset Natural History and Archaeological Society; City of Birmingham Museum; the Governing Body of the Queen's College, Oxford; Aerofilms Ltd; B. T. Batsford Ltd and Mr Peter Baker; Dorchester Studios; *Illustrated London News:* National Monuments Record.

More personally, I should like to thank a number of people for their help in various ways: Mr J. Stevens Cox, editor of the *Toucan Press Monographs* and *Thomas Hardy Year Books*, for so generously lending me photographs, some of them taken by Hardy's friend Hermann Lea; Miss Lois Deacon for reading the Appendix about Tryphena, and allowing me to reproduce her photograph; Miss Evelyn Hardy for the photograph of Horace Moule; the Rev. E. V. Tanner for lending me the photograph of Hardy's grave; Mr Charles Woolf of Newquay for taking photographs of St Juliot, and Wing Commander A. R. G. Bax for permission to photograph the Rectory; Miss Pamela Chandler of St Ives for two photographs; the Librarian and his Assistants of the Dorset County Library; Mr T. R. Wightman, Hon. Secretary of the Thomas Hardy Society, for valuable information; Mr and Mrs Winchcombe, Curators of the Birthplace, for their hospitality; and finally, the Curator of the Dorset County Museum, Mr R. N. R. Peers, and the Assistant Curator, Miss E. M. Samuel, for whom no trouble has been too much.

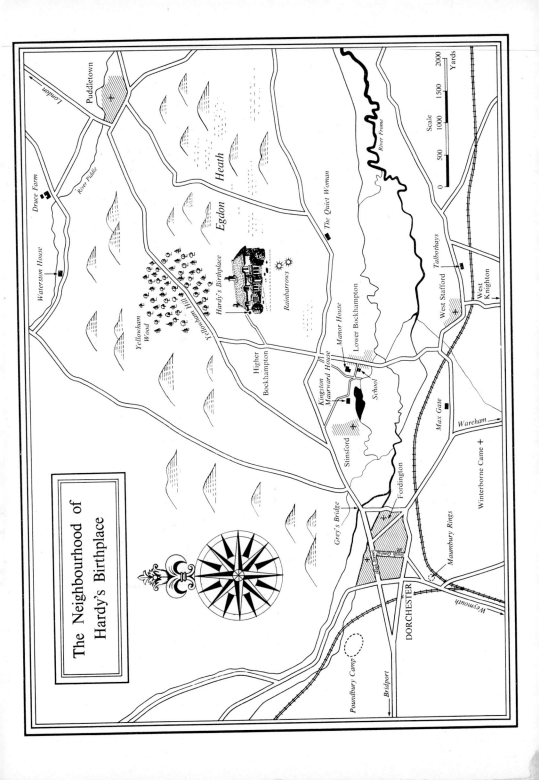

The Neighbourhood of Hardy's Birthplace

1. Higher Bockhampton. Hardy's drawing of his birthplace: 'a long low cottage with a hipped roof of thatch.' Built for his grandfather in 1800.

2. Lower Bockhampton and bridge over the Frome. Behind the cottages on the left was the first school attended by Hardy.

Preface

This book was really begun 40 years ago, when Mrs Hardy invited my wife and myself to tea at Max Gate. We were very young, and she was very kind; she told us how the war had almost shattered her husband's belief in the gradual improvement of the world; showed us sketches of uniforms that he had made for The Trumpet Major *and* Dynasts, *and the manuscript of* The Woodlanders, *the first novel to be written at Max Gate, nearly a quarter of it in the hand of the first Mrs Hardy; and she told us stories of the dog Wessex: how the stamping of a letter excited him, for that meant a walk to the post.*

That was in 1930, two years after Hardy's death, and I wrote a poem—FEH to FEH—on his ninetieth birthday, celebrated in Stinsford churchyard. I also wrote a paper that I read to a literary society, and filed so carefully that I lost it. Since then, scores of books have been written about Hardy, many of which I have read, but this book is essentially a development of that hour-long essay of 40 years ago: an account of his life and work.

'The ultimate aim of the poet,' he wrote, 'should be to touch our hearts by showing his own.' And this is just what he did; not only in his verse but also in his prose, and it is the goodness and compassion of the heart he so shyly revealed, with its memories and conflicts, that make the man so endearing, his poetry so consolatory, and add the quality of greatness to his best novels. The full appreciation of his work depends on a knowledge of his life: they so interpenetrate that they must be treated together.

The Tryphena episode illustrates this. He was much given to loving and losing, and in his late twenties fell in love, though not desperately, with his young cousin, but left her for Emma Gifford. The marriage was an unhappy one, and with Tryphena's death came the full realisation of what might have been. He lived in the past, and like Pearston in The Pursuit of the Well-Beloved, *which he then wrote, 'loved the woman dead as he had never loved her in life . . . no spark of passion existing.' He then wrote* Jude, *with its bitter attack on the marriage laws that tied man and wife together for life. When Emma died twenty years later, however, the pattern was repeated. He loved the woman dead as he had never loved her since the early days of their marriage, and to the ghost of the young woman of St Juliot he wrote some of the greatest love poems in the language.*

Because of this interpenetration of life and work, illustrations are perhaps more helpful for the understanding of Hardy than for the understanding of any other great writer.

F.E.H.

St Ives
Cornwall
September 1971

CHAPTER ONE

Childhood and Schooldays
1840–56

Towards the end of his life Hardy drew up a family pedigree in which he traced the descent of the Dorset Hardys from the French le Hardys of Jersey, one of whom, John, son of Clement le Hardy, crossed the Channel in the late fifteenth century and settled in the region of Eggardon near Bridport. A century later his grandson, the Elizabethan Thomas Hardy of Melcombe Regis (Weymouth), founded and endowed Dorchester Grammar School, and more than two centuries later still another Thomas Hardy fought at Trafalgar as captain of the *Victory* and, created baronet, promoted admiral, was commemorated by a monumental column on the summit of Black Down overlooking his home at Portisham.

A frequent theme in Hardy's novels is that of the decline and decay of old families—notably of the aristocratic Turbervilles of Bere Regis into the peasant Durbeyfields of Marnhull—and by the late eighteenth century the Dorset Hardys as a whole had lost whatever importance they once possessed. At this time there was living in Puddletown a John Hardy who, as a wedding present for his son Thomas, built a small house in the country between Puddletown and Dorchester. That was in 1800, and in the following year Thomas took his bride, Mary Head of Fawley, Berkshire, to his new home, where he set up in business as a builder, with a profitable side-line as smugglers' agent.

Thomas I and Mary Hardy had two sons: James who became a watchmaker in Dorchester, and Thomas II, born 1811, who

1

joined his father in the building business. Thomas I died in 1837, and two years later, in December 1839, Thomas II married Jemima Hand, a young woman of 26. Six months after their marriage their first child Thomas III, the future poet and novelist, was born in the house built for his grandfather 40 years before.

It is a small, thatched house, little more than a cottage, with a kitchen, sitting-room and office, and three bedrooms above. Originally there were stables and outbuildings, essential for a builder who sometimes employed a dozen men or more, but these have gone, the gravel-pits are overgrown, and all that remains is the house and garden. In his earliest extant verses, blank verse in the manner of Wordsworth's *Prelude* written shortly after his grandmother's death in 1857, Hardy described how she had told him what the place was like when she and her husband moved into the house in 1801:

> Our house stood quite alone, and those tall firs
> And beeches were not planted. Snakes and efts
> Swarmed in the summer days, and nightly bats
> Would fly about our bedrooms. Heathcroppers
> Lived on the hills, and were our only friends;
> So wild it was when we first settled here.

Since then, more cottages have been built along the short country lane, forming the hamlet of Higher Bockhampton, and when Hardy was a boy the beech-boughs swept the thatch, honeysuckles climbed the walls as though they wished to over-top the appletrees, 'If we may fancy wish of trees and plants,' and nearby grew an oak, sprung from a seed 'Dropped by a bird a hundred years ago.'[1] The two lines are characteristic, for Hardy felt intuitively the past within the present, and the kinship that links all forms of living things.

He was always deeply attached to his birthplace, where he lived for the first 22 years of his life, but even more important than the house was its situation. He never used the word 'Dorset' in his novels, preferring the vaguer 'Wessex', the country of the West Saxons a thousand years and more before his time, lying south of the Thames between the Sussex of the South

Saxons to the east and Cornwall of the Celts to the west. Yet his essential Wessex is Dorset, and the outlying regions that play a minor part in his work, from eastern Oxford and Winchester to western Tintagel, he called Upper, North, Mid, Outer, and Lower Wessex.

It is important to appreciate the nature of Dorset, for Hardy so identified himself with this small area of England, not only in extent but also in depth, that the scene is more than mere background; it is rather a pervasive element of sights and sounds and whispered history, which moulds his imaginary characters, influences their thoughts, and in part determines their actions. Giles Winterborne, for example, is the personification of the woodlands and cider-making region of Blackmore Vale, imagined by Grace Melbury as 'the fruit-god and the wood-god in alternation: sometimes leafy and smeared with green lichen, as she had seen him among the sappy boughs of the plantations: sometimes cider-stained and starred with apple-pips, as she had met him . . . with his vats and presses beside him.'

From Lyme Regis the coast of the county sweeps south-east, bulwarked for miles by the uncannily straight line of the Chesil Bank, to the almost-island of Portland, which, with the slender neck that links it to the northern mainland, so strangely resembles a miniature version of the American continent. Then, from Weymouth the coast runs east to Durlston Head, where it turns north to Swanage and Poole on the Hampshire border. Parallel to the coast, and some eight miles inland, flows the river Frome, from its source near the Devonshire border, through Maiden Newton to Dorchester, where it is joined by the Cerne from the north, then mazily eastward through meadows to Wareham, shortly after which it enters the great harbour of Poole. Another, and rather bigger river, the Stour, rises just outside the northern border and flows almost parallel to the Frome 15 miles away, through Sturminster Newton, Blandford and Wimborne Minster, after which it crosses the Hampshire border and joins the Avon, which finds the sea at Christchurch. The Frome and Stour, therefore, divide Dorset into three approximately equal parts running from north-west to south-east;

but the county is more significantly divided into very different regions that cut across them.

From the Overworld of *The Dynasts* the ancient Spirit of the Years no doubt explained the essential structure of the shire to his younger companions. It is as though four tides have swept in from the east, each lower than its predecessor, and leaving its own distinctive deposit; and something like this did in fact happen when aeons ago the sedimentary rocks of England were laid down under the sea. First, a deposit of limestone, which was almost obliterated by a layer of clays and sandstone, itself half-covered by a tongue-like layer of chalk, which in turn has been half-covered by a tongue of sands on either side of the Frome.

The sands and heaths that cover most of Hampshire cross the border on a 20-mile front between Cranborne and Studland, just south of Poole harbour, advancing within converging lines to form a triangle with its apex near Dorchester. It is the Egdon Heath of Hardy:

This obscure, obsolete, superseded country figures in Domesday. Its condition is recorded therein as that of heathy, furzy briary wilderness—'Bruaria' ... 'Turbaria Bruaria'—the right of cutting heath-turf—occurs in charters relating to the district. 'Overgrown with heth and mosse,' says Leland of the same dark sweep of country.

This triangular area of heath overlies part of the chalk wedge that enters Dorset south of Shaftesbury and spreads over half the county. From under the heath the chalklands rise gently to the northern escarpment that runs south-west from Melbury Hill to Bulbarrow, High Stoy and Beaminster Down, where it turns to run eastward and form the heights of Eggardon, Black Down and Bincombe Down south of Dorchester, before narrowing into a ridge that reaches the sea in the chalk cliffs flanking the geological complexities of Lulworth Cove; then, as the Purbeck Hills, arched like an eyebrow, the chalk sweeps to the coast at the Foreland. Many of these heights are crowned with earth-works thrown up by the Bronze Age men who built Stonehenge, and studded with barrows within which they lie buried.

At the base of the chalk lie the clays and sandstone that make the third main region of Dorset. The northern escarpment overlooks the fertile Vale of Blackmore, Hardy's 'Vale of Little Dairies', of woodlands and orchards, and there in the valley, after the huge fields and low hedges of the downs

the world seems to be constructed upon a smaller and more delicate scale; the fields are mere paddocks, so reduced that from this height their hedgerows appear a network of dark green threads overspreading the paler green of the grass. . . . Arable lands are few and limited; with but slight exceptions the prospect is a broad, rich mass of grass and trees mantling minor hills and dales within the major.

In the south-west, between the chalk and Lyme Bay, lies Marshwood Vale, another fertile valley of dairies where a corner of Devonshire has strayed over the border. Out of the clays rise sandstone heights such as the northern hill on which, like a Tuscan hill-town, Shaftesbury stands, Pilsdon Pen to the west, and Golden Cap on the coast near Bridport.

On the most southerly part of the coast are outcrops of the underlying limestone. The Isle of Portland is a solid block of limestone four miles long, from which has been quarried the stone of St Paul's Cathedral and other great buildings of England, and with a people, in Hardy's youth at least, distinct from those of the mainland, inbred like the Pierstons and Caros of *The Well-Beloved*, and speaking their own strange dialect. The limestone reappears in the cliffs on either side of Lulworth Cove, and again in the Isle of Purbeck, hardened into the blue-grey almost-marble that was chiselled and polished into slender columns by the builders of thirteenth-century Gothic churches.

Such would be Dorset as seen by the Spirits of the Overworld: a fringe of limestone along the southern clays that run round the wedge of chalk that enfolds the sands and heath. Near the centre, at the tip of the tongue of heathland, in the middle of the Frome valley, is Dorchester, the Durnovaria of the Romans, where their roads met and crossed one another.

The traveller from south to north, therefore, from Weymouth to Sherborne, leaving behind the limestone island of Portland, climbs the chalk escarpment at Upwey and follows the straight gently-falling road flanked by barrows that were ancient long before the Romans made it, and on the left the multiple ramparts of the finest prehistoric fortification in the country, Maiden

Castle, a mile-and-a-half in circumference. On the outskirts of Dorchester is another and even stranger earthwork, Maumbury Rings, again prehistoric, but adapted by the Romans to make a provincial Colosseum, an amphitheatre for the staging of gladiatorial combats. After crossing High Street and the Frome, which skirts the town at the bottom of the hill, the Roman road forks left towards Ilchester, and a later road runs north up the valley of the Cerne, climbing the easy slope of the downs through Cerne Abbas with its fertility-cult giant cut in the chalk, to High Stoy, where it falls steeply out of the brick-and-flint country into that of *The Woodlanders*, and so across the Vale of Blackmore to the stone-built town of Sherborne and its Abbey.

The London road that enters Dorset by the coast at Lyme Regis runs east among the sandstone hills fringing Marshwood Vale, but soon after Bridport climbs on to the chalk, where the scene is barer and slopes are gentler, beyond Winterborne Abbas joining the straight stretch of Roman road that falls slowly towards Dorchester. When Hardy was a boy, Dorchester, the Casterbridge of his novels, 'was the complement of the rural life around; not its urban opposite. Bees and butterflies in the corn-fields at the top of the town, who desired to get to the meads at the bottom, took no circuitous course, but flew straight down High Street without any apparent consciousness that they were traversing strange latitudes.' High Street is not greatly altered; here the road runs more steeply down the chalk, on the right the lodgings of Judge Jeffreys of the Bloody Assizes, on the left St Peter's Church and the great bow-window of the King's Arms, through which Elizabeth-Jane first saw Michael Henchard. At the bottom of the hill, where the Frome is crossed by the first of two bridges, town and country make a complete break, and soon the road forks, the main road to Puddletown and London to the left, the Roman road going straight on through Stinsford until lost in the fields and heath. The two are linked, however, by a country lane in the middle of which a smaller lane breaks away eastwards: 'Cherry Alley', at the end of which is Hardy's birthplace. 'It faces west', towards Dorchester and the chalk downs; at its back, where the lane ends, is Rainbarrow and the tip of Egdon Heath.

*　　　*　　　*

When Thomas Hardy was born, in the morning of 2 June 1840, the doctor pronounced him dead, but the nurse, feeling a flicker of life, cried, 'Stop a minute! He's alive enough, sure!' Alive, but delicate, and not expected to grow up; nor did he wish to grow up. One of his earliest memories was of lying on his back in the sun, like little Jude Fawley gazing through the chinks of the straw hat pulled over his face, and vaguely reflecting that growing up brought responsibilities; he had no ambition, and did not want to be a man. Then no doubt, 'like the natural boy', like Jude, 'he forgot his despondency, and sprang up'.

He had a brother and two sisters: Mary, born in 1841, Henry in 1851, and Kate in 1856. Mary, therefore, was the companion of his childhood, the two younger children belonging almost to another generation. None of them married; the two girls became schoolmistresses, and when Henry was old enough he joined his father in the building business.

Tommy, as he was called, was very precocious, and could read almost as soon as he could walk, for his mother was a great reader and ambitious for her son. She had inherited her love of books from her mother, Betty Swetman, who had collected a small library and was well versed in the classics of the seventeenth and eighteenth centuries, from Milton and Bunyan to the essays of Addison and Steele, and novels of Richardson and Fielding. Unhappily, she so offended her father by secretly marrying a servant, George Hand, that he disinherited her, refusing to see her again, and when her husband died she was left impoverished with a family of several young children. One of them was Jemima, Hardy's mother, for whom recollection of her early life was always a source of distress. However, she found solace in her mother's books, and support in needlework and cooking, until her youthful troubles ended with her marriage. The unhappiness of her youth no doubt accounted for her peasant fatalism, which almost inevitably she communicated to her son. 'Mother's notion (and also mine),' he was to write at the age of thirty, 'that a figure stands in our van with arm uplifted, to knock us back from any pleasant prospect we indulge in as probable.'

From his father, a delightful, easy-going man, Tommy

inherited a passionate love of music. When Thomas I, his grandfather, lived at Puddletown before his marriage, he was one of
a small band of strings, clarinets and serpents that used to play
in the gallery of the church, and when he moved to Higher
Bockhampton in the neighbouring parish of Stinsford, finding
the church music sadly neglected, he at once began to reform it.
From 1801 to his death in 1837 he played his 'cello every Sunday
in the west gallery of Stinsford church, where he was eventually
joined by his sons James and Thomas, who sat behind him to
play their violins. It was here, according to 'A Church Romance',
that Jemima Hand and Thomas II fell in love 'c. 1835':

> She turned in the high pew, until her sight
> Swept the west gallery, and caught its row
> Of music-men with viol, book and bow
> Against the sinking sad tower-window light.
> She turned again; and in her pride's despite
> One strenuous viol's inspirer seemed to throw
> A message from his strings to her below,
> Which said: 'I claim thee as my own forthright!'
> Thus their hearts' bond began. . . .

An extension of the playing of hymns in church was the
playing of carols out-of-doors at Christmas, when they visited
their neighbours in Stinsford parish, as so lovingly described in
Under the Greenwood Tree. And Hardy and Sons were inevitably
in demand for more mundane rural festivities, such as dances
and club-walking of the kind in which we first meet Tess. In
The Return of the Native is a humorous, though legendary,
description of Thomas I at work, for he died three years before
his grandson was born:

Whenever a club walked he'd play the clarinet in the band that
marched before 'em, as if he'd never touched anything but a clarinet
all his life. And then, when they got to church-door he'd throw down
the clarinet, mount the gallery, snatch up the bass-viol, and rozum
away as if he'd never played anything but a bass-viol. Folk would
say—folk that knowed what a true stave was—'Surely, surely that's

never the same man that I saw handling the clarinet so masterly by now!'

Although Thomas II abandoned church-playing soon after Tommy was born, he did not abandon church-going, nor did he abandon his music. An enthusiastic dancer, of an evening he would fiddle hornpipes, jigs and country-dances, to which the little boy, moved to tears by some of the airs, danced a solitary accompaniment. He was only four at this time, only four when his father gave him a small accordion, and not much older when he learned to tune a violin and to play, after a fashion, from the music-books compiled by his father and grandfather.

The parish church of Stinsford is halfway between Higher Bockhampton and Dorchester, more than a mile across the fields, and there the small impressionable boy became familiar with the hymns, music and splendid words of the Anglican ritual, with the Psalms, Prayer Book and Authorised Version of the Bible. He had a tenacious memory, and in his novels biblical quotations and allusions, particularly from the dramatic stories of the Old Testament, came quite naturally to his pen. The church is dark, but when his young eyes grew accustomed to the gloom he could see on the north wall the Grey monument, at the bottom of which were two weeping cherubs and a winged skull, a sight that long haunted his imagination. He learned by heart every word of the inscription commemorating Angel Grey, and 40 years later gave his first name to the hero of *Tess*. There was another memorial that fascinated him because of the story attached to it : two oval plaques linked by hearts, the one to William O'Brien, the other to his widow Susanna. Susanna, or Lady Susan, was a daughter of the Earl of Ilchester, who, according to eighteenth-century standards, disgraced herself by secretly marrying an actor, albeit a distinguished one. Her father forgave her, however, on condition that O'Brien left the stage, and he gave them Stinsford House, adjoining the church, as their home. They were a devoted couple, and when her husband died in 1815, Lady Susan commissioned the local builder, Hardy's grandfather, to make a vault below the church 'just large enough for our two selves only'. He and his men constructed the vault (consuming— Hardyan touch—'nineteen quarts of beer over the job'), added

Lady Susan to it 13 years later, and set up the memorial on the chancel wall. Lady Susan and her story occur a number of times in Hardy's writings.

Brought up on the edge of Egdon, in the isolation of Higher Bockhampton and an atmosphere of music, sacred as well as profane, with weekly expeditions to the medieval church with which his family was so closely associated, it is no wonder that the imaginative boy was transported by its magic. If a Sunday morning were too wet for him to go to church, he would himself conduct a service at home, where, wrapped in a tablecloth and standing on a chair, he would read prayers to the congregation of his grandmother before preaching her a sermon of fragments remembered from the vicar's discourses. And no wonder he had thoughts of becoming a parson, and even when an unbeliever remained 'churchy', so strongly drawn by memories of his childhood that in old age he wrote:

> . . . I feel
> If someone said on Christmas Eve,
>   'Come; see the oxen kneel
> In the lonely barton by yonder coomb
>   Our childhood used to know,'
> I should go with him in the gloom,
>   Hoping it might be so.

It is almost true to say that a church lies at the centre of all Hardy's novels, and it is true that many of his most memorable scenes take place in a church or churchyard.

From Stinsford churchyard a drive runs eastward through a park to Kingston Maurward House, an early-Georgian mansion overlooking a lake formed by the Frome. In 1845 the estate had been bought by Francis Martin, and his wife Julia Augusta at once began to busy herself with good works, one of her first being the building of a local school 'for the education of the children of the labouring classes.' It was at the eastern end of the park, between the original, but then derelict, Tudor manor house and the hamlet of Lower Bockhampton, where a bridge crosses the Frome. It was to this little school, more than a mile south of his home, that Tommy was sent when it opened in

1848. He was then eight, but still very small—'fresh, pink, crisp-curled'—and the first pupil to arrive in the new schoolroom, where he waited tremulously for the formal entry of the master and mistress with the other children.

He was fortunate, for in 1848 only about half of the children in the country had the chance to go to school, and it was to be another 20 years before the state provided elementary education for all. It was an age of general illiteracy and ignorance—not the same thing as lack of intelligence—when the majority passed their lives within a few miles of their homes, intermarrying and perpetuating superstitions and traditions immemorially old. The decade of the Hungry Forties was also one of social unrest, and 1848 a year of revolution throughout Europe, though England experienced nothing more dangerous than the climax of the Chartist movement for further parliamentary reform. Even this proved to be an anti-climax, for better times were on the way, the repeal of the Corn Laws ushering in Free Trade and the prosperous 'fifties that began with the Great Exhibition of 1851. Trade Unions, however, were not yet legalised, and Hardy's father must have known the Lovelace and Stanfield brothers of neighbouring Tolpuddle, who broke the law trying to organise a Friendly Society of Agricultural Labourers. It was innocent and harmless enough, pledged to non-violence, more like a children's charade in which there was dressing-up, blindfold swearing on a Bible, skulls and a skeleton holding a scythe. Yet at the Dorchester Assizes in 1834 the Lovelaces, Stanfields and two others were found guilty of sedition and illegal conspiracy, and sentenced to seven years' transportation. It is odd that Hardy never brought the grotesque story of the Tolpuddle Martyrs into his novels.

As a boy he was used to grotesque stories and sights. He saw men sitting in the stocks, and was taken by his father to see the burning in effigy of the Pope and Cardinal Wiseman in Maumbury Rings during the No-Popery riots that followed Newman's secession to Rome in 1845. Not long before his time old women, supposed witches, were burned alive in this Roman amphitheatre, and in 'The Mock Wife' he was to tell the story of Mary Channing, a young mother of nineteen, who in 1705 was strangled and burned on the unproved charge of murdering her husband. The gallows stood there as a public spectacle until 1767, when they were erected outside Dorchester gaol, and there, while still a schoolboy, Hardy saw a woman hanged, on the previous evening having watched the hangman eat his supper in his cottage, and early next morning standing close to the gallows. Not long afterwards he saw another execution through a telescope from the Egdon heights behind his home.

There were other sights less gruesome and almost as exciting. In 1848 he could cheer the stage coaches racing along the London road half-a-mile to the north of his home, and half-a-mile below his school cheer the trains that had just brought Dorchester within two or three hours of London. The weekly *Dorset County Chronicle* then had to compete with the daily national newspapers; orally transmitted ballads and their centuries-old tunes were 'slain at a stroke by the London comic songs that were introduced'; and for the greater part of Hardy's life the roads were almost deserted, as were coaching-inns like The Three Tranters in *Desperate Remedies*, where horses had been changed, and passengers had eaten and slept. At the turn of the century cyclists had the roads to themselves, though the motor-car was to alter all that.

At school Tommy was taught the Three R's: reading, writing and arithmetic, as well as geography, and at home his reading was supplemented by his mother, who gave him Dryden's translation of Virgil, Johnson's *Rasselas*, and Saint-Pierre's sentimental *Paul and Virginia*, though the boy probably preferred *Tales about Sons of the Sea* and *A History of the Wars*, an old periodical taken by his grandfather, who had been a volunteer during the wars against Napoleon. Mrs Martin also took an interest in his education. Having no children of her own, she was passionately attached to the precocious little boy who had been the first pupil in her school, and would take him on her lap and fondle him while he sang to her. It was, therefore, a great grief to her when, after a year, his parents decided to send him to a more advanced school in Dorchester.

This was not the Grammar School founded by the Elizabethan Thomas Hardy, nor the school in South Street conducted by the poet, the Rev. William Barnes, but the Nonconformist school of Isaac Last, whose fees were low and reputation high. So, at the age of nine the boy began his day with a three-mile walk over the fields to Stinsford, and then along the road to the two bridges across the Frome and up Dorchester High Street, where on market-day 'Horses for sale were tied in rows, their forelegs on the pavement, their hind legs in the street, in which position they occasionally nipped little boys by the shoulder who were passing to school.'[2] Then at the end of the day he walked the three miles back to Higher Bockhampton.

The exercise did him good, and though he was, as he confessed, rather an idle schoolboy, he was quick, and at the age of 12 began to learn Latin and to read Caesar and Eutropius. These simple histories appealed to his innate feeling for the past and kindled an interest in Roman Dorchester, and Roman Dorchester stimulated his interest in Latin. 'Casterbridge announced old Rome in every street, alley, and precinct,' he was to write later,

It looked Roman, bespoke the art of Rome, concealed dead men of Rome. It was impossible to dig more than a foot or two deep about the town fields and gardens without coming upon some tall soldier or other of the Empire, who had lain there in his silent unobtrusive rest for a space of fifteen hundred years.

Long-buried Romans were a familiar sight to the people of Dorchester, but the boy would gaze in wonder at these ghosts in a scoop of the chalk.

His taste in fiction was for history, among his favourite books being the romances of Ainsworth, Scott and Dumas. He also read the tragedies of Shakespeare, not for their poetry but for their plots, and was disappointed by *Hamlet*, in which the ghost fades with the crowing of the cock in the first act. He was a born bookworm, but in addition to reading there was music, and sometimes he would accompany his father to play the fiddle at some rural festivity, like the boy in the story of *The Three Strangers*, 'about twelve years of age, who had a wonderful dexterity in jigs and reels, though his fingers were so small and short as to necessitate a constant shifting for the high notes, from which he scrambled back to the first position with sounds

13

not of unmixed purity of tone.' Then, when he was 15 he began to teach at Stinsford Sunday School which he had attended as learner not long before, among his pupils being a plump little dairymaid who was to appear as Marian in *Tess*, perhaps one of the uneducated girls whom he helped to write their love letters. And he himself fell in love from time to time: with sweet Lizbie Browne who scorned him as too young, with Louisa Harding to whom he spoke only two words, a shy 'Good evening' in the lane: two girls whom he never forgot.

He was now 16 and had to think of a profession. He did not wish to join his father as a builder—his brother Henry could do that when he grew up—and everybody was agreed that he ought to be a parson. Sometimes he thought so too. But his father knew a Dorchester architect and church-restorer, John Hicks, for whom he had carried out work, and for a premium of £40 Hicks offered to take the boy as a pupil for three years. The boy agreed; and so, like Shakespeare, Thomas Hardy left school at the age of 16.

CHAPTER TWO

Architect's Pupil
1856–62

Hardy used to say that he was 'a child till he was sixteen, a youth till he was five-and-twenty, and a young man till he was nearly fifty.' Yet when he left school at 16 to learn architectural drawing and surveying with Hicks, although inexperienced and perhaps physically immature, mentally he was well abreast of his years. Bookish to a degree, with an exceptional knowledge of the Bible, well grounded in Latin and mathematics and with a smattering of French, he was a promising candidate for an

3. Puddletown ('Weatherbury') Church. The west gallery in which Hardy's grandfather used to play the violin before his marriage and move to Stinsford parish.

4. Music manuscript used by the 'Mellstock Quire.' The signature is either that of Hardy's father or his grandfather.

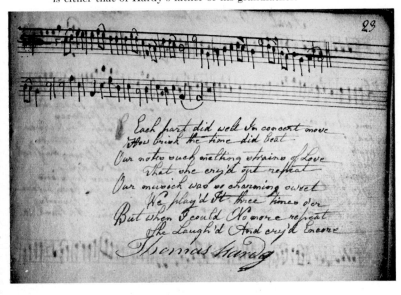

5. Dorchester Station as seen from Maumbury
Rings at the opening of the railway in 1847.

6. Stinsford ('Mellstock') Church. 'Thomas was
kept strictly at church on Sundays, till he
knew the Morning and Evening Services
by heart.'

7. The British School, Greyhound Yard, Dorchester: the
   nonconformist school that Hardy attended 1849-56.

8. Dorchester as it was when Hardy was a schoolboy. Looking east down High St. from St Peter's Church towards the King's Arms and bridges over the Frome.

9. Cornhill, the Antelope Hotel, and St Peter's on the far side of High St. Hardy probably walked along here on the day this photograph was taken, *c.* 1860 on his way to Hicks's office at 39 South St.

academic career, for university and ordination. But circumstance, an ironic and tragic word in his later vocabulary, was against him; his father was merely a builder and master-mason, more interested in music than the making of money, and could better afford to have his son trained in an architect's office than in an Oxford or Cambridge college; and to have a son who was an architect was in the nature of a partnership. In any event, the boy probably preferred the familiarity and security of the home that he celebrated in his early verses, 'Domicilium', written at about this time, to the strangeness of the unknown. Although not unsociable, he preferred solitude; and he was shy, so sensitive that he disliked being touched, his handshake rarely being more than a reluctant civility. This aloofness may have been partly the result of his early isolation on the edge of Egdon, and his small knowledge of life outside his immediate surroundings. His father would sometimes take him further afield on his building expeditions, but he had only once been out of Dorset, when his mother took him, aged nine, to visit a sister in Hertfordshire, a journey partly by coach, partly by train on the new Dorchester–London line. The boy and his mother were good companions, enjoyed playing together, and one day she took him to see another sister, probably Maria Sparks, walking across the heath to Puddletown disguised by cabbage-nets pulled over their faces.

His new occupation led to some extension of his travels, for though his daily walk to Hicks's office in Dorchester's South Street was the same as that he had pursued for the last seven years as a schoolboy, surveying and sketching involved visits to distant villages, from Rampisham to Bettiscombe on the Devonshire border, both of which were restored or rebuilt by Hicks while Hardy was with him. More locally, there was restoration work to be done in Stinsford church and St Peter's, Dorchester, where there is a framed plan of the church drawn by Hardy in his first year with Hicks. The craze for church restoration was then at its height, and Hardy was later to say some bitter things about the work in which he had been unwittingly engaged. Some old churches were simply pulled down and rebuilt; those exhibiting two or three periods of Gothic were reduced to one uniform style; irregularities were smoothed away, chancel-arches and monuments moved, medieval tracery replaced by caricatures in new stone, and old oak pews and pulpits by new-fangled deal. The first entry in his Architectural Notebook is a short article on 'Pine Timber', possibly dictated by Hicks.

'Restoration' meant replacement rather than repair, and if Hardy had been a practising architect he would never have undertaken such work. For him an old building was primarily the hands that had shaped it, the feet that had worn its floors; human interest was more important than the architectural, the associative influences more valuable than the aesthetic: 'The protection of an ancient edifice against renewal in fresh materials ... is the preservation of memories, history, fellowship, fratern-ities. Life, after all, is more than art.'[3] His historical sense, his feeling for continuity and the beauty of association were in-tensified by his architectural studies, and they lie at the root of his novels and poems, almost, it might be said, they are the roots: 'The beauty of association is entirely superior to the beauty of aspect, and a beloved relative's old battered tankard to the finest Greek vase.' And again: 'An object or mark raised or made by man on a scene is worth ten times any such formed by unconscious Nature. Hence clouds, mists, and mountains are unimportant beside the wear on a threshold, or the print of a hand.' The full appreciation of Hardy, the man as well as his work, depends on the reader's response to this intense feeling for people, for the dead as well as, perhaps even more than, the living.

In addition to an extension of the Dorset scene, and to a dawning awareness of the relationship between architecture and literature, work with Hicks meant an extended knowledge of life. He knew as well as any other boy of his age the workfolk among whom he had lived, and still lived, but now he was to meet more educated professional men. There was Hicks himself, a kindly genial man, something of a classical scholar, who did not overwork his pupils. For Hardy was not the only one. When he arrived he found another articled pupil in the office, Robert Bastow, a well educated boy some two years older than himself with a taste for the classics. The two began to read Latin poetry together—Virgil, Horace, Ovid—though most of Hardy's reading was done at home between five and eight in the morning, when he left for the office. He led what he called a triple existence: the scholar's in the early morning, the professional architect's during the day, and the rustic's at night, when he would sometimes take his fiddle, perhaps with his father, to play country-dances at some village festivity that went on into the small hours. Encouraged by Bastow he also began to learn Greek, and here Hicks, too, was useful, for he prided himself on his Greek. The boys had little respect for his Latin, however, and when there was a dispute about grammar Hardy would appeal to the master of the school next door, William Barnes.

So Hardy met the Dorset poet, amateur archaeologist, and philologist with a passion for the pure Saxon of Wessex. Born in the Vale of Blackmore, and since 1835 a schoolmaster in Dorchester, he was at this time a man of nearly sixty, and about to publish another volume of verse: *Poems of Rural Life in the Dorset Dialect*. Hardy heard him recite his humorous verse in public with droll delivery and mild smile, but preferred the more serious poems that appeared in the *Dorset Chronicle*. The blend of nature and everyday cottage life appealed to him strongly, as well it might, for it was to be the subject of his own best work, and was an important influence on the impressionable boy. But Barnes lacked Hardy's profundity, and his poems are little more than descriptions inspired by memory rather than imagination, almost devoid of imagery and owing much of their charm and pathos to variations on a refrain, as in 'The Wife A-Lost', one of Hardy's favourites, and also tragically prophetic:

> Since I noo mwore do zee your feäce,
>   Up-steärs or down below,
> I'll zit me in the lwonesome pleäce,
>   Where flat-bough'd beech do grow;
> Below the beeches' bough, my love,
>   Where you did never come,
> An' I don't look to meet ye now,
>   As I do look at hwome.
>
> Since you noo mwore be at my zide,
>   In walks in summer het,

> I'll goo alwone where mist do ride,
> Droo trees a-drippen wet;
> Below the raïn-wet bough, my love,
> Where you did never come,
> An' I don't grieve to miss ye now,
> As I do grieve at hwome . . .

The vocabulary is almost entirely Old English in derivation, latinisms being confined to a few nouns and verbs: 'face', 'place', 'grieve'. Hardy might have profited from this, for although his best work has a similar homeliness of diction—one thinks of the last paragraph of *The Woodlanders*—in his workaday prose his characters do not 'see', but 'perceive', 'observe' or 'discern'; they do not 'understand', but 'comprehend'; they 'assist' rather than 'help', 'endeavour to ascend' rather than 'try to climb'; events do not 'begin before', but 'commence previous to' or 'prior to' or 'anterior to'; and a 'group of buildings' is a 'congeries of edifices'. These are the pedantries of a self-educated stylist (his split infinitives on the other hand seem to be a deliberate protest against pedantry), and one curious solecism may be mentioned here, one that persists from *Desperate Remedies* to *Tess*, from 'neither of the five seem' to 'neither of the [sixteen] men moved.' Hardy remembered Barnes affectionately as 'an aged clergyman, quaintly attired in caped cloak, knee-breeches, and buckled shoes,' as he is still to be seen in bronze at the top of Dorchester High Street. He also remembered the old man's indignation at the name 'bicycle' for the new-fangled machine that Hardy so liked riding, among his last words being, 'Why didn't they call it "wheel-saddle"?'

Hardy's object in taking up Greek was to read its literature, and he had already embarked on the *Iliad* when his course was deflected by Bastow's announcing that he was going to be baptised, and advising him to follow his example. He had been brought up as a Baptist, Hardy in the Church of England, and the result was fierce disputes about infant and adult baptism, Bastow being reinforced by two young Scottish graduates, sons of the local Baptist minister, Perkins. As the Perkins brothers could quote the Greek of the New Testament, Hardy, in the unequal struggle of one against three, laid aside his Homer and took up the Greek Testament before going to work in the morning. He found little authority there for infant baptism, but stuck to his guns until Bastow left the office in 1859, by which time he had come to the conclusion that the matter was of little importance, and he returned to the *Iliad*. Although disagreeing with them, he admired the Perkins family for the simple sincerity of their lives, and the father was later to appear as the Baptist minister in *A Laodicean*.

As Bastow's departure meant more work for Hardy, whose period of apprenticeship had been extended beyond the original three years, he began to sleep in Hicks's house instead of walking home to Bockhampton. In this way he met the Rev. Henry Moule, Vicar of Fordington, the unsavoury slum parish that lay between South Street and the marshes of the Frome, the Mixen Lane area of *The Mayor of Casterbridge*. By this time Henry Moule was something of a hero for the part he had played in the great cholera epidemic of 1854 when, like the parson in *A Changed Man*, he and his wife had worked alone to check the plague and reduce mortality. As Hicks's home, above his office, was almost within Fordington parish, Hardy attended his church of Fordington St George, and so got to know not only the vicar but also some of his seven sons. One of these was Horace Moule, recently down from Queen's College, Cambridge, and about to start his career as writer and critic. As he was eight years older than Hardy, and a good Greek scholar with a happy gift of imparting knowledge, it was only natural that the boy who had left school at 16 should revere this cultured man, and seek his opinion and advice. One thing had worried him for some time: if he was going to be an architect, was he justified in spending so much time reading Homer and Greek tragedy, the study of which he had just begun? Moule would have liked to encourage the scholar, but his considered opinion was that he should concentrate on his profession, and from that moment Hardy virtually abandoned his Greek.

There were compensations. Moule's business was the reviewing of newly published books, and it was he who introduced Hardy to current English literature. There was no lack of important new books to be discussed between the years 1859 and 1861, when Browning left Italy for England after the death of his wife Elizabeth Barrett. The first instalment of Tennyson's *Idylls of the King* appeared in 1859, as did one of the first and best of Meredith's novels, *Richard Feverel*, followed by *Evan Harrington*. Then in 1860 came George Eliot's *Mill on the Floss*, the opening autobiographical chapters of which must have enchanted Hardy, who would also read *Great Expectations*, *Framley Parsonage*, Wilkie Collins's sensational *Woman in White*, and *Lovel the Widower*, which appeared in the newly founded *Cornhill Magazine* with Thackeray himself as editor. A more controversial book for discussion with Moule was *Essays and Reviews*, a symposium by seven authors who claimed the right to free inquiry in matters of religion. These 'Seven against Christ', one of whom was a future Archbishop of Canterbury, were violently attacked by Bishop Wilberforce, thousands of the clergy affirmed their belief in eternal punishment, and the book was officially condemned by the Church. Far more important and controversial was Darwin's *Origin of Species*, published in November 1859. Here was a very different account of man's origin and history from that given in the Bible; man had not been created by God in his own image, but, like other animals, had evolved from lower forms of life by a process of natural selection. 'Nonsense!' Wilberforce fulminated, 'Pigeons have always been pigeons, and men have always been men.' But Hardy was not so sure as the Bishop of Oxford.

CHAPTER THREE

Architecture in London
1862–67

Hardy came of age in the summer of 1861, and after five years of architectural training it was time that he began to support himself. Horace Moule had widened the horizon for him, and instead of trying to find work in Dorchester, in April 1862 he set out for London to seek his fortune. Perhaps his decision was influenced by another unsuccessful love affair. He had just, apparently, proposed to and been rejected by a Dorchester girl, Mary Waight, some years older than himself, and may have wished to avoid the pain of seeing her. He was still not very sure of himself, and bought a return ticket in case his venture should prove a failure. But he also carried two letters of introduction to architects. He was lucky, for one of them was able to introduce him to another architect who was looking for just such a man as Hardy, a young Gothic draughtsman who knew something about the designing and restoration of churches.

The architect in search of an assistant was Arthur Blomfield, only about ten years older than Hardy, yet already so well established in his profession that he had just been elected President of the Architectural Association. He liked Hardy who —less than three weeks after leaving Dorchester—on a Monday morning in May began work in a London drawing-office in St Martin's Place, facing the National Gallery. In the autumn, however, Blomfield moved to grander premises in Adelphi Terrace overlooking the Thames, where Hardy was to work for the five years of his stay in London. The Adelphi had been built by the Adam brothers just 100 years before, in a style very different from Blomfield's Victorian Gothic; here Garrick had lived and entertained his old friend Johnson, and here Hardy and his young companions drew caricatures on the classical marble mantelpieces.

What these pupils of Blomfield's thought of Hardy we do not know. Companionable yet aloof, with a Westcountry burr in his speech—for it must be remembered that he had lived all his life at Bockhampton—some of them may have smiled at his occasional dialect words, such as West Saxon 'fall' for the imported gallicism 'autumn'. And if he felt homesick, as he must have done at times, from the office he could see Portland in the stone of Somerset House a few hundred yards down the river, of St Paul's on the hill behind it, and Purbeck in the paving-stones of the streets. Every bridge across the Thames was visible, and during his stay he saw the building of the Embankment below, and of Charing Cross railway-bridge and station on the south side of the Terrace. His lodgings were on the then westerly outskirts, at 16 Westbourne Park Villas, so that his walk to Blomfield's office—half of it through Hyde Park—was almost as far as that across the fields from Bockhampton to Hicks's office in Dorchester. Or if it were wet he might take the horse omnibus 'to London', or even for part of the way the newly-built underground railway.

He had no friends in London, but soon after his arrival Horace Moule paid him a visit, and gave him supper after taking him to a Roman Catholic service, which he found very impressive. Moule had coached him in the writing of English, and now began to carry on a sort of correspondence course with him. Thus, in reply to a query from Hardy he wrote from Dorchester explaining the proper use of the subjunctive, and Hardy, who studied Defoe, Addison, Gibbon and other acknowledged masters, even the *Times* leaders, for their style, sent him analyses of their prose. But Moule replied that the best way to learn to write well was 'to generate something to say'. Don't read anybody for his style, but for his thoughts, for 'you must in the end write *your own* style.'

One day he called on Mrs Martin, the lady of Kingston Maurward manor, who had built the school at Bockhampton and become as fond of her little Tommy as he had been of her. They had not met since he was a small boy, for she and her husband had left Stinsford for London ten years before, and the visit was not a great success, the young man with a moustache having little in common with the pretty child she used to kiss. However, she asked him to call again, but he soon became so engrossed in the new exciting life he was leading that he never returned.

He was working hard in his spare time. The Royal Institute of British Architects had offered a medal and prize of £10 for the best essay on 'The Application of Coloured Bricks and Terra Cotta to Modern Architecture', and here Blomfield was helpful, for he had just built a church in Shoreditch of these materials: red, yellow and blue bricks. In March 1863 Hardy was pronounced the winner and awarded the medal, but not the money, as it was considered that he had 'scarcely gone sufficiently into the subject.' Soon afterwards he won £3 for a design for a country mansion, and with the money bought a number of English versions of Greek and Latin classics.

Although Blomfield found time to sing glees with Hardy and his pupils during office hours, he was a busy man. Unlike Hardy, he started with advantages: educated at Rugby and Trinity College, Cambridge, his father had been Bishop of London, which probably accounts for the number of churches that he was commissioned to build or rebuild in the neighbourhood of the Bishop's Palace in Fulham. He was also thought to be the right man to supervise the removal of bodies from graveyards when a railway secured the right to cut through them. When, therefore, navvies began to dig into St Pancras churchyard, Blomfield appointed a watchman to see that coffins were not rifled by body-snatchers, or bones carried off to be ground into powder; and to make doubly sure, deputed Hardy to watch the watchman. The bodies were removed to other burial grounds after nightfall, the graveyard from which they were taken being lit by flare-lamps. It must have been a grotesque scene as crumbling coffins and rattling bones were carried out of the flickering glare into the dark, and one evening when Blomfield called to see that Hardy was at his post, one of the coffins fell apart to reveal a skeleton with two skulls—the final Hardyan touch.

In this age of communication, of tape-recorder, television and colour photography, it is not easy to appreciate how limited were the cultural sources within Hardy's reach before he exchanged Bockhampton for London. Although there was a museum in Dorchester there was no public library, so that his books were virtually restricted to those of his mother at home, those of the two small circulating libraries in the town, the few he could afford to buy, and those he was able to borrow. Hence the great importance of Moule, who had put the library of Fordington Rectory at his disposal as he approached manhood. Music there had been in plenty, but it was mainly that of the church and country revels: hymns, carols, ballads, jigs and reels, some of it very beautiful, but nevertheless limited in range. It is improbable that young Hardy ever heard a Beethoven quartet, and he certainly never heard a Beethoven symphony or Mozart opera. There was an assembly-room but no theatre in Dorchester, though Weymouth, some 12 miles from Bockhampton, had more to offer, and he would occasionally see a play performed by a travelling company of actors. As there were no art galleries, he can have seen very few good pictures, and his knowledge of important painting would be confined to engraved reproductions, of original sculpture to carvings and effigies in churches. The only visual art with which he was well acquainted was architecture, fine examples of which were numerous in Dorset, from Puddletown church and Sherborne Abbey to Georgian Kingston Maurward House and classical-Gothick Milton Abbey. Yet he had never seen anything like the dome of St Paul's Cathedral before he went to London.

As a maker of architectural sketches, fine and delicate as his handwriting, Hardy was himself an artist in a modest way, and we can understand why the picture-starved young man so eagerly frequented the National Gallery. Blomfield's first office was just across the road, and Adelphi Terrace only a quarter of a mile away, and for months he went there for 20 minutes after lunch every day it was open, studying the work of one painter at a time. It is not surprising, therefore, that in his first published novel he wrote of his heroine: 'Those who remember Greuze's "Head of a Girl" have an idea of Cytherea's look askance at the turning'; and 'a narrow bony hand that would have been an unmitigated delight to the pencil of Carlo Crivelli'; and 'The reflection from the smooth stagnant surface tinged his face with the greenish shades of Correggio's nudes.' And then—'He modulated into the Pastoral Symphony.'[4]

He had at last heard a Beethoven symphony. But, brought up on the choral singing of the church, he seems to have preferred oratorio and opera to orchestral music: especially Italian opera which, for a time at least, he went to hear at Covent Garden or Her Majesty's two or three times a week. Then there was the theatre, or rather, Shakespeare. Charles Kean was still producing his lavish spectacles with a text so mangled that Hardy, who took a copy of the plays with him, must have closed his book in despair. It was easier to follow Phelps's simpler productions at Drury Lane. The tercentenary of Shakespeare's birth was celebrated in 1864 and, but for a misunderstanding, Phelps should have been at Stratford, whose loss was Hardy's gain, for he was able to see a series of the plays with that touchy celebrity in the principal roles. More frivolously, and less frequently, there was dancing at the Argyle and 'gay Cremorne', and better still at Willis's, the former Almack's haunted by Georgian phantoms, where he could foot the Lancers and Caledonians to the original tunes he loved so well: occasions remembered nostalgically in 'Reminiscences of a Dancing Man'.

Opera, Shakespeare and the Lancers; Hardy's evenings appear to have been fully occupied, yet in August 1862 he wrote to his sister Mary:

I have not been to a theatre since you were here. I generally run down to the Exhibition for an hour in the evening, two or three times a week; after I come out I go to the reading room of the Kensington Museum.

The Great Exhibition of 1851 in Hyde Park had been such a success that the Prince Consort promoted another on a Kensington site just south of the Park, where a huge group of cultural buildings was planned. This was the Exhibition referred to by Hardy, when the South Kensington Museum was merely a glass and iron structure known as the Brompton Boilers, the reading-room of which he visited in search of material for the prize essay he was then writing. To the inconsolable grief of Queen Victoria, the Prince Consort died shortly before the opening of the Exhibition, and Hardy would see the beginning of the spiky Albert Memorial, and of the great round of the Albert Hall that faced it.

When the excitement of exploring London and the enchantment of its entertainments had a little worn off, Hardy's thoughts turned again towards literature, and by the end of 1863 he was spending most of his time after office hours reading. There was neither scope nor stimulation for his imagination, nothing creative, in making architectural drawings for Blomfield's designs, and he thought of trying to link architecture to literature by becoming an art critic. Meanwhile he read, and sometimes gave short talks to Blomfield's pupils on what he had read, as well as telling Mary what she ought to read. 'About Thackeray. You must read something of his,' he wrote in December 1863,

He is considered to be the greatest novelist of the day—looking at novel writing of the highest kind as a perfect and truthful representation of actual life—which is no doubt the proper view to take.

He warned her, however, that because his works were so truthful they had anything but an elevating tendency. '*Vanity Fair* is considered one of his best.' By the time Mary read the letter, Thackeray was dead. Dickens remained, and Hardy heard him give his celebrated readings from his novels in the Hanover Square Rooms. And there was Trollope, whose Barchester novels were coming out at this time; Hardy sent his sister a copy of *Barchester Towers*.

Of even more importance to his development than the Victorian novelists was the work of John Stuart Mill, whose treatise *On Liberty* had recently been published. Hardy knew almost by heart this logically argued plea for the liberty of expressing and publishing opinions, so fettered by Victorian hypocrisy and prudery, and for free play for the reformer and thinker, 'who must follow his intellect to whatever conclusions it may lead.' For him Mill was one of the profoundest thinkers of the century, and one afternoon in 1865 he heard this least demagogic of men address an uncomprehending audience in Covent Garden when he was a candidate for Parliament: 'He stood bareheaded, and his vast pale brow, so thin-skinned as to show the blue veins, sloped back like a stretching upland, and conveyed to the observer a curious sense of perilous exposure.' Mill was a rationalist, and Hardy's acceptance of his teaching made him unable to accept the religious opinions of Newman in his *Apologia*, much as he would have liked to accept them because of his early memories, and for the sake of Moule who admired both the man and the book; but though the style was charming and the argument very human, there was 'no first link to his excellent chain of reasoning, and down you come headlong.'

26

Perhaps as a preliminary to becoming an art critic, but primarily for the amusement of Blomfield's pupils, Hardy wrote a short story which he sent to *Chambers's Journal*, where it appeared in March 1865 as 'How I Built Myself a House'. As this, apart from a few juvenilia in the *Dorset Chronicle*, was the first of his works to be published, its opening is of more than common interest, and tragic in the unforeseen Hardyan irony of its vision of a happy married life with children: 'My wife Sophia, myself, and the beginning of a happy line, formerly lived in the suburbs of London, in the sort of house called a Highly-Desirable Semi-detached Villa.' It is a light-hearted cautionary tale in which the young couple contract with an architect for the building of a house for a specified sum, but run into far greater expense by 'getting into extras', and finding many of the fittings not included: patent bell-pulls, a kitchen range, and ventilators 'which worked vigorously enough, but the wrong way round.'

Palmerston, who had been Prime Minister for the last ten years, died a few months later, and Hardy saw his funeral from the triforium of Westminster Abbey. His death marked the end of an epoch in English history, as Hardy realised when he wrote to Mary: 'Only fancy, Ld. P. has been connected with the govt. off and on for the last 60 years, and that he was contemporaneous with Pitt, Fox, Sheridan, Burke, etc. I mean to say his life overlapped theirs so to speak.' And, so to speak, did Hardy's. He had heard Palmerston in the House of Commons, where he had first spoken shortly after the Battle of Trafalgar, and Palmerston he must have felt was another link between himself and the Napoleonic Wars. That year, 1865, was also the end of a phase in Hardy's life.

In spite of this modest start to a literary career, he was not happy, and in May made the note: 'The world does not despise us; it only neglects us.' And again, on 2 June:

My 25th birthday. Not very cheerful. Feel as if I had lived a long time and done very little. Walked about by moonlight in the evening. Wondered what woman, if any, I should be thinking about in five years' time.

The thought of some woman was partly responsible for his despondency that evening; but then, 'Feel as if I had done very little.' At his age Shakespeare was writing plays for the London theatre, and Keats was only 25 when he died, yet after nine years' training he was merely an architect's draughtsman; and he did not wish to be an architect. He wanted to write, not so much prose as verse—poetry. Poetry was his first love, and he abandoned the idea of combining prose with architecture as an art critic for that of poetry with the Church, as a parson—like Newman and Barnes. If he were a country curate he would have money enough to live on and time enough in which to write his poetry. It would mean going to a university, but his father would lend him the necessary money until he was ordained. He would like to be a parson: old churches and their histories, their music, their liturgy and readings from the Bible all called him, yet he could not conscientiously accept ordination; the biological revelations of Darwin, the rationalism of Mill, the agnosticism of Huxley ('agnostic' was a word of his coining), had shaken his belief. He was torn between feeling and reason, faith and fact; he wanted to believe, but he could not. Besides,

To succeed in the Church, people must believe in you, first of all, as a gentleman, secondly as a man of means, thirdly as a scholar, fourthly as a preacher, fifthly, perhaps, as a Christian—but always first as a gentleman.[5]

And he was the poor man, no gentleman—not even, strictly, a Christian. The only course seemed to be to persevere with architecture and write poetry when he could find the time.

He had written occasional verse since his schooldays, no doubt even earlier, but now in 1865 he began to write in earnest, with a view to publication; and to steep himself in what he considered 'the essence of all imaginative and emotional literature' he read nothing but poetry for the next two years, apart from newspapers and reviews; not the regular, rational verse of Dryden and Pope and their classical school, but the wilder imaginings of the romantics, from the Elizabethans to the Victorians of his own day. The *Golden Treasury* had appeared in 1864, and from this, for him, priceless anthology he was able to select most of the poets whose work he wished to pursue: Shakespeare, of course, but also the gruesome tragedies of Webster and their poetry of skeletons and skulls. Then to the next great period of English poetry: Wordsworth, Coleridge and Scott, whose poems he preferred to his novels, and once assured T. E. Lawrence in all seriousness that the *Iliad* was 'in the *Marmion*' class'. Wordsworth's famous Preface to the *Lyrical Ballads* would interest and encourage him, and may well have been an important influence on his development as poet and novelist:

The principal object, then, proposed in these Poems was to choose incidents and situations from common life, and to relate or describe them throughout, as far as was possible, in a selection of language really used by men. . . . Humble and rustic life was generally chosen, because in that condition the essential passions of the heart find a better soil in which they can attain their maturity. . . . The language, too, of these men has been adopted . . . because, from their rank in society and the sameness and narrow circle of their intercourse, being less under the influence of social vanity, they convey their feelings and notions in simple and unelaborated expressions.

Even more exciting was the second generation of Romantic poets—Byron: certain cantos of whose *Childe Harold* he considered to be among the finest in English descriptive poetry, notably his description of Lac Leman, not of its sights by day, but of its sounds by night; Shelley: greatest of English lyrists, whose 'O world, O life, O time' was one of his favourite poems; Keats: humbly-born as himself, the pathos of whose life and early death seems to have moved Hardy as much as his poetry.

The young Tennyson had been Keats's true successor, but the middle-aged celebrity had declined into the genteel Victorianism of *Idylls of the King*, not to be compared with his early work, nor with the harsh realism of Crabbe's tales in verse. Nor with the more romantic tales and dramatic monologues of Browning, who had just published his *Dramatis Personae*, poems about people, about men and women, especially about women, 'with such hair too', in verse unpretentious and colloquial:

> Some people hang portraits up
> In a room where they dine or sup:
>   And the wife clinks tea-things under,
> And her cousin, he stirs his cup,
>   Asks, 'Who was the lady, I wonder?'

Among the Americans there was the haunting poetry of Edgar Allan Poe, with its hollow echoing assonance and rhymes, as in 'Ulalume', and the bracing unconventional poetry of Whitman in *Leaves of Grass*. Then, in 1866 came the *Poems and Ballads* of Swinburne, little more than Hardy's age, whose intoxicating music sent the undergraduates of Oxford chanting 'Dolores' down the High; and Hardy never forgot the excitement with which he read his lines in London:

> O that far morning of a summer day
> When, down a terraced street whose pavements lay
> Glassing the sunshine into my bent eyes,
> I walked and read with a quick glad surprise
>   New words, in classic guise.

It was not only the winged alliterative movement of the lines that gave him this glad surprise, it was also the revolutionary liberating ideas of this young poet who sang with certainty of the things that tormented him with doubt:

> It was as though a garland of red roses
> Had fallen about the hood of some smug nun
> When irresponsibly dropped as from the sun,
> In fulth of numbers freaked with musical closes,
> Upon Victoria's formal middle time
>   His leaves of rhythm and rhyme.

Hardy had been brought up to believe in a life eternal, but that was not the message of 'The Garden of Proserpine': 'Only a sleep eternal/In an eternal night.' Swinburne did much to confirm Hardy in his agnosticism.

So, without Swinburne's opportunities—aristocratic parentage, Eton and Oxford—Hardy wrote his poetry at night in the

10. The architect's pupil. Hardy aged 19.

11. Horace Moule (1832-73), 'the scholar and critic of perfect taste', who did so much to help and encourage Hardy as a young man.

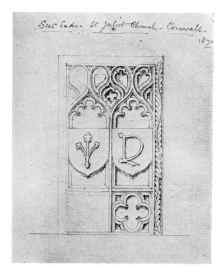

12 Two drawings from Hardy's 'Architectural Notebook': Stinsford Church, left and St Juliot, above.

13. Adelphi Terrace, London, where Hardy worked as assistant to the architect Arthur Blomfield, 1862-67.

loneliness of London lodgings: 'Amabel', with its tolling, Poe-like iteration of the name; 'She to Him', the beginning of a sonnet sequence in the manner of Shakespeare—'When you shall see me in the toils of time'; 'Revulsion', in which he expressed the hope that never again would he love a woman. 'For winning love we win the risk of losing,/And losing love is as one's life were riven.' The susceptible young man was much given to loving and losing. 'Hap':

> If but some vengeful god would call to me
> From up the sky, and laugh: 'Thou suffering thing,
> Know that thy sorrow is my ecstasy,
> That thy love's loss is my hate's profiting!'
>
> Then would I bear it, clench myself, and die,
> Steeled by the sense of ire unmerited;
> Half-eased in that a Powerfuller than I
> Had willed and meted me the tears I shed.
>
> But not so. How arrives it joy lies slain,
> And why unblooms the best hope ever sown?
> —Crass Casualty obstructs the sun and rain,
> And dicing Time for gladness casts a moan.
> These purblind doomsters had as readily strown
> Blisses about my pilgrimage as pain.

Unless Hardy altered this sonnet before it was published 30 years later, it shows that by the time he was 26 he had developed the philosophy which, with modifications, was to underlie all his later work. Man's ills are not the doings of some supernatural sadistic power, nor does he owe his joys to any beneficent Being: 'All is fortune,' hap, chance, luck, circumstance, casualty, Crass Casualty, or whatever we choose to call it. The dice were not loaded against him, the chances were even, but for the moment at least he was playing a losing game.

He sent his verses to magazines, but always they were returned and, out of diffidence or respect for editors' opinions, he rarely sent them twice. He thought of writing blank-verse plays, and even tried to gain experience of the stage, but this came to no more than a walking-on part in a pantomime at Covent Garden. In the ten years of his professional career he had won a medal

for an essay, £3 for a design and £3 15*s* for a short story. He had
failed as a lover, failed as a poet, failed as an architect, and his
health too was failing. He had been home for short holidays from
time to time, but five years of London smoke and fog, of stench
from the river below Adelphi Terrace, of six hours' reading every
night, had weakened him. Blomfield suggested a long holiday
in the country, and when Hardy opportunely received a letter
from Hicks asking if he could recommend an assistant for his
office in Dorchester, he offered to go himself for a time. Moule,
who was then a master at Marlborough College, wrote to say
that he was delighted to hear 'of yr. intended move in our
direction,' and towards the end of July 1867, leaving most of
his belongings, including books and manuscript poems, at
Westbourne Park, he returned to Bockhampton.

CHAPTER FOUR

Dorset again
1867–69

At home Hardy would find his brother Henry, now sixteen, of
an age to join his father in the building business, and his young
sister Kate aged eleven. Mary, after attending Salisbury Training
College, had become a schoolmistress in Dorchester. He had
kept in touch with them all while he had been away, writing often
to Mary, who had also visited him, and sending small presents
to Harry and Kate. His parents, now in their middle fifties,
were well, though his mother, so ambitious for his success, must
have felt some anxiety about his health, and disappointment at
his own lack of ambition and the little progress he had made in
his profession.

So Hardy resumed the routine of five years before: sleeping

at Bockhampton and walking the three miles across the fields to Hicks's office in Dorchester, though now as his paid assistant instead of paying pupil. The exercise and his native air soon restored his health and energy, and he began to wonder how he could best develop his bent for writing. There was, apparently, nothing to be gained by writing verse, but prose was a possibility. He had an intimate knowledge of country life in Dorset, ten years' experience of architecture, and five years' experience of London; by combining the three strands he might write a novel that a publisher would accept and the public buy. He did not work for Hicks regularly, so one day in the early autumn of 1867 he sat at a table in his bedroom at Bockhampton and began the story of *The Poor Man and the Lady: by the Poor Man.* Then, finding that he needed his books and manuscripts, he paid a hurried visit to London and brought back the things he had left there.

By this time, or soon afterwards, he would have renewed acquaintance with his young cousin Tryphena Sparks, who had been only a child when he went to London early in 1862, but was now a girl of sixteen and a half. Her mother was his mother's eldest sister Maria, who had married James Sparks, a cabinet-maker of Puddletown, their first child Rebecca having been born 21 years before Tryphena, who was eight years younger than her favourite brother Nathaniel. She had been educated at Athelhampton village school, about a mile from her home, and was now a student-teacher at Puddletown school preparatory to entering a training college at eighteen. She was an attractive girl, with a mass of dark chestnut hair, dark firmly-drawn eyebrows, brown eyes and a determined mouth, and the young man of 27, so given to falling in love, was attracted by this young cousin.[6]

Hardy was a secretive man, and in his autobiography, *The Life of Thomas Hardy*, ostensibly written by his second wife but clearly written or dictated by him, he makes no mention of Tryphena, save once as 'a cousin' about whom he wrote the poem beginning 'Not a line of her writing have I,' which was published as 'Thoughts of Phena'. But there can be little doubt that sometime before 1870, when Tryphena was 19, he was in love with her, perhaps engaged to her, and that she was an important influence on his life and work, especially after her death.

By the end of 1867 he had finished the rough draft of *The Poor Man and the Lady*, and during the first five months of 1868, in the intervals of working for Hicks, he revised and made a fair copy of his novel, though when he had finished he was in no cheerful mood, and made the note: 'Cures for despair: To read Wordsworth's "Resolution and Independence". Stuart Mill's "Individuality". Carlyle's "Jean Paul Richter".' His depression may have had something to do with the fortunes of Tryphena. On 16 January 1868 the Puddletown School log-book has the entry: 'Reproved pupil teacher for neglect of duty— parents very angry in consequence—determine to withdraw her a month hence.' Four days later another girl was appointed pupil-teacher 'in T. Sparks's place', Tryphena being transferred to the boys' section of the school.[7] There is, however, no further record of her work there; perhaps, though not necessarily, because the original threat was carried out, and she was dis- missed in February. If Hardy's poem of 1890, 'In a Eweleaze near Weatherbury' refers to Tryphena, and they had been meeting on the heath and pastures between Bockhampton and Puddletown, she may occasionally have been late for school, and he have felt responsible for her disgrace and the jeopardising of her career.

He finished the fair copy of his manuscript on 9 June, but it was 25 July before he sent it to the publishing house of Macmillan. The novel was never published, but we have an outline of the plot from Edmund Gosse, to whom Hardy once related it.[8]

The action took place in Dorset in the nineteenth century, and the story was told in the first person by the Poor Man, Will Strong, son of a labourer on the estate of a squire. Will showed such talent at the village school that the squire and his wife took an interest in him, and paid for his further education as an architect's draughtsman. The young Poor Man and the squire's beautiful daughter and heiress, the Lady, fell in love, but when the squire discovered this he compelled Will to go to London, where he became assistant to an eminent architect, made great progress and won a prize, which was withdrawn. (There was a grotesque account of another architect whose mistress, a music-hall dancer, helped him by designing pulpits, altars, crucifixes and other church furniture.) The lovers, considering themselves betrothed, wrote to each other until the squire discovered what was happening, and forbade their correspondence. In his resentment Will took to radical politics.

The squire and his family then left Dorset for London, and one day when Will was passionately addressing a crowd in Trafalgar Square, the Lady drove by in her carriage, and stopped to listen. Offended by his socialism, she broke off all relations with him. Soon afterwards they happened to attend the same concert, when the Lady sat in the back row of the best seats, Will in the front row of the cheaper ones. They were both moved by the music, and he contrived to hold her hand till the end of the performance. As they walked away together she asked him to call openly at their house. He called, but the Lady was out, and he was angrily and contemptuously received by her mother. He lost his temper; the mother fainted; he revived her by pouring water on her face, and the rouge ran down her cheeks. Her rage redoubled, and when her husband came in he ordered the footman to throw him out of the house. The squire and his family then returned to Dorset, and there were no more lovers' letters.

When Will heard that the Lady was about to marry the heir of a neighbouring landowner he hurried down to Dorset, and on the night before the wedding entered the churchyard, where he saw a muffled figure go into the church. He followed, and found himself alone with his Lady. At first she was angry, but then confessed that he was the only man she had ever loved. Hardy himself could not remember if she married the man of her father's choice, but she fell ill, and at her request her father sent for Will. She died, and her father erected a memorial to her, designed by the Poor Man.

Three weeks after posting his manuscript Hardy received a letter from Alexander Macmillan. He had read the novel carefully and much of the writing seemed to him admirable: 'The scene in Rotten Row is full of power and insight,' and 'Will's speech to the working men is full of wisdom.' But there were qualities fatal to the success of the book. The satire was too sweeping: of the upper class, London society, middle-class, Victorian Christianity and morality, politics and church restoration. The 'black-wash' would be taken for ignorant misrepresentation, as would 'the utter heartlessness of *all* the conversations . . . in drawing-rooms and ballrooms about the working-classes.' Thackeray made fun about the upper classes, but 'you mean mischief.' A socialistic novel was not a book for the house of Macmillan, though its author seemed to be, 'at least potentially, of considerable mark, of power and purpose. If this is your first book I think you ought to go on,' Macmillan concluded, and he enclosed the opinion of John Morley, who agreed with him. 'Much of the writing is strong and fresh,' particularly the opening scene on Christmas Eve in the tranter's house. But the story was too loosely constructed and some of the scenes so wildly extravagant that 'they read like some clever lad's dream.'

No doubt this was true enough: there *is* a dreamlike, sometimes nightmarish, quality about some of Hardy's scenes. In his next book, *Desperate Remedies*, there is the midnight scene in which Manston carries the body of his murdered wife in a sack to bury it in a wood, followed by a detective, followed by the murderer's mother, followed by his mistress. Hardy is not a novelist and poet of sunrise and morning, but of sunset, twilight and darkness. Even as a very small boy he would sit on the stairs at home, where the walls were painted venetian red, waiting for the evening sun to intensify the colour, when he would recite to himself the hymn, 'And now another day is gone.'

There were other characteristic elements in *The Poor Man* besides darkness and graveyards. Hardy was not given to boasting, but he did tell Gosse that 'it showed a wonderful insight into female character,' 'I don't know how that came about!' he added. But women attracted him; time and again he had loved and lost, and a capricious woman is at the heart of most of his novels. Then, the theme of the Poor Man and the Lady is that of his first four books, and of some of his later ones, and Hardy himself was the Poor Man of the first. Although he maintained that there was far more autobiography in his poetry than in his novels, his Poor Man is called Strong, and 'strong' is a synonym of 'hardy'. He is the son of workers on a Dorset estate (Kingston Maurward), attends the village school (Lower Bockhampton), where the lady of the manor (Julia Augusta) takes an interest in him; is trained as a draughtsman (Hicks's office) before going to London where he becomes assistant to an architect (Blomfield), and even wins a prize that is not awarded. It is not that the Poor Men are self-portraits; like many other novelists Hardy incorporated his own experiences in his early work, but there was probably more of Hardy and his opinions in Will Strong than in the others. His indignation must have been roused by the appalling condition of the poor in London and, like his hero, shocked into radicalism by what he saw and heard. His later novels, however, were not to be concerned with political satire and, save towards the end, man's inhumanity to man, but with satires of circumstance, and the inhumanity of forces more—or less—than human.

He must have worked very hard between August 1867 and June 1868 to have written and transcribed a novel in the intervals of working for Hicks, and in the autumn he found time to rewrite parts of it in the light of Macmillan's criticism. When he took his manuscript to London in December, however, Macmillan repeated that he could not accept it, but suggested that some other publisher might well do so, and gave him an introduction to Frederick Chapman. So he left it with the firm of Chapman and Hall, and returned to Bockhampton.

As he did not hear from them he went to London again in January 1869 and waited until a letter arrived asking him to call at their shop in Piccadilly. There he had a glimpse of one of his heroes, Carlyle, before Chapman told him they would publish the book if he would guarantee £20 against loss. He agreed, and again left London. But in March he had another letter, asking him to call and meet 'the gentleman who read your manuscript.' To his surprise he found that the gentleman was no less a person than the handsome and theatrical George Meredith, literary adviser to Chapman and Hall, who told him that, though the firm was prepared to publish as agreed, he would be well advised not to 'nail his colours to the mast' in a first book, as it would be so violently attacked by reviewers that his prospects would be injured. Better, he said, rewrite it in a less violent and aggressive manner or, better still, scrap it and write another novel 'with a purely artistic purpose' and a stronger plot. Hardy was so impressed by this man, twelve years his senior, author of half-a-dozen well-known novels and two volumes of poetry, that he took his manuscript away to consider what he should do. At length he decided to make a third attempt, and sent it to the firm of Tinsley Brothers, who promptly returned it.

Another failure. And there was no more work to be had from Hicks. He had died while Hardy was in London, and his practice had been bought by a Weymouth architect, G. R. Crickmay. As, however, Crickmay was no specialist in Gothic, he asked Hardy to help him for a time in finishing the drawings left by Hicks in his Dorchester office; then, his work proving so satisfactory, he offered him a position in his Weymouth office for a period of at least three months. In June, therefore, Hardy moved into lodgings in Weymouth, where he swam in the sea in the early morning and rowed in the bay almost every evening, sometimes, perhaps, with Tryphena: 'They thus sat facing each other in the graceful yellow cockle-shell, and his eyes frequently found a resting-place in the depths of hers.'

That quotation is from the early pages of *Desperate Remedies*, in which a young architect 'of rather humble origin' takes the young lady Cytherea for a row in Budmouth (Weymouth) Bay. For Hardy had begun another novel, and when he had finished his work for Crickmay, and Tryphena, now 18, had gone to Stockwell Training College in London, he remained in his Weymouth lodgings to write the sensational story of Aeneas Manston, 'quite below the level of *The Poor Man and the Lady*,' he thought cynically. Tinsley's had just published Wilkie Collins's new thriller *The Moonstone*, and if thrills were what publishers and the public wanted, they should have them.

14. Kingston Maurward House, Stinsford, the home of Julia Augusta Martin, and 'Knapwater House' of *Desperate Remedies*.

15. Hardy's cousin, Tryphena Sparks, aged 22, when she was a schoolmistress in Plymouth.

16. Emma Lavina Gifford, aged 29, when she met Hardy.

18. (*Opposite*) St Juliot Rectory. 'They sank lower and lower . . . swept round in a curve, and the chimneys and gables became darkly visible.' (*A Pair of Blue Eyes.*)

17. Hardy in 1870, when he met Emma Lavina Gifford at St Juliot Rectory. 'He had a beard ... and quite a business appearance.'

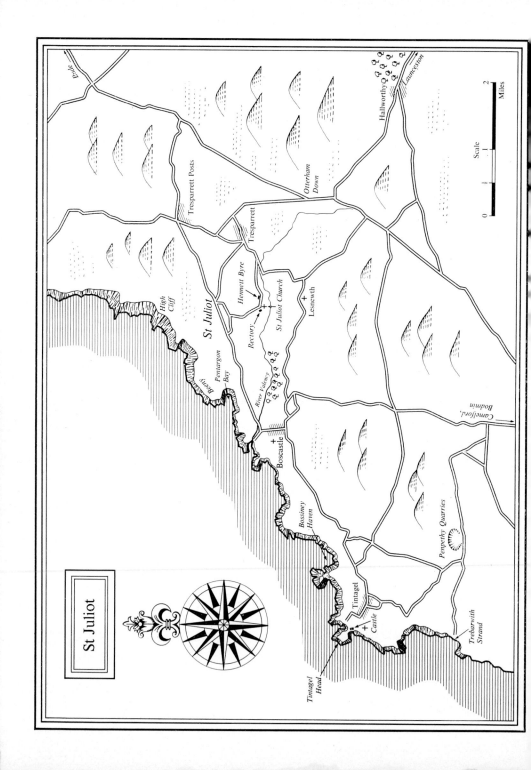

St Juliot

Bude
Tresparrett Posts
Otterham Down
Hallworthy
Launceston
High Cliff
St Juliot
Hennett Byre
Tresparrett
Rectory
St Juliot Church
Lesnewth
Beeny
Pentargon Bay
River Valency
Boscastle
Camelford, Bodmin
Bossiney Haven
Penpethy Quarries
Tintagel
Castle
Tintagel Head
Trebarwith Strand

Scale
0 1 1 2
Miles

CHAPTER FIVE

St Juliot

1870

In the winter of 1869 Hardy had been drawn into a company of gay young dancers in Weymouth, and to escape the distractions of the town and finish his novel he returned to the quiet of Bockhampton at the beginning of February. A few days later he received a note from Crickmay: 'Can you go into Cornwall for me, to take a plan and particulars of a church I am to rebuild there?' The place was St Juliot, which Hicks had visited shortly before his death, and Hardy remembered the romantic name; but as he was writing the last section of his book he declined Crickmay's request. However, another letter persuaded him to change his mind, so, having posted all but the last few chapters of his manuscript to Macmillan, he prepared to make his first excursion into Cornwall.

St Juliot is a high wind-swept parish on the north coast, where it plunges into the sea down the great cliffs that bulk between Beeny and the little port of Boscastle. There is no village, only a few scattered houses, and the church and rectory lie on the steep northern slope of the wooded valley of the little Valency river that scurries towards the sea at Boscastle. Even today the scene is remote, remote as it is beautiful, and for Hardy in 1870, in the early days of the railway, his journey was an adventure into the unknown.

Starting by starlight on the morning of Monday, 7 March, he reached Plymouth in the afternoon, and by four o'clock had crossed the Tamar into Cornwall and was at the White Hart

Hotel in Launceston. There he hired a dogcart to take him the last 16 miles, by Halworthy and Otterham to St Juliot Rectory, a drive that he was soon, and accurately, to describe in the second chapter of *A Pair of Blue Eyes*:

When two or three additional hours had merged the same afternoon in evening, some moving outlines might have been observed against the sky on the summit of a wild lone hill in that district. They circumscribed two men, having at present the aspect of silhouettes, sitting in a dogcart and pushing along in the teeth of the wind. . . .

Fourteen of the sixteen miles intervening between the railway terminus and the end of their journey had been gone over, when they began to pass along the brink of a valley some miles in extent. . . . Another oasis was reached; a little dell lay like a nest at their feet, towards which the driver pulled the horse at a sharp angle, and descended a steep slope which dived under the trees like a rabbit's burrow. They sank lower and lower. . . . They emerged from the bower, swept round in a curve, and the chimneys and gables of the vicarage became darkly visible. Not a light showed anywhere. They alighted; the man felt his way into the porch, and rang the bell.

Meanwhile, Hardy made a brief note in his diary: 'The dreary yet poetical drive over the hills. Arrived at St Juliot Rectory between 6 and 7. Received by young lady in brown.'

The young lady in brown had blue-grey eyes and a mass of corn-coloured hair. She was Emma Lavinia Gifford, daughter of a former solicitor of Plymouth, where she had been born in November 1840, a few months later than Hardy. When the elderly Rev. Caddell Holder married her sister Helen she had escaped from an unhappy home near Bodmin by accompanying them to St Juliot, where she helped with the work of the parish and played the harmonium in the crumbling church. She was lonely, for there was little or no society in the neighbourhood, and she did not like the Cornish peasants as much as those of her native Devonshire; but she was a fine horsewoman and found compensation in galloping over the hills on her beloved mare Fanny, her bright hair streaming in the wind. On the evening of Hardy's arrival her brother-in-law, the Rector, had been taken ill with gout; while her sister was tending him the door-bell rang, and she had to receive the unknown architect alone. Hardy was to describe this momentous meeting as she might have experienced it:

> On that gray night of mournful drone,
> Apart from aught to hear, to see,
> I dreamt not that from shires unknown
>   In gloom, alone,
>   By Halworthy,
> A man was drawing near to me . . .
>
>   Where Otterham lay,
> A man was riding up my way . . .
>
> The man had passed Tresparret Posts . . .
>
>   By Hennett Byre
> The man was getting nigh and nigher.
>
> There was a rumble at the door,
> A draught disturbed the drapery,
> And but a minute passed before,
>   With gaze that bore
>   My destiny,
> The man revealed himself to me.

In her 'Recollections', a manuscript found after her death, Emma gave her own version of the meeting:

I was immediately arrested by his familiar appearance, as if I had seen him in a dream—his slightly different accent, his soft voice; also I noticed a blue paper sticking out of his pocket. . . . I thought him much older than he was. He had a beard, and a rather shabby greatcoat, and had quite a business appearance. Afterwards he seemed younger. . . . The blue paper proved to be the MS. of a poem, and not a plan of the church, he informed me, to my surprise.

That night, after dinner and a visit to the Rector's room, there was music.

On the next morning, Tuesday, Hardy walked down the road to the church, where he would find the little walled churchyard brimming with snowdrops. While he was measuring and drawing there was a funeral, and a man tolled a bell by lifting the clapper and letting it fall against its side. The tower was cracked, and the bells had been removed and placed upside down in the dilapidated transept. On Wednesday, Mrs Holder took him and Emma for a drive along the coast, from Boscastle to Tintagel and Trebarwith Strand, then inland to Penpethy quarries, where he selected greenish-coloured slate for roofing the church. He treasured the vision of the fair young woman against the slate background, and 50 years later celebrated the visit in the poem 'Green Slates'. There was music again in the evening, when the sisters sang duets.

On Thursday, Hardy took a holiday. In the morning 'Went with E.L.G. to Beeny Cliff. She on horseback.' And in the afternoon the sisters walked part of the way to Boscastle with him, though 'E.' provokingly read as she walked. Before dinner they sat in the garden overlooking the Valency valley, and afterwards there was more music.

Friday, 'March 11. Dawn. Adieu. E.L.G. had struck a light six times in her anxiety to call the servants early enough for me. The journey home.' Many years later Hardy described their parting in 'At the Word "Farewell"'. He had to drive the 16 miles back to Launceston to catch his train, and candles were alight on the breakfast-table when he entered the dining-room, the french window of which opened on to the lawn, where he could just see Emma, 'like a bird from a cloud'. Probably he would never see her again, but irresistibly impelled he stepped through the casement:

> Even then the scale might have been turned
>   Against love by a feather,
> —But crimson one cheek of hers burned
>   When we came in together.

The poem may have been a composite recollection, the first kiss given at a later parting, but it seems clear that Hardy was already attracted by the 'so living' young woman with the fair hair and blue eyes. Certainly the poem 'When I Set out for Lyonnesse', written sometime after his return, rings with the authentic triumph of a love lyric:

> When I came back from Lyonnesse
>   With magic in my eyes.

All marked with mute surmise
My radiance rare and fathomless,
When I came back from Lyonnesse
With magic in my eyes!

Radiance must have been tinged with anxiety by this turn of events, but meanwhile there was work to be done, and he moved from Bockhampton back to Weymouth lodgings to report to Crickmay and prepare detailed drawings for the restoration of St Juliot church—and await news about his novel. It came on 5 April, when his manuscript was returned; the sensational *Desperate Remedies* was no more to the liking of Macmillan than the satirical *Poor Man and the Lady*. So he packed up the pages again and sent them to Tinsley's, a firm much more likely to publish such a book, and waited. A month later he had a reply, stating the terms on which they were prepared to accept it, provided he sent them the last few chapters, of which they had only a synopsis.

By this time he was finishing his work for Crickmay, and in the middle of May he went to London, though there was no obvious reason for his going. He seems to have done nothing about Tinsley and the remaining chapters of his novel, and in the *Life* we are told that 'he went sadly, for he had left his heart in Cornwall,' and that 'it is not clear what he was waiting for there.' Two days after his arrival he visited the Royal Academy and admired Gérôme's painting of 'The Death of Ney', then renewed contact with Blomfield whom he helped to finish some drawings; and Blomfield introduced him to Raphael Brandon, a champion of English Gothic as opposed to French, and for him he also worked desultorily for a time. Then, Horace Moule was in London, still a regular critic for the *Saturday Review* and *Literary Gazette*, but now an Inspector of Workhouses in East Anglia, and he told him of his 'vague understanding' with Emma. Possibly his reason for lingering for three months in London was to see Tryphena, then enduring the spartan regime of Stockwell Training College, just across the river in Clapham. Yet all this time he and Emma were exchanging letters, and he wrote a 'Ditty' for 'E.L.G.' at St Juliot, 'That no spot on earth excels/Where she dwells!' If Tryphena's holiday began in August, he did not go back with her to Dorset, but on the sixth took the train for Plymouth, Launceston and Lyonnesse.

At St Juliot he found the young lady in brown transformed into a young lady in blue, a colour matching her eyes, and much more becoming her fair complexion and hair. The Rector and his wife took them for drives along the coast, notably to Tintagel and its fabled Castle of King Arthur. And they walked together. down the Valency valley, where they sketched, talked of books, and picnicked, one day losing a tiny tumbler under a waterfall of the stream. On longer expeditions Emma rode on Fanny while Hardy walked beside her, to Pentargon and Beeny and High Cliff beyond. It was the summer of the Franco-Prussian War, and on 18 August, when the battle of Gravelotte was fought, they were reading Tennyson together in the Rectory garden, and watching a man and his horse harrowing a field in the valley below where couch-grass was burning: an incident which, remembered 45 years later, was to inspire a poem of another war: 'Only a man harrowing clods/In a slow silent walk.'

Before leaving St Juliot he must have given final instructions to a builder about the demolition and rebuilding of the tower and north aisle of the church, and restoration of the remainder, of which he had made careful drawings. And he must have talked to Emma about his novel, for on his return to Dorset he wrote the last chapters, revised the earlier part, and sent it to her in instalments, of which she made fair copies. In rewriting he added a remark that she had made about Beeny, applying it to a barren down where 'it never looked like summer': and the eighteen-year-old heroine, Cytherea, who may originally have been the dark-haired Tryphena, became, in appearance at least, the young lady of St Juliot:

Her hair rested gaily upon her shoulders in curls and was of a shining corn yellow in the high lights, deepening to a definite nut-brown as each curl wound round into the shade. She had eyes of a sapphire hue. . . .

In December he returned his revised and completed manuscript to Tinsley, who demanded an advance of £75 as a guarantee against loss; and in his copy of *Hamlet* Hardy wrote the date

'December 15, 1870' against the passage: 'Thou wouldst not think how ill all's here about my heart.'

There were other reasons for despondency besides this risking of half his capital on the success of his novel. The fair young lady of thirty who had 'opened the door of Romance' to him was displacing his dark-haired, dark-eyed cousin of nineteen. Yet he was not in a position to marry: he had no money, and little prospect of making any. Soon after his return from Cornwall he had made the note about the figure that stood in front with arm uplifted, ready 'to knock us back from any pleasant prospect we indulge in as probable,' and was no doubt thinking of the difficulties that lay before him if he were to choose Emma rather than Tryphena. She was the Lady, daughter of a solicitor, albeit bankrupt, and niece of a Canon of Worcester, but poor as himself, the Poor Man, son of a working-builder, a 'low-born churl' as her father was to call him, and it was not easy for the poor and low-born to marry into the family of a Victorian gentleman.

CHAPTER SIX

Two Novels

1871–73

Hardy was in London in January 1871, when he paid Tinsley his £75—in cash—before returning to Bockhampton to correct the proofs of his novel. At the same time he was collecting what remained of the fast-dying country ballads from the lips of old people who remembered them from the days before the arrival of city culture with the railway, and which he had heard sung when a child. During his verse-writing years of 1866–67 he had himself written a ballad in the traditional manner—'The Fire at

Tranter Sweatley's', a modestly bawdy tragi-comedy about a girl whose uncle compels her to marry a drunken old carrier, who accidentally sets fire to his house and himself on his wedding-night, while the girl is rescued by her young lover:

> Her cold little buzzoms half naked he views
>   Played about by the frolicsome breeze;
> Her light-tripping totties, her ten little tooes,
> All bare and besprinkled wi' Fall's chilly dews,
> While her great frightened eyes through her ringlets so loose
>   Sheened like stars through a tangle o' trees.[9]

It is delightfully done, and helpful for the understanding of Hardy; for many of his short stories, and even his novels, are basically romantic ballads in prose. Moreover, the episode of the fire and tell-tale bone was used again in *Desperate Remedies*, which was published anonymously on 25 March.

The essential characters are: the wealthy lady of the manor Miss Aldclyffe, her illegitimate son Aeneas Manston, the young architect Edward Springrove, and Cytherea Graye, orphaned daughter of a man who loved but lost Miss Aldclyffe when she was a girl. The essential action is the rivalry of Springrove and Manston, aided by his mother, for Cytherea. As Manston is married, he gets rid of his wife, marries Cytherea, is suspected first of bigamy then of murder, is discovered, and hangs himself in gaol. Miss Aldclyffe dies, leaving her estate to Cytherea, who marries Edward Springrove.

Hardy laboured under two difficulties. The standard Victorian novel was a three-volume, 'three-decker', affair of some 900 pages, too many for the matter of most authors. Then, he became involved in serial publication in magazines, and had to bowdlerise his stories for family reading. *Desperate Remedies*, however, was not a serial story, but it would be much more effective if only half the length, and some of the finest of the later novels, *The Woodlanders* for example, would have been even better if he had not been obliged to pad.

As *Desperate Remedies* is Hardy's first published novel, it is worth considering in some detail. The theme is taken from *The Poor Man and the Lady*, Edward Springrove now playing the

19. St Juliot Church, showing the tower and north aisle,
formerly the nave, rebuilt under Hardy's direction.

20. A group at St Juliot Rectory in 1870. Emma Gifford
standing between her sister Helen, Mrs Holder, and
the Rev. Caddell Holder.

21. 'Vallency Valley / With stream and leafed alley.'

22. Boscastle Harbour, at the mouth of the River Valency.

part of the Poor Man, Cytherea that of the Lady; and there are obvious outcrops of *The Poor Man*, such as the satirical, 'They went along Pall Mall on foot, where in place of the usual well-dressed clubbists—rubicund with alcohol—were to be seen, in linen pinafores, flocks of house-painters pallid with white lead.' Then, the scene is that of *The Poor Man*: Hardy's native parish of Stinsford. Miss Aldclyffe lives at Knapwater House (i.e. Kingston Maurward), 'regularly and substantially built of clean grey freestone throughout, in that plainer fashion of Greek classicism which prevailed at the latter end of the last century.' Nearby is the original Tudor manor house, 'an Elizabethan fragment, consisting of as much as could be contained under three gables and a cross roof behind.' Naturally, Hardy delighted in architectural detail: 'The mullioned and transomed windows, containing five or six lights. . . .' The garden slopes down to a narrow river (the Frome), beyond which is the footpath (from Lower Bockhampton to Stinsford and Dorchester) where Edward Springrove meets Cytherea on the evening of her marriage with Manston.

There is autobiography in this background, with every inch of which Hardy had been familiar since his childhood, and there is more detailed autobiography in the career of Edward Springrove. Cytherea's brother, Owen, describes him:

He is a thorough artist, but a man of rather humble origin . . . the son of a farmer, or something of the kind. . . . He's about six-and-twenty . . . a thorough bookworm . . . knows Shakespeare to the very dregs of the foot-notes. Indeed, he's a poet himself in a small way . . . an impulsive fellow who has been made to pay the penalty of his rashness in some love affair.

(Edward is already engaged when he meets Cytherea.) He is a draughtsman (like Will Strong, like Hardy) in the office of a Weymouth architect, and rows with Cytherea (Tryphena?) in the bay before—here Hardy reverses events—going to London 'to advance his profession.' Springrove's opinions, too, are Hardy's:

But I shan't advance . . . worldly advantage from an art doesn't depend upon mastering it. I used to think it did: but it doesn't.

Those who get rich need have no skill at all as artists. .... From having already loved verse passionately, I went on to read it continually: then I went rhyming myself. If anything on earth ruins a man for useful occupation ... it is the habit of writing verses on emotional subjects.

And the author himself adds the comment that, while poetry develops the capacity for married love of the highest and purest kind, it precludes its realisation, for it does not afford the means. 'The man who works up a good income has had no time to learn love to its solemn extreme; the man who has learnt that has had no time to get rich.' He had no desire to get rich, but he had to have money enough to marry; that is why he had abandoned verse and turned to the next best thing, prose, the writing of novels. Tennyson was an exception, and lived by his poetry, but Meredith by his prose; and if Thackeray, Dickens, George Eliot, Trollope and Wilkie Collins could make a living out of writing novels, so might he—and perhaps marry Emma Gifford.

This comment on poetry and marriage is a revelation of Hardy's difficulties at this time, as is this of his sensitivity: 'Now it is a noticeable fact that we do not much mind what men think of us, or what humiliating secret they discover of our means, parentage, or object, provided that each thinks and acts thereupon in isolation.' It is the gossiping about the skeletons in our cupboards that is intolerable. But in this first book Hardy felt that he should, like other Victorian novelists, introduce aphoristic reflections of a more general nature to show his knowledge of the world, such as: 'What is Wisdom really? A steady handling of any means to bring about any end necessary to happiness.' And, 'The sudden withdrawal of what was superfluous at first, is often felt as an essential loss.' And, 'The chief pleasure connected with asking an opinion lies in not adopting it.' Then there are the little selfconscious pedantries introduced to impress the reader: comparisons with paintings in the National Gallery, literary allusions—'like Beatrice accusing Dante from the chariot', 'as Coleridge happily writes it'—and a seasoning of Latin quotations. These things are not characteristic, however. In his later and best work he does not thus clumsily intrude, but becomes an unseen, pervasive presence of which we are always half-consciously aware, a quality that he shares with Shakespeare and others of the highest rank in the hierarchy of literature.

There are other elements in this first novel, however, that are characteristic of his later work, though here, as we should expect, generally in a cruder and exaggerated form. Aeneas Manston, for example, is an illegitimate son, and illegitimacy was something of an obsession with Hardy. Although he was not himself illegitimate, he was born less than six months after his parents' marriage, and he fiddled with his family pedigree to obscure any aberrations. And whenever a child, generally a boy, is introduced as a character in his novels and short stories the chances are that there is something odd about his birth, like the small boy in 'The Withered Arm', and Father Time in *Jude*.

Night, if not an obsession, was always a fascination, and in *Desperate Remedies* there must be as many scenes by night as there are by day; not the kind of night when the sky is pierced by the light of planets and stars, as prosaically observed by Gabriel Oak when he wants to know the time, or more scientifically and poetically by Swithin St Cleeve when he observes the constellations from the top of his tower, but an enveloping blackness made even more obscure by the light of a candle, a lantern or a fire. From under 'the dense shadow of inky boughs' Manston watches a train approaching from the blackness of a cutting: a fountain of sparks, a red glare, a rapid flashing of illuminated windows, through one of which he sees the profile of his detested wife. He thanks God on his knees when she has been burned, as he thinks, in the fire that consumes the inn, and after murdering her hides the body by the light of a candle. Fire by night is far more dramatic than fire by day, and night fires are a frequent occurrence, from the burning of Bathsheba's ricks to the beacons on Rainbarrow in *The Return of the Native* and *The Dynasts*.

Here, too, in *Desperate Remedies* are the first of the innumerable church and churchyard scenes of the novels. Manston takes the reluctant Cytherea into Carriford church: 'Everything in the place was the embodiment of decay: the fading red glare from the setting sun, which came in at the west window, emphasising the end of the day and all its cheerful doings' (one thinks of the small boy sitting on the stairs with their venetian-red walls, and reciting, 'Now another day is gone'), 'the mildewed walls, the uneven paving-stones, the wormy pews' (memories of a church restorer) . . . 'and the dank air of death which had gathered with the evening.' After their marriage, by the light of candles streaming from the vestry, Cytherea sees Edward, or his spirit, almost hanging to a monument 'sculptured in cadaverous marble'. And last scene of all, a more cheerful, though somewhat mysterious one, takes place on Midsummer Night, 1867, in the belfry.

The book is a sequence of such grotesque and melodramatic incidents. There is the strange Lesbian scene in which Miss Aldclyffe persuades Cytherea to come into her bed. They have nightmares, and Cytherea hears a rattle that reminds her of her mother's death. Manston plays the organ in the crumbling manor house to the accompaniment of thunder and lightning. As the fire consumes the inn and adjoining cottages, 'the church clock opposite slowly struck the hour of midnight, and the bewildered chimes, scarcely heard amid the crackling of the flames, wandered through the wayward air of the Old Hundred-and-Thirteenth Psalm.' Manston tries to drug the woman who is posing as his murdered wife and, after being discovered in the act of burying her body, breaks into Cytherea's house, chases her until she faints, and has a desperate struggle with Edward before being captured and hanging himself.

Melodrama is heightened by coincidence. Cytherea unwittingly becomes the companion of the woman who was her father's first love and, by chance, Owen hears a strange story of her girlhood from a man, then a Londoner, but now employed in the neighbourhood. Brother and sister discuss these coincidences in the garden, and happen to be overheard by a woman behind the hedge. Hardy's novels are full of these ingeniously contrived accidents, and coincidence, or chance, is a major determinant of the fortunes and misfortunes of his characters: as when Mrs Yeobright visits Eustacia while Clym is asleep and Wildeve in the house, and Tess slips her written confession under Angel's door and, as luck would have it, under the carpet as well—an almost impossible feat.

Overhearing, as distinct from eavesdropping, is a matter of chance: as when Manston overhears two drunken poachers behind the high settle of an inn discussing himself and his actions on the night of the fire. Hardy's hearing appears to have been abnormally acute—'Every word was clear and distinct, in the still air of the dawn, to the distance of a quarter of a mile'— and this sensitivity accounts for the prominent part played by sound in description, imagery and atmosphere; in *The Return of the Native*, the rubbing of reeds 'like a congregation praying humbly,' the 'worn whisper, dry and papery' of the wind in myriads of mummied heath-bells. Throughout *Desperate Remedies* the scene is haunted by two sounds, sometimes near, more often remote, but always there: one is the sound of a waterfall, the other of a pumping-engine, a whistling creak of cranks, with a sousing noise between each creak. It is to the rush of the waterfall and creak of the engine that Manston kills his wife, and between the two that he buries her. The sleepless Cytherea hears the distant whistle and metallic creak, 'like a plough, or a rusty wheelbarrow', and the gloomy murmur of the waterfall evokes its midnight image: 'Black at the head, and over the surface of the deep cold hole into which it fell; white and frothy at the fall; black and white, like a pall and its border.'

More frequently, of course, the imagery is evoked by the thing seen rather than heard, Thus, 'Like Nature in the tropics, with her hurricanes and the subsequent luxuriant vegetation effacing the ravages, Miss Aldclyffe compensated for her outbursts by excess of generosity afterwards.' And her solicitor 'surveyed everybody's character in a sunless and shadowless northern light.' Each is a vivid character-sketch in a few words, but there is little of the imagery that makes Hardy's later descriptive writing so memorable, and that of the hot evening sky at Lulworth is exceptional: 'The light so intensified the colours that they seemed to stand above the surface of the earth and float in mid-air like an exhalation of red.'

Occasionally the atmosphere of mystery and gloom is relieved by the commenting chorus of rustics, Clerk Crickett, Gad Weedy and the rest: ''Tis jest the house for a nice ghastly hair-on-end story, that would make the parish religious.' This comic relief is, of course, borrowed from Shakespeare, and there is much of Elizabethan, or rather Jacobean, melodrama in the plot and atmosphere of *Desperate Remedies,* and a touch of its poetry, too. But it is of Webster rather than of Shakespeare that the novel reminds us. The villain of *The White Devil* dies to the words 'I am i' the way to study a long silence,' and the last words of Manston's confession read: 'I am now about to enter on my normal condition. For people are almost always in their graves. When we survey the long race of men, it is strange and still more strange [that comes from *Measure for Measure,* most Websterian of Shakespeare's plays] to find that they are mainly dead men [an echo of the echo in *The Duchess of Malfi*: 'Thou art a dead thing.'] who have scarcely ever been otherwise.'

Desperate Remedies is ingenious—Hardy classed it among his Novels of Ingenuity—but by no means a great novel. Nor was it one that he wished to write; he was only following Meredith's advice to attempt a novel with a stronger plot in the hope of producing a best-seller. As he told Macmillan, his object was 'simply to construct an intricate puzzle,' the characters being merely pegs on which to hang the plot, about as real as those in a fairy-story. It is more than this; Cytherea is real enough, the first of his heroines, an adumbration of the easily hypnotised Grace Melbury; but although it gives us glimpses of what was to come, it lacks the essential elements of his art: his profound appreciation of the Dorset scene, and unique experience of country life and the country folk among whom he had been born and bred. A week after its publication the reviews began to appear. The *Athenaeum* considered it a powerful story, though in some respects unpleasant and coarse in expression; the rustic characters were exceedingly good, and it predicted a bright future for the unknown author. The *Morning Post* pronounced it an eminent success, but the *Spectator* was shocked by the writer's audacity in suggesting that an unmarried lady could be the mother of a child: 'The law is hardly just which prevents Tinsley Brothers from concealing their participation also.' After the first shock Hardy could afford to ignore such nonsense, but one remark stung him: the suggestion that it was 'a desperate remedy for a desperate purse.' It was true. He had written the book to make money, but, though he did not forfeit the whole of his guarantee, he was £15 poorer than when he began, and the prospect of marriage as remote as ever. Moule tried to comfort him, and wrote an encouraging article in the *Saturday Review*, too late however to make the book a success.

Hardy was at this time working for Crickmay in Weymouth, primarily, no doubt, to keep in touch with St Juliot, which he visited on his behalf in May, when he would have found the old church tower, north aisle and transept demolished, and re-building begun. 'The rarity of the visits made them highly delightful to both,' wrote Emma, 'We talked much of plots, possible scenes, tales and poetry, and of his own work.' But any magic that he may have carried with him from Lyonnesse was dimmed when he saw copies of his novel remaindered for half-a-crown on a bookstall at Exeter station; and in July he marked the passage in *Macbeth*: 'Things at the worst will cease, or else climb upward/To what they were before.'

He was determined to make them climb upward if he could. He had followed Meredith's advice and failed, but there remained Morley's opinion of *The Poor Man*: 'The opening pictures of the Christmas-eve in the tranter's house are really of good quality.' So, while helping Crickmay with his gothic drawings in the summer of 1871, he took the tranter scenes and poorman-and-lady theme from his rejected novel and wove them into an imaginary account of the musical exploits of his father and grandfather in Stinsford before he was born. His first title for the book was *The Mellstock Quire*, but this he changed to *Under the Greenwood Tree*, and in August sent his manuscript to Macmillan. It was read by John Morley, who praised it for its delicacy and harmony of treatment. But the opening scenes were too long, the writer lacking 'sufficient sparkle and humour'—an odd criticism; but then Morley was not remarkable for sparkle and humour—to carry off such an extended description of a trifle. Nor was the book likely to have much of a sale. Yet, 'it is good work, and would please people whose taste is not ruined by novels of exaggerated action or forced ingenuity.' Morley knew who was the author of *Desperate Remedies*. The report was not sufficiently encouraging for Macmillan, who told Hardy that he could not publish the book just then, and returned the manuscript.

Having been abused for his coarseness, it was something to be praised for his delicacy, but Hardy threw the manuscript into a box with his unpublished poems, and wrote to Emma to say that he had abandoned writing as a career. She replied that she had every faith in him as a writer, and begged him to go on, even if it meant a further postponement of marriage. Moule, too, advised him not to give up writing altogether. But in the last months of 1871 Hardy worked steadily for Crickmay, and at the beginning of 1872 returned to London and the Westbourne Park lodgings to resume the architectural work that he had left in 1867 to make his excursion into novel-writing.

It was just at this critical time in his career that Tryphena finished her two-year course at Stockwell Training College. She had done very well and, though she was only twenty, applied for the post of Headmistress of the Girls' Department of Plymouth Public Free School. Evidently her 'neglect of duty' as a pupil-teacher at Puddletown school was not taken very seriously, for she was appointed, and at Christmas 1871 moved into the school-house and took up her duties. At the beginning of 1872, therefore, by one of life's little ironies, positions were reversed. Instead of Hardy in Dorset, between Tryphena in London and Emma in Lyonnesse, he was now in London and Tryphena in Plymouth on the border of Cornwall, only 30 miles from St Juliot. Moreover, by a further irony, he was engaged in designing schools. Before 1870 elementary education had been provided for some children by the Churches, but in that year the State assumed the duty of educating the remainder. It was not entirely free, nor was it compulsory, but this revolutionary Education Act of 1870 meant the erection of a vast number of new schools for the Boards who managed them, and the architect with whom Hardy had found employment, Professor Roger Smith, was preparing designs for the London School Board.

It was while working for Smith, and occasionally for Blomfield in the evening, that one day in the Strand he met Tinsley, who asked him when he was going to let him have another novel. 'Never,' Hardy replied; but when pressed he admitted that he had recently written a short novel, though he was not sure where it was. As Tinsley urged him to find it, he wrote to his parents, telling them where to look, and asking them to send it. At the beginning of April, therefore, he delivered the manuscript to Tinsley, who offered him £30 for the copyright. Hardy agreed, and casually mentioned that he had outlined another novel, which he might go on with. His resolution to stick to architecture was breaking down.

Tinsley worked quickly, for *Under the Greenwood Tree*: 'A Rural Painting of the Dutch School by the Author of "Desperate Remedies",' was published towards the end of May, shortly before Hardy's thirty-second birthday. The title, of course, was taken from the song in *As You Like It*:

> Under the greenwood tree,
> Who loves to lie with me,
> And turn his merry note
> Unto the sweet bird's throat,
> Come hither, come hither, come hither:
> Here shall he see
> No enemy
> But winter and rough weather.

And the novel strikes the unmistakable Hardy note at once:

To dwellers in a wood almost every species of tree has its voice as well as its feature. At the passing of the breeze the fir-trees sob and moan no less distinctly than they rock; the holly whistles as it battles with itself; the ash hisses. . . .

On a cold and starry Christmas-eve within living memory a man was passing up a lane towards Mellstock Cross in the darkness of a plantation that whispered thus distinctively to his intelligence. . ..

Trees, sounds, night, a road, and a solitary man. A few years later the lines might have been prelude to some sombre story, but here they introduce a rural comedy of two young lovers and their neighbours, where there is no rough weather and winter is no enemy. What had most pleased the reviewers of *Desperate Remedies* had been the rustic characters, who, however, played a very minor part, but here all are countryfolk except the parson; and though the scene is again Hardy's native parish, it is without the manor house and grounds, and virtually confined to Bockhampton, Stinsford church and vicarage, and the path between, with occasional excursions to Weymouth and Yellowham Wood near Puddletown. It is the first of the Novels of Character and Environment, and what makes it so endearing is that the characters and environment are those of Hardy's childhood; as though he were the youngest of the Dewy children, the four-year-old Charley, wonderingly absorbing the impressions that he was to describe nearly 30 years later.

The characters are not portraits, neither are they caricatures, but lovingly created and real as those who once sat and chatted with Justice Shallow in his Cotswold orchard; Tranter Reuben, genial and easy-going as Hardy's father; grandfather William, whose two passions are the bass-viol and cleaving apple-tree wood; the diminutive bootmaker, Mr Robert Penny, with his flashing spectacles; Elias Spinks, who walks 'perpendicularly and dramatically' and talks in hints like Corporal Nym: 'I know little, 'tis true—I say no more . . . Maybe I've read a leaf or two in my time.' The tranter's cottage is the Hardy home: 'a long low cottage with a hipped roof of thatch, having dormer windows breaking up into the eaves, a chimney standing in the middle of the ridge, and another at each end.' On the left of the entrance was the living-room, with a beam bisecting the ceiling, just as it does today; and how good was the talk within it on that Christmas Eve of more than a century ago. Here is Reuben on the subject of truth: 'My sonnies, all true stories have a coarse touch or a bad moral, depend upon't. If the story-tellers could ha' got decency and good morals from true stories, who'd ha' troubled to invent parables?' And old William on the degeneracy of church music:

They should ha' stuck to strings. Your brass-man is a rafting dog—well and good; your reed-man is a dab at stirring ye—well and good; your drum-man is a rare bowel-shaker—good again. But I don't care who hears me say it, nothing will spak to your heart wi' the sweetness of the man of strings! . . . But clarinets was death. And harmonions—harmonions and barrel-organs be miserable—what shall I call 'em? —miserable dumbledores!

The lovers, naturally, are somewhat apart from their elders. Dick Dewy is a staunch, diffident young fellow of twenty, who is sometimes driven almost distracted by the girlish vanity and coquetry of Fancy Day. As part of the novel seems to have been written before Hardy met Emma, there may be something of Tryphena in Fancy: of more than average height, flexible and graceful, she has plentiful knots of dark-brown hair, and dark eyes arched by brows 'like two slurs in music'. And, like Tryphena, she is a newly appointed headmistress who moves into her school-house at Christmas.

The writing is light and delicate as the idyll itself, the prose of a poet to whom images come spontaneously: stars twinkle so vehemently that their flickering seems 'like the flapping of wings', and a limp rasher of bacon hangs down between the bars of a gridiron 'like a cat in a child's arms'. The one brief shadow of trouble is when Fancy, secretly engaged to Dick, succumbs to ambition and accepts the vicar's offer of marriage. She soon repents, however, withdraws her acceptance, and asks him to keep her indiscretion for ever a secret. He agrees, but adds: 'Tell him everything; it is best. He will forgive you.' But the story ends:

> From a neighbouring thicket was suddenly heard to issue in a loud, musical, and liquid voice—
> 'Tippiwit! swe-e-et! ki-ki-ki! Come hither, come hither, come hither!'
> 'O, 'tis the nightingale,' murmured she, and thought of a secret she would never tell.

No doubt Dick and Fancy lived happily ever after, but Parson Maybold's advice, if followed, would have saved some of Hardy's later heroines from tragic consequences.

The *Pall Mall Gazette* complained that this episode with the vicar marred the simple character of the tale, but was full of praise for everything else, particularly for the descriptions and conversations of the choir, and in the *Saturday Review* Moule called it 'the best prose idyl that we have seen for a long time past.' Although sales were slow, reviews were so encouraging that Tinsley asked Hardy how much he would want for a story

to run as a serial for about twelve monthly issues of *Tinsleys'*
Magazine. As his three novels, the first one unpublished, had
brought him in a total of £15, Hardy was cautious. He had
already drafted another story and it would not take him long to
write, but it must pay better than architecture. When he said he
would do it for £200 Tinsley readily, too readily, agreed, and
Hardy spent that night studying the law of copyright. Tinsley
was taken aback when he told him the next day that the £200
was for the serial rights only, not the volume edition, but again
agreed, provided he should have the right of publishing the
book. In this way Hardy began his career as a writer of serials,
as profitable as it was frustrating, for he had to be careful to
write nothing that would offend the family circle or Mrs Grundy.

He had only a fortnight in which to supply his first instalment
for the September issue of the magazine, so telling Professor
Smith that he would like a holiday, he returned to his lodgings
and began to write. He worked quickly, for on 7 August he
sailed from London to Plymouth, whence he went to Kirland
House, near Bodmin, where Emma was staying with her father.
The poem 'Near Lanivet'—Lanivet is a village a few miles west
of Bodmin—makes it clear that the visit was an unhappy one,
as does 'I Rose and Went to Rou'tor Town', the sombre converse
of 'When I Set out for Lyonnesse'. 'She' speaks:

> I rose and went to Rou'tor Town
>   With gaiety and good heart. . . .
>
> When sojourn soon at Rou'tor Town
>   Wrote sorrows on my face. . . .
>
> The evil wrought at Rou'tor Town
>   On him I'd loved so true
>   I cannot tell anew:
> But nought can quench, but nought can drown
> The evil wrought at Rou'tor Town
>   On him I'd loved so true!

They drove the 20 miles to St Juliot, a name inevitably suggestive
of the youthful star-crossed lovers, Romeo and Juliet, and the
scene of his novel, *A Pair of Blue Eyes*.

It may have been now that he found to his dismay that the contractor in charge of the church restoration had replaced an Early English window with a meaningless Victorian one, and a fifteenth-century rood-screen with one of varnished deal. 'Well,' said the generous builder, 'I said to myself, "Please God, now I am about it, I'll do the thing well, cost what it will!"' 'Where's the old screen?' Hardy asked appalled. 'Used up to boil the workmen's kittles; though 'a were not much good at that!' Soon afterwards the restored church was opened by the Bishop of Exeter, but Hardy was not there. Journeys from London or Bockhampton were expensive for a poor man.

He seems to have been in no hurry to get back to London after this August visit of 1872, for he returned by way of Bath. Then, finding London debilitating, in September he returned to Bockhampton, where he finished the novel by the end of the year. By May 1873 it had run through ten issues of the magazine, and in the last week of the month it was published in three volumes: '*A Pair of Blue Eyes*. A Novel. By Thomas Hardy, Author of "Under the Greenwood Tree", "Desperate Remedies", Etc.' It was the first time his name had appeared as the author.

After his first visits to St Juliot in 1870, it was only natural that he should have thought of writing a novel about such a romantic region, have drawn up an outline, and even written parts of it, before throwing the script aside when Macmillan declined *Under the Greenwood Tree*. Up to a point, therefore, *A Pair of Blue Eyes* is an account of what bechanced at Lyonnesse in that memorable year, a continuation of his autobiography. It is true that Stephen Smith, the young Adonis with bright curly hair, is not Hardy; but he is an architect, and the son of a mason. Nor is Elfride Swancourt, an immature girl of 19, Emma Gifford; but she has blue eyes, corn-coloured hair, and is devoted to riding on her mare Pansy. We meet her in the first chapter, when she is waiting in the vicarage of Endelstow, a remote parish on the Cornish coast, for an architect who is coming to make drawings for the restoration of the church. Her father, the vicar, is in bed, suffering from gout. The second chapter describes Stephen's drive from Launceston to the vicarage, where he is received by the fair-haired, blue-eyed young lady. After a meal he goes upstairs to see the vicar, and then Elfride plays and sings to him. The next day he inspects the church, and the vicar drives them to Pentargon and along the coast. As they climb the hill from Boscastle to the vicarage, the horse adopts a 'deliberate stalk' and the young couple jump out to ease the load, an incident remembered long afterwards in the poem 'At Castle Boterel':

> . . . Myself and a girlish form benighted
>> In dry March weather. We climb the road
> Beside a chaise. We had just alighted
>> To ease the sturdy pony's load
>> When he sighed and slowed.
>
> What we did as we climbed, and what we talked of
>> Matters not much, nor to what it led. . . .
>
> It filled but a minute. But was there ever
>> A time of such quality, since or before,
> In that hill's story? To one mind never. . . .

Next morning they breakfast by candlelight, and Stephen leaves by the grey light of dawn. He returns in August, when he walks beside Elfride on her pony Pansy to Beeny and beyond. Then, like Emma's father, Elfride's is a bankrupt snob, who dismisses Stephen when he discovers his lowly origin.

Up to this point the novel is a fairly accurate account of Hardy's first two visits to St Juliot, though Stephen and Elfride are ten years younger than were he and Emma when they met, as Henry Knight, 'a man of thirty', is ten years younger than Horace Moule, obviously the original of, though very different from, Stephen's adored and patronising patron, the celebrated reviewer. Moule never met Emma and, apart from a few episodes such as the sea voyage from London Bridge to Plymouth, autobiographic incident dissolves into romance and fantasy. Stephen goes to India to make his fortune, Knight falls in love with Elfride, but abandons her when he learns that she once spent a night in a train with Stephen. Elfride marries Lord Luxellian and dies of a broken heart. Her body is brought back to Cornwall by the train in which Stephen and Knight, by chance, are travelling, and in the last scene her three lovers meet in the vault below Endelstow church, where she lies in her coffin.

Hardy did not class *A Pair of Blue Eyes* among his Novels of Character, but among those of Romance and Fantasy. Indeed, there is little to be said about the characters. Knight, like Angel Clare, is an intellectual Puritan, one who has never kissed a woman in his life, except his mother and Elfride. 'Aren't you glad to hear it?' he asks, and expects her never to have kissed a man, except her father and himself. He is a spinsterish prig who fascinates, dominates, snubs, bullies and ruins the lives of the two young lovers. Stephen is little more than a romantic boy, though staunch as any of Hardy's heroes, and Elfride in the hands of Knight like a terrified, fluttering bird. It is no more a tragedy of character than *Romeo and Juliet*, with which early play of Shakespeare's this early novel of Hardy's has obvious affinities: poetry, and the faithful Stephen-Romeo returning to find his love lying in a vault.

When he was at St Juliot in October 1871 Hardy had written to Tinsley that 'owing to the representation of critic-friends who were taken with D.R.' he had begun another novel, 'the essence of which is plot, *without crime*—but on the plan of D.R.' He carried over the melodrama of *Desperate Remedies* into *A Pair of Blue Eyes*, and as the plot of the one had much to do with churchyards, so does that of the other centre on the churchyard of St Juliot. Stephen talks to Elfride of his early life and his love while they sit by night on the tomb of the young farmer who was said to have died for her love. Knight talks to her of his love while they sit on the altar-steps from which the tomb is visible by moonlight, through the gap made by the fallen tower. When Stephen returns from India he first meets Elfride again when, with Knight, she is reluctantly inspecting the Luxellian vault, which is soon to be the scene of their parting. Stephen's father, the mason, is in charge of its repair, and there, much as in *Hamlet*, the rustic chorus assembles to comment on events: Martin Cannister, who considers two-inch black borders on notepaper an excess of mourning: 'I'm sure people don't feel more than a very narrow border when they feels most of all'; the shrivelled mason who got the better of the last Lord Luxellian by thinking 'What a weight you'll be, my Lord, for our arms to lower under the aisle of Endelstow church some day!'; William Worm, who has such a noise in his head that ' 'Tis just for all the world like people frying fish: fry, fry, fry, all day long in my poor head.' What matter though the dialect be Dorset, not Cornish; they are genuine Hardy countryfolk.

Sensational in another way is the scene in which Elfride rescues Knight from the top of the cliff-face to which he is clinging. It is Hardy's first extended piece of dramatic, descriptive writing:

He reclined hand in hand with the world in its infancy. . . . By one of those familiar conjunctions of things wherewith the inanimate world baits the mind of man when he pauses in moments of suspense, opposite Knight's eyes was an imbedded fossil, standing forth in low relief from the rock. It was a creature with eyes. The eyes, dead and turned to stone, were even now regarding him. It was one of the early crustaceans called Trilobites. Separated by millions of years in their lives, Knight and this underling seemed to have met in their death . . .

Time closed up like a fan before him. He saw himself at one extremity of the years, face to face with the beginning and all the intermediate centuries simultaneously. . . .

It is a vivid and memorable episode, inspired by Hardy's own recognition of the past in the present, history in current events. He felt his kinship with the strange fossils of Portland and Purbeck, much as he felt his kinship with the prehistoric makers of Maiden Castle, the Romans of Durnovaria, the builders of Stinsford Church, and members of its choir who, not long before his birth, played and sang in its gallery.

Two of Hardy's comments in this scene are worth remark, as prologue to the omen coming on. One is on pitiless Nature, who scatters 'heartless severities or overwhelming generosities in lawless caprice'; the other on 'inexorable circumstance' which, like the figure in our van seems to thwart the striver for a prize, but throws it at him if he surrenders and no more tantalising is possible. Knight surrenders and is saved by Elfride, but she is not saved by Knight. She is the first of Hardy's heroines to suffer for not telling.

Beeny Cliff (Aug. 22. '70)

The Figure in the Scene.

.....". I stood back that I might pencil it
With her amid the scene;
Till it gloomed & rained."

(Moments of Vision.)

23. Emma on Beeny: 'only her outline shown / With rainfall marked across.'

24. Bathsheba revives Gabriel Oak: 'a striking illustration' by Helen
Paterson in the *Cornhill Magazine* for January 1874.

25. Waterston House, Puddletown: Bathsheba's farmhouse, 'a hoary
building, of the early stage of Classic Renaissance.'

A Pair of Blue Eyes was well received by the reviewers, including Moule, who called it a 'tragedy of circumstance', by which he meant 'the power of mere events on certain kinds of character.' And in a letter to Hardy he wrote: 'You understand the *woman* infinitely better than the lady—but how gloriously you have idealised here and there.' It is significant that it appealed especially to poets: Tennyson liked it best of Hardy's novels, and Coventry Patmore wrote to say how much he had enjoyed it, though he could not help regretting that a work of 'such unequalled beauty and power' had not been written in verse. It was a temptation to turn again to his first love, poetry, but he was already engaged on another novel. Towards the end of 1872 Leslie Stephen had written to say what pleasure *Under the Greenwood Tree* had given him, and asked if he would write a similar story, though with more incident, as a serial for the *Cornhill Magazine* of which he had recently become the editor. Hardy had agreed, and in March began to write a pastoral tale about a young woman farmer, a shepherd and a cavalry sergeant. But in June, shortly after publication of *A Pair of Blue Eyes*, he took a holiday.

He went to London and showed his young brother Henry the sights. He also dined with Moule, who was on his way to Ipswich as Poor Law Inspector, and on the 20th they met again in Cambridge, a place that Hardy had never seen but often dreamed of. He stayed in rooms in Moule's college, Queen's, and next morning they climbed to the roof of King's College Chapel from which, across the Fens, they could see the gleaming octagon of Ely Cathedral: 'a never-to-be-forgotten morning'. Moule accompanied him to the station and saw him off for London—'His last smile,' Hardy noted in his diary. From London he went to Bath, where Emma was staying with a friend. To begin with he made local excursions 'with the ladies': to Bristol and the south Cotswolds, where he noted the curly fleeces of the sheep; then farther afield with Emma alone: one day to Clifton and Brunel's recently completed suspension bridge across the Avon Gorge, another to the Wye valley and Tintern Abbey, where they repeated the famous lines that Wordsworth had written there just 75 years before. But 1873 was a year in a very different age from that of 1798, and Hardy's comment on the ruined abbey was: 'Compare the age of the building with that of the marble hills from which it was drawn.'

The next day he returned to Bockhampton, where he spent the rest of the summer writing *Far from the Madding Crowd*. He liked to write in the place he was describing, and on 21 September walked to Woodbury-hill Fair, the Greenhill Fair of the novel, and scene of Sergeant Troy's exploits as Dick Turpin towards the end of the book. Then, a few days later came the news of Moule's death. On the evening of the day on which Hardy had walked to Woodbury Hill, Moule had cut his throat in his college bedroom at Cambridge. He was 41, and had for some years been subject to fits of depression which affected his work, or so he thought, which again increased his depression. The body was brought back to Dorchester, and Hardy awaited his friend's arrival, sitting on 'the eve-lit weir' below Fordington church. His death was a severe shock and a great loss to Hardy, who owed more to Moule than to any other man. Since the time when he was a boy apprenticed to Hicks, he had helped, advised and encouraged him, and if it had not been for this 'scholar and critic of perfect taste' he might not then have been standing on the threshold of success.

Fortunately—and despite one crushing misfortune, Hardy was so often fortunate—there was another man of exactly the same age as Moule waiting to help him, the man who had commissioned his pastoral tale, Leslie Stephen. An Etonian and Cambridge graduate, Stephen had married a daughter of Thackeray, and in addition to being editor of the *Cornhill Magazine* was himself a writer of distinction, and an enthusiastic mountaineer, one of the first Presidents of the Alpine Club. He was to become editor of the *Dictionary of National Biography* and, by a second marriage, father of Virginia Woolf and Vanessa Bell. When Hardy met him in 1873 he had just published his *Essays on Freethinking*, another important book that influenced Hardy.

At the end of September he sent Stephen as much as he had written of his novel, about a quarter, and then spent the remainder of the autumn writing its continuation and helping his father with the cider-making. In December he went to St Juliot, and at Plymouth station on his return journey bought a copy of the *Cornhill*, at the beginning of which he found the first instalment, the first five chapters, of *Far from the Madding Crowd*, with a 'striking illustration' by Helen Paterson. It was the last day of the old year, 1873.

CHAPTER SEVEN

Marriage
1874

The year 1874 was to be a memorable one for Hardy. It began auspiciously on 3 January with an article in the *Spectator*, congratulating readers of the *Cornhill* on the first instalment of an anonymous story 'so clever and so remarkable' that either it was written by George Eliot or 'some new light among novelists' had appeared. And on the 8th Leslie Stephen wrote to congratulate him on the reception of the first number, even though he was confused with George Eliot because he knew the names of the stars. Although the career of serial novelist was not the one that Hardy would have chosen, it was preferable to architecture, and might be equally rewarding; and now that he was beginning to make money he was at last in a position to marry.

It is clear from the two poems, 'Thoughts of Phena' and 'The Wind's Prophecy', to be considered later, that Hardy was in love with his cousin Tryphena some time after his return from London in 1867, but how deeply we do not know. He might have married her even though, as Jude Fawley was to say, 'It was not well for cousins to fall in love'; but then came his visit to St Juliot in March 1870 and the dawn of another love. He and Emma Gifford had a number of things in common: she was fond of music, sketched, talked of books, and she encouraged his writing and made fair copies of his manuscripts. As she herself wrote: 'I found him a perfectly new study and delight and he found a "mine" in me he said.' Then, a woman in her thirties who had exchanged an unhappy home for isolation in a remote Cornish parish, urged perhaps by her sister,[10] she may have set out to captivate the man who could carry her off to a brighter future than the one that seemed to be in store for her. And Hardy, the poor man, may not have been unwilling to be captivated by the lady. It seems probable that by 1870 he was no longer deeply attached to Tryphena, and that, gradually perhaps, he exchanged the old love for the new. It may be that he became formally engaged to Emma on his visit to St Juliot at the end of 1873, and told Tryphena what had happened when he passed through Plymouth on his way home. If so, he probably never saw her again.

Before he could marry he had to finish his novel; so, returning to Bockhampton he wrote as rapidly as he could. We can follow his progress from the letters that Stephen wrote to him as the instalments came in. Thus, on 12 March 1874: 'I have ventured to leave out a line or two in the last batch of proofs, from an excessive prudery of which I am ashamed; but one is forced to be absurdly particular. May I suggest that Troy's seduction of the young woman will require to be treated in a gingerly fashion. . . .' Then, a month later: 'The cause of Fanny's death is unnecessarily emphasized . . . I have some doubts whether the baby is necessary at all. . . .' Hardy, thinking of his marriage, replied that circumstances made him quite willing, even anxious, to modify the magazine-version of his novel to please its readers, that for the present he wished 'merely to be considered a good hand at a serial.' 'Perhaps,' he added, 'I may have higher aims some day.'

He finished the book in July and then went to London, where he took lodgings in Westbourne Park to make arrangements for the wedding. There he revised the last part of his manuscript and sent it to Stephen before Emma arrived to stay with her brother. They were married on Thursday, 17 September in St Peter's, Elgin Avenue, Paddington, the ceremony being performed by Emma's uncle, Dr Gifford, a Canon of Worcester and future Archdeacon of London. None of Hardy's relations was there, the only other people present being his landlady's daughter and Emma's brother, who signed the book as witnesses. The next day, however, Hardy wrote from Brighton to tell his brother and the rest of his family about the wedding, and that he was on his way to Paris for material for his next story. And Emma began a diary: 'Brighton. Rough sea on Friday. Saturday 19th. Aquarium . . . Tom bathed. Sea rough . . . Dieppe . . . Rouen.'[11]

They were away for little more than a fortnight, and early in October took rooms in Surbiton, a pleasant residential area on the south bank of the Thames, some 12 miles west of London. A month later *Far from the Madding Crowd* was published in two volumes by Smith, Elder, and by the end of the year Smith was able to report that the first edition of 1000 copies was almost exhausted. The reviews were favourable, but not ecstatic. The *Spectator* found it an original and amusing story, but complained that the admittedly very humorous dialogue was too subtle and intellectual for the peasants of Dorset. More interesting was the comment from America, where the novel had been published at the same time as in England. The reviewer was Henry James, a younger man than Hardy, and a novelist of a very different kind. Almost all novels are too long, he wrote, and *Far from the Madding Crowd* is inordinately long, distended by conversational and descriptive padding. Certainly there is much felicitous description of rural England, but 'the only things we believe in are the sheep and the dogs.'

In the serial version of *A Pair of Blue Eyes* Hardy had written that 'fiction has taken a turn—for better or for worse—for analysing rather than depicting character and emotion.' Hardy was a depicter, James an analyser, and a novelist of drawing-rooms with little understanding of, or interest in, countryfolk; but Hardy was of them, knew them and loved them, and in this pastoral tale drew life-size portraits of his characters—or rather, larger than life, for there is an epic quality about Gabriel Oak, homely and blunt-spoken though he is: something elemental and eternal, as though he were the representative, personification of all shepherds since the coming of the Saxons into Wessex. And despite her vanity and fickleness there is a similar grandeur about Bathsheba, who 'was of the stuff of which great men's mothers are made. She was indispensable to high generation.'

James was right about the inordinate length of the Victorian novel, and most of Hardy's novels *are* too long, but *Far from the Madding Crowd* is one of the exceptions, and there are very few pages that we would willingly let go. This is mainly because of the consistency of content and its treatment; without intruding gentry, it is a leisurely tale of the countryside where, as in the Forest of Arden, 'they fleet the time carelessly, as they did in the golden world.' There is a Homeric quality of timelessness— 'in Weatherbury three or four score years were included in the mere present'—of breadth and spaciousness about it, symbolised by the lengthy description of the medieval, church-like barn, and Bathsheba's singing of a ballad at the shearing-supper to the piping of Gabriel's flute, while 'the shearers reclined against each other as at suppers in the early ages of the world.' And there is something of the same quality in Bathsheba's instructions for the decking of Fanny Robin's coffin—sweets to the sweet, like the flowers for Ophelia—box, and yew, and boy's love: 'completely bury her in them. And let old Pleasant draw her, because she knew him so well.'

As for the chorus of rustics, it is true that when Hardy wrote *Far from the Madding Crowd*, only three or four years after the Education Act of 1870, half of them, probably most, would be illiterate, with a vocabulary of only a few hundred simple words. But he was not a realist, concerned with the accurate, tape-recorder reproduction of dialogue; he was a poet condemned to write prose for a living, and descriptions of nature and dialect speech were the two nearest approaches to poetry open to him. Here is Henery Fray's comment on Bathsheba: 'Pride and vanity have ruined many a cobbler's dog. Dear, dear, when I think o' it, I sorrows like a man in travel!' Here Jan Coggan on the subject of Church and Chapel: 'I bain't such a fool as to pretend that we who stick to the Church have the same chance as they, because we know we have not. But I hate a feller who'll change his old ancient doctrines for the sake of getting to heaven.' And here Joseph Poorgrass on drink and a multiplying eye: 'Yes;

I see two of every sort, as if I were some holy man living in the times of King Noah and entering into the ark ... I feel too good for England: I ought to have lived in Genesis by rights.' Apparently Poorgrass had been coached by Moule in the proper use of the subjunctive, and if Wessex peasants never talked like Hardy's—or Warwickshire clowns like Shakespeare's—so much greater the debt of our gratitude to their creators.

The opening scene is high up in the sheep pastures of the chalk plateau beyond Maiden Newton, but after the disaster to Gabriel's flock it changes to Weatherbury, Hardy's name for Puddletown, near the northern edge of Egdon Heath. Almost all the action takes place between the village and Dorchester, some six miles away, but most of it is concentrated within the small area between the farmhouses of Bathsheba and Boldwood. The original of Bathsheba's house is Waterston Manor to the west of the village, 'a hoary building of the early stage of Classic Renaissance', which Hardy fondly describes in detail, taking particular delight in the finials and other features that still retained traces of their Gothic extraction. Boldwood's house is probably Druce Farm, on the other side of the stream, and here is the scene of the sheep-washing, in the pool near which Boldwood makes Bathsheba an offer of marriage.

For the plot, as in all Hardy's major novels save one, is that of a woman, the central character, and two or more men— Bathsheba, Oak, Troy, Boldwood—and it is interesting to note how Hardy, with his own marriage approaching, emphasised, either consciously or unconsciously, the words 'marriage' and 'marry'. It is true that all the novels have much to do with marriage, but here the key-words are those that Bathsheba so recklessly printed on the Valentine she sent to Boldwood: MARRY ME: two words that he constantly sees before him on his mantelpiece, and speaks to himself aloud: 'Marry me.' They are also the key-words of the non-marriage sub-plot, so en-treatingly repeated by Fanny to Frank Troy: 'You said lots of times you would marry me ... tomorrow? ... shall it be tomorrow?' She writes to tell Oak that she is going to be married; and Oak in his prosperity calls to see if Bathsheba would 'like to be married', but is repulsed with 'I shan't marry—at least yet.' Troy marries her, however, and it is not long before he tells her that 'a ceremony before a priest doesn't make a marriage,' and Bathsheba warns Liddy: 'If ever you marry—God forbid that you ever should! you'll find yourself in a fearful situation; but mind this, don't you flinch. Stand your ground, and be cut to pieces.' Troy is supposed drowned, and Boldwood renews his suit: 'If you marry again ... marry me!' Troy returns, Boldwood shoots him, and Gabriel's turn has come again; but it is Bathsheba who coaxes him to ask 'whether you would allow me to marry you after all.' It is a happy ending to a pastoral romance of minor tragedy, and Coggan voices the opinion of the Chorus: 'Hurrah! God's above the devil yet.' Shortly after writing that, the Poor Man married the Lady.

He was now 34, slightly built and below medium height, dark-eyed and dark-bearded, with a quiet voice and unassuming manner. Like his parents, he spoke two languages: the dialect of the countryfolk among whom he had been brought up, and in which he still conversed with them, and standard English, which had become his normal speech as an architect, though still with a trace of Dorset in his accent. Although he had a keen sense of humour, an ability to laugh, or rather to smile, at himself as well as at the absurdities of others and the incongruities of life, his natural melancholy was intensified by a feeling of frustration, a tension between his powerful emotions and equally powerful intellect. He wanted to concentrate on poetry, but had to concern himself with prose. He wanted to believe in what he had been taught to believe in Stinsford church: in the Bible, the supernatural, the Christian God, but his reason revolted, and he read Darwin, Huxley, Mill, Spencer, and the Positivist philosophy of Comte: abandon the quest for the unknowable, and exchange the service of an unknown God for the service of Man. Such thinking was unpopular and, sensitive as he was, added to his reserve and feeling of isolation as something of a misfit in polite Victorian society. Yet, companionable rather than sociable, friendly when in company but not seeking society, society was now seeking him as a rising celebrity. Besides, he had an attractive wife who, after lonely years in Cornwall, was eager for society. And Miss Thackeray, Leslie

Stephen's sister-in-law, assured him that a novelist must, of course, enjoy society. He would try.

At Christmas 1874, a newly-married man with a recently published, very successful novel, he was in more cheerful mood, though piqued at being mistaken for George Eliot, or an imitator of that great novelist. He had no intention of confining his writing to rural subjects; he had been to Paris and Rouen in search of material for a new story, and he would now study a higher grade of London society than the lowly one he had known in his twenties as an obscure architectural draughtsman. Leslie Stephen and his publisher George Smith were asking for another novel, so, putting aside a story about the woodlanders of Blackmore Vale, he began to write 'a somewhat frivolous narrative': *The Hand of Ethelberta*.

CHAPTER EIGHT

London and Sturminster Newton

1875–78

At the beginning of 1874 Hardy had been a struggling and virtually unknown novelist, a man with no social or educational advantages, who had just lost the friend who had helped him to the modest position he had gained. At the beginning of 1875 his name was known to almost all the reading public, he had married a woman of good family (or, as his father-in-law is said to have put it, he was the 'low-born churl who had presumed to marry into my family'), and London society was eager to receive him. But London society could not be studied in Surbiton, as he told George Smith at the beginning of the year: 'We are coming to Town for three months on account of Ethelberta.'

So, storing all their possessions—books, linen and 'sundries'—in four small cases, they moved to rooms in Westbourne Grove, near the lodgings he had occupied in his Blomfield days, and there they followed the usual social round of dinner-parties and visits to theatres, concerts, galleries, museums, and events such as the University Boat Race.

Soon after their move Hardy was able to send the opening chapters of his new serial to Stephen, who asked him to call at his house one evening. He found him in his library, 'a tall thin figure wrapt in a heath-coloured dressing-grown,' and after some talk about the serial Stephen changed the subject. When he had been a Fellow of Trinity Hall some 20 years before, he had taken holy orders, but by the recent Clerical Disabilities Act he was entitled to renounce them without forfeiting the civil rights, such as sitting in Parliament, that he had lost as a clergyman, and knowing that Hardy would sympathise with his decision, he asked him to witness his Deed of Relinquishment. Hardy did so, and stayed to talk about theology and the new science, about evolution and the structure of the universe.

In June, the July number, the first of twelve monthly instalments of *The Hand of Ethelberta*, appeared in the *Cornhill*, and also in the *New York Times*; and on the 18th, the sixtieth anniversary of the Battle of Waterloo, Hardy took Emma to Chelsea Hospital to visit the veterans of the campaign. He had always been fascinated by the Napoleonic Wars, which were comparatively recent history when he was a boy, and he now made the note: 'A Ballad of the Hundred Days. Then another of Moscow. Others of earlier campaigns—forming altogether an Iliad of Europe from 1789 to 1815.' It was the seed from which *The Dynasts* was to spring 30 years later.

A routine of museums and picture galleries by day and 'crushes' by night left little time for writing, and after a three-months' study of London society on account of Ethelberta he made for Dorset to chronicle her history, and to find a house. From Shaftesbury they went to Blandford, then followed the railway to Wimborne and Bournemouth, where they were stranded in their lodgings on St Swithin's Day, 15 July, when 'the rain came down like silken strings,' as described in 'We Sat at the Window', a strangely desolate poem of failure to appreciate one another. From Bournemouth they sailed across Poole Bay to Swanage, where they found rooms in the house of a captain of a fishing-boat, and Hardy settled down to finish the adventures of Ethelberta, who was soon to arrive at the same place.

They were finished in January 1876; in March the couple moved to Yeovil, still in search of a house, and in April *The Hand of Ethelberta: A Comedy in Chapters* was published by Smith, Elder. It was received with little enthusiasm. The *Saturday Review* thought it would make a better comedy in scenes than in chapters, a better play than novel; and the author 'must abandon such out-of-the-way subjects.' One critic, however, hailed it as 'the finest ideal comedy since the days of Shakespeare.' But Stephen was disappointed: 'You have a perfectly fresh and original vein,' he wrote, but it was not exploited in *Ethelberta*, and this was his last contribution to the *Cornhill*, though not the end of his friendship with Stephen.

The Hand of Ethelberta was a return to the novel of ingenuity instead of a continuation of the novels of Character and Environment, of characters like Bathsheba and Gabriel Oak in the Dorset countryside, and it might be called 'The Poor Woman and Four Gentlemen.' Ethelberta is an adventuress, an altruistic Becky Sharp. The daughter of a butler, she is left a widow while still a girl, and educated by her titled mother-in-law, who dies, leaving her a house in London. She lets part of the house, in which she employs her numerous brothers and sisters as servants, writes verses, and tales in the manner of Defoe, which she recites to public audiences. Hardy had been re-reading Defoe, whose prose he admired, and had written *The Poor Man and the Lady* in the 'affected simplicity' of his style; and there are obvious fragments of the first novel in the satirical portrayal of London society in which the 'complete divorce between thinking and saying is the hall-mark of high civilisation.' The squirrel-haired Ethelberta's hand is sought by four men; she will not marry the young musician Christopher Julian until he gets rich, flirts with a young painter and with a man-about-town, but chooses a disreputable old viscount, the staircase of whose house near Swanage alone is worth her hand. Sol, her sturdy carpenter brother, accuses her of 'creeping up among the useless lumber of our nation that'll be the first to burn if there comes a flare,' and his republican sentiments are another echo from *The Poor Man*. Her brother, father, young lover and, for very different reasons, the viscount's brother, all set out from London on a chase to Bournemouth and Swanage in an attempt to prevent her marriage. They meet 'by the sorcery of accident' just before they reach the church, but are too late, finding only the young painter who has watched the ceremony unseen, as Edward Springrove had watched the marriage of Cytherea Graye and Aeneas Manston.

In spite of some imaginative flashes, and a few of the minor characters such as Ethelberta's sister Picotee and brothers Sol and Joey, the book is little better than the ordinary run of Victorian novels, and Hardy either did not realise, or was unwilling to admit, that as a novelist his scope was limited, that his knowledge of middle- and upper-class society was superficial, acquired comparatively late in life, and that it was Dorset where he had been bred, and its country characters among whom he had been brought up, that inspired him to write as no other man could. Yet *Ethelberta* is interesting for its glimpses of the first year of his married life. Apart from a prelude in Wareham and Bournemouth, the scene of the first half of the book is London, where there are dinner-parties, an excursion to see the Boat Race, visits to the British Museum, Royal Academy and Cripplegate church. When the scene changes to Swanage, where Hardy wrote the last part of the book, the poet takes over for a few pages. 'Knollsea was a seaside village lying snug within two headlands as between a finger and thumb,' and the captain's cottage where he and Emma stayed is fully and affectionately described: 'By anyone sitting in the room that commanded this prospect, a white butterfly among the appletrees might be mistaken for the sails of a yacht far away on the sea; and in the evening when the light was dim, what seemed like a fly crawling upon the windowpane would turn out to be a boat in the bay.' Then there were the walks they took together, notably along the chalk ridge of Nine Barrow Down to Corfe Castle—but there Ethelberta meets her viscount, and we are back in society. There is, however, a visit to Rouen, where Hardy and Emma, like Ethelberta, climbed to the base of the cathedral *flèche* and watched the morning mist clearing below them; and their sail across Poole Bay is repeated by Sol and the viscount's brother.

In addition to these autobiographical incidents, there is something of self-portraiture in the descriptions of Christopher Julian. Hardy always protested that he never put himself into his novels, yet he more than once said of himself what Ethelberta says of Julian: 'ambition—a quality in which I fear you are very deficient.' His sister calls him fondly 'the most melancholy man God ever created,' and he gives the reason why: 'an under-feeling I have that at the most propitious moment the distance to the possibility of sorrow is so short that a man's spirits must not rise higher than mere cheerfulness out of bare respect to his insight.' Another way of describing the figure in our van with arm uplifted.

In the spring of 1876, however, Hardy was not in melancholy mood, and in May the couple left their Yeovil lodgings for a tour of Holland and the Rhine. From Rotterdam they went to The Hague and Scheveningen, a fishing-village among the dunes that was being developed as a holiday resort, then up the Rhine to Heidelberg, which they loved, Baden and Strassburg, and back through Metz and Gravelotte, which must have revived memories of an August afternoon at St Juliot six years before. From Brussels Hardy went to explore the field of Waterloo and, back in London fresh from the scene of the battle, on its anniversary again visited its thinning ranks of survivors at Chelsea Hospital. Then, soon after their return to Yeovil, they heard of a house to be let on the river at Sturminster Newton. This they took and, as their only furniture was a bookcase and a door-scraper, they hastily bought what was necessary, and on 3 July, nearly two years after their marriage, took possession of their first home 'Riverside Villa', just outside the town, overlooking a reach of the Stour. It was the prelude to a two-years' idyll.

Black's Guide to Dorset for this year, 1876, has the entry:

STURMINSTER NEWTON (population, 1916. *Inns:* The Crown and the Swan), on the projected Dorset Central Railway, a market-town of great antiquity, built on a gentle slope which declines to the rushy Stour. . . . Beyond the river (spanned by a good stone bridge) rises a richly wooded upland abounding in game; and at the foot of the bridge a pleasant orchard, covering a mound, and encircled by a dry fosse, marks the site of an ancient Castle.

It was the perfect place for a prolonged second honeymoon, and in the evenings they rowed on the Stour below their house, where they were saluted by mowers behind the palisades of rushes that bordered the river. And there were walks to neighbouring villages, including Marnhull, where Tess was later to come from, and, like Tess at the beginning of her story, girls danced on the green by Riverside Villa. But Hardy was not writing *Tess*, he was working, oddly enough, on *The Return of the Native*: 'oddly' because he had laid aside a story about the woodlanders of Blackmore Vale to write *Ethelberta*, and he was now living in the Vale, while the scene of his new novel was Egdon Heath, 20 miles away, beyond the chalk plateau. Yet he was himself the native of Egdon, one who had known the heath since childhood, and in the opening chapter described it as no other man could, adding:

Haggard Egdon appealed to a subtler and scarcer instinct, to a more recently learnt emotion, than that which responds to the sort of beauty called charming and fair. . . .

The time seems near, if it has not actually arrived, when the chastened sublimity of a moor, a sea, or a mountain will be all of nature that is absolutely in keeping with the moods of the more thinking among mankind. And ultimately, to the commonest tourist, spots like Iceland may become what the vineyards and myrtle-gardens of South Europe are to him now; and Heidelberg and Baden be passed unheeded as he hastens from the Alps to the sand-dunes of Scheveningen.

Autobiography again—and a remarkable anticipation of post-impressionist painting; but then, Hardy was before his time in so many ways. He made the point more briefly in his notebook: 'Paradoxically put, it is to see the beauty in ugliness'; four years later Van Gogh was to write: 'Good Lord, how beautiful that was . . . places which, although as hideous as possible, are for an artist a paradise.'

Hardy had shown the beginning of his novel to Leslie Stephen, who liked it, but feared that the relations between Eustacia, Wildeve and Thomasin might develop into something too dangerous for the *Cornhill*, and would not consider it unless he could see the whole. So Hardy offered it to Chatto and Windus, who accepted it for their monthly magazine *Belgravia*, in which it was to appear throughout 1878.

By this time Hardy was beginning to feel that, as a novelist, he was living too far from the social and cultural centre of England, and Emma hankered after something more interesting than life on the outskirts of a tiny Dorset town, almost as isolated as St Juliot. She loved the country as a change, but wanted to live in London. So, in February 1878 they took a three-years' lease of a house in London, and prepared to leave Riverside Villa. They had been very happy there, but even at Sturminster there had been periods of despondency, as when he wrote: ' "All is vanity," saith the preacher. But if all were only vanity, who would mind? Alas, it is too often worse than vanity; agony, darkness, death also.' And there had been the episode of their maid-servant. One night they saw her entering the house with a man who fled when Emma ran downstairs and ordered the girl to her room. Next morning she was gone, and two months later Hardy made the note: 'August 13 [1877]. We hear that Jane, our late servant, is soon to have a baby. Yet never a sign of one is there for us.'

There was still no sign when they left Riverside Villa: 'March 18 [1878]. End of the Sturminster Newton idyll,'—'Our happiest time,' he added later. The move was a tragic mistake, as he was to write in 'A Two-Years' Idyll', though perhaps nowhere could it have been much further prolonged:

> Yes; such it was;
> Just those two seasons unsought,
> Sweeping like summertide wind on our ways;
> Moving, as straws,
> Hearts quick as ours in those days;
> Going like wind, too, and rated as nought
> Save as the prelude to plays
> Soon to come—larger, life-fraught:
> Yes; such it was. . . .

> What seems it now?
> Lost: such beginning was all;
> Nothing came after: romance straight forsook
> Quickly somehow
> Life when we sped from our nook,
> Primed for new scenes with designs smart and tall.
> —A preface without any book,
> A trumpet uplipped, but no call;
> That seems it now.

On 22 March they moved into The Larches, 1 Arundel Terrace, Trinity Road, Upper Tooting, near Wandsworth Common. 'And it was in this house that their troubles began.'[12]

CHAPTER NINE

London

1878–81

After his two years' rustication Hardy resumed the social life of London, although the scene of the novel he had in mind was Dorset. He was elected a member of the Savile Club; dined with the publishers Alexander Macmillan and Kegan Paul; met Thomas Huxley, and influential hostesses such as the widow of the poet 'Barry Cornwall', Mrs Procter who knew everybody, and Mrs Sutherland Orr, sister of Sir Frederick Leighton, the new President of the Royal Academy; and he visited art exhibitions and theatres, meeting Henry Irving after a performance at the Lyceum. He was shy of making new acquaintances, but beginning to enjoy society.

Meanwhile *The Return of the Native* was being serialised in *Belgravia*, and Chatto and Windus were so pleased with it that they asked him for a short story for another magazine of theirs.

26. Lulworth Cove, with 'two projecting spurs of rock which formed the pillars of Hercules to this miniature Mediterranean.'

27. Swanage ('Knollsea'), where Hardy and Emma lived July
1875–March 1876, and where he finished *The Hand of Ethelberta*.

28. The Stour at Sturminster Newton, scene of the two years' idyll,
July 1876–March 1878, when Hardy wrote *The Return of the Native*.

He agreed, and in July *An Indiscretion in the Life of an Heiress* appeared in the *New Quarterly*. It was long for a short story, some 60 pages, but Hardy was able to produce it quickly, for it was a shortened version of *The Poor Man and the Lady*, from which he extracted material that he had not already used in his five published novels.

In this story Will Strong the architect has become the schoolmaster Egbert Mayne who saves the Lady, Geraldine Allenville, from being killed by a new-fangled threshing-machine. Her father, squire of Tollamore and patron of the village school, is grateful, and gives him the use of his library. Egbert falls in love with Geraldine, watching her as she sits below a marble monument of two weeping cherubs and a winged skull. She visits him at the school and at his cottage, and in one episode lays the foundation-stone of a tower. He goes to London for five years, and there writes an unsucessful novel, followed by a successful one. On reading in the paper that Geraldine is to marry a peer, he returns to Tollamore, meets her in the church before the wedding, and she agrees to run away from home and marry him. After their marriage she goes to seek reconciliation with her father, while Egbert waits for her in the grounds of the house. But she is taken ill, and dies a few days later.

It is *The Poor Man* over again, with abbreviations and variations. Tollamore church with its marble monument is Stinsford, the squire's house is Kingston Maurward, and the school the one that Hardy attended at Bockhampton. Egbert's career is much the same as his up to the time of writing *Under the Greenwood Tree*, the most interesting additional incident being Geraldine's laying the foundation-stone of a tower, for this is what Emma had done when the tower of St Juliot church was rebuilt. 'In due time,' she wrote in her 'Recollections', 'I laid the foundation stone, with a bottle containing the record of the proceedings, the school-children attending. I plastered it well, the foreman said. Mr Holder made a speech to the young ones to remember the event . . . I wonder if they do remember it and me.' *An Indiscretion* is interesting as semi-autobiography, but it was merely a pot-boiler, and Hardy neither mentioned it in his *Life* nor included it in the collected edition of his works.

The Return of the Native was another matter. It finished its run as a serial in November, when Smith, Elder published it in three volumes, with a map of Egdon Heath drawn by Hardy himself. The *Times* protested that it could not be greatly interested in people whose lives were so extraordinary; that the reader was taken even farther from the madding crowd. Some reviewers compared it unfavourably with that novel, and the *Athenaeum* pronounced it 'distinctly inferior'. Eustacia Vye was another Madame Bovary, and we did not want women of that sort imported from France into England. There was a deplorable lack of gentry, and the peasants talked a language that was never spoken by man, certainly not by Victorians (Hardy replied that he merely gave a general idea of the speech of intelligent peasants; that to insist on all its pronunciations and mispronunciations would distract attention from the characters themselves). The *Academy* also found it 'very French', and the story too dependent on a series of accidents. For the *Spectator*, however, it was 'a story of singular power and interest', though there was a tendency to treat tragedy as mere 'drearness', 'a deeper tinge of the common leaden-colour of the human lot.' The novel sold only slowly, but it was more successful in America, where it was serialised and published at the same time as in England.

Whatever faults reviewers might find in the story, they were united in their praise of Hardy's descriptions, particularly of nature, and in *The Return of the Native* nature means Egdon Heath. In no other novel is the scene so localised, confined to one place, and we follow the succession of the seasons throughout a year in the first decade of Hardy's life, for the action is supposed to take place some time between 1840 and 1850. We first see the heath at twilight on 5 November, 'colossal and mysterious in its swarthy monotony . . . suggesting tragical possibilities.' In March, season of a timid animal world of tadpoles, toads, young ducks and bumble-bees, it awakens from winter's trance 'in almost feline stealthiness'. By May the moist hollows have passed 'from their brown to their green stage', and lizards, grasshoppers and ants appear. July, when the sun has fired the heather from crimson to scarlet, is 'the one season of the year when the heath is gorgeous,' but it declines into August, when the heat cracks the earth and fills the air with stinging insects. And so we return to autumn and another November—to the climax on the evening of the 6th. We are always aware of the heath as a background, and more than a background: as a presence that influences the thoughts and actions of the men and women who inhabit it. Clym loves Egdon, Eustacia hates it, and that is at the root of the tragedy.

On his visits to the National Gallery Hardy had been impressed by Hobbema's painting of 'The Avenue', in which he felt how the presence of a human figure infuses emotion into quite commonplace objects; and to describe a scene, then add a solitary figure, was a favourite way of introducing his characters. Thus, *The Return of the Native* begins with the sombre splendour of his landscape painting of Egdon, across which a Roman road runs straight to the horizon, and—'along the road walked an old man.' It is Captain Vye, only a minor figure in the drama, but his daughter Eustacia is introduced in a similar way: as a motionless form against the evening sky on the summit of Rainbarrow, rising from the mound 'like a spike from a helmet'.

When the novel appeared as a serial each of the twelve instalments had an illustration by Arthur Hopkins, brother of Gerard Manley Hopkins, and for his guidance Hardy wrote to tell him the order of importance of the characters: '1 Clym Yeobright, 2 Eustacia, 3 Thomasin and the reddleman, 4 Wildeve, 5 Mrs Yeobright.' This is surprising, for many readers would place Mrs Yeobright no lower than third. Thomasin is merely the good conventional heroine, a sweet but colourless girl who seems 'to belong rightly to a madrigal.' The reddleman, Diggory Venn, is a sterling character of the breed of Gabriel Oak, but a flitting, shadowy figure, a nocturnal worker behind the scenes for Thomasin's good. As for Wildeve, he is only a necessary pawn in the game, a young lady-killer who is there to marry Thomasin and run away with Eustacia. The basic drama is that of a mother's love for her son, of a son's love for his mother, and of the estrangement that follows his infatuation with a beautiful voluptuous girl, which leads to the death of both 'women. If Mrs Yeobright is not the chief character, she is the central one—and probably a near-portrait of Hardy's own mother.

Hardy was an artist, a poet, though not always a reliable craftsman, but here the story is constructed and developed with consummate skill, the main episodes coinciding with the seasons. In the first Book, November, we are introduced to the three women: Thomasin, concerning whom 'all similes and allegories ended with birds'; Mrs Yeobright, a shrewd middle-aged woman in whose face is concentrated the solitude of the heath; Eustacia, whose beauty is gradually revealed as she walks by twilight, a solitary figure, then fully in a chapter devoted to this Queen of Night: full-limbed, soft-bodied, with the passions that make a model goddess, but not quite a model woman. Then in Book Two, December, the thoughtful-looking native, Clym Yeobright, returns from Paris, and meets Eustacia when she plays a man's part in the Mummers' Play. It is the fateful meeting from which all else follows. Book Three, Spring, is that of Clym's fascination and marriage with Eustacia, and consequent breach with his mother. All is now poised for the tragedy of Book Four in high summer; first, the *peripeteia*, or reversal of fortune: Clym's near-blindness and reduction to a common furze-cutter; then the catastrophe of Mrs Yeobright's attempted reconciliation, apparent rejection, and death. This Book of 'The Closed Door', when the strong-willed, broken-hearted mother staggers back across the heath under the blazing August sun, muttering to little Johnny Nunsuch, is one of the finest Hardy ever wrote, and among the most memorable in English fiction. There follows the autumnal *anagnorisis* of Book Five, Clym's discovery that Eustacia had closed the door on his mother; his fury; the pathos of his tying her bonnet-strings before she leaves him; her flight with Wildeve, and the drowning of both in the weir. 'She is the second woman I have killed this year,' Clym cries. 'I was a great cause of my mother's death; and I am the chief cause of hers.'

Hardy intended the story to finish with Venn's disappearance from the Heath, silently and mysteriously as in all his former flittings, and his marriage with Thomasin is something of an anti-climax, added to satisfy the demand of serial-readers for a happy ending. The careworn Clym, however, remains as a preacher of moral lectures devoid of creeds, not only on Egdon, but carrying his message into the surrounding countryside and towns.

On reading *The Return of the Native* one thinks instinctively in terms of Greek tragedy and Aristotle's analysis of plot, with its reversal of fortune and recognition scene, of the tragic incident as one that occurs between those who are dear to one another, 'as when a mother kills her son, or a son his mother.' And there is a classical concentration, a unity, induced by the constant background of the heath and correspondence of the seasons to the acts of a tragedy, the final catastrophe taking place exactly a year and a day after the opening twilight scene, the placid pool where Eustacia and Wildeve met becoming the roaring weir that drowns them. That Hardy was thinking in terms of Greek tragedy seems clear from his allusions to Aeschylus, Prometheus and Oedipus, but like Shakespeare he was essentially a romantic, and he seasoned tragedy with the comic relief of another rustic, unclassical, chorus: 'For my part,' said Timothy Fairway, 'I like a good hearty funeral as well as anything. You've as splendid victuals and drink as at other parties, and even better. And it don't wear your legs to stumps in talking over a poor fellow's ways as it do to stand up in hornpipes.' Nor could he resist an occasion for the grotesque. Here, however, it is not the customary melodrama of charnel-houses and churchyards, for in this semi-pagan story the church is barely mentioned, but of lingering superstitions like Susan Nunsuch's making a wax model of the 'witch' Eustacia, sticking it with pins, and melting it slowly over the fire. But perhaps most grotesque of all scenes in Hardy is that of Wildeve's gambling on the heath, first by lantern-light with the half-witted Christian Cantle, then with the crimson reddleman by the light of glow-worms. It is one of Hardy's Rembrandtesque scenes, like nearly all those in which Diggory appears. Others are the fires on Rainbarrow and in Eustacia's garden, and when she first sees Clym his fire-lit face is against the background of a dark-tanned settle, a spectacle 'in Rembrandt's intensest manner'. The artist's violent chiaroscuro fascinated Hardy, and so many of his scenes recall his paintings, bright red and gold emerging from brown-black shadow, especially in this novel, most Rembrandtesque of all.

Thomas Hardy

The Return of the Native is one of the really great Hardy novels, though it is sometimes marred by his early encumbrances of style. Biblical reference and quotation came quite naturally to him, such as Mrs Yeobright's 'issues from a Nebo denied to others', though it may be questioned if many readers understand the metaphor, and 'Jareh, Mahalaleel' will puzzle more. But most of these out-of-the-way allusions are contrived elaborations: Albertus Magnus, Candaules' wife, Tarentine, Zenobia, Sallaert, and the rest. Then, there are the colourless latinisms: 'the female domestic'; Clym 'perceived a recumbent figure'; and Mrs Yeobright 'from her elevated position . . . could perceive the roof . . . of the little domicile.' This sort of writing comes strangely from the man who admired Defoe and Barnes of Wessex, but occasional clumsiness is outweighed by innumerable felicities. There is the quiet close to Mrs Yeobright's anguish: 'While she looked a heron arose on that side of the sky and flew on with his face towards the sun. . . .' And there is always 'the imperturbable countenance of the heath, which having defied the cataclysmal onsets of centuries, reduced to insignificance by its seamed and antique features the wildest turmoil of a single man.' That has the rhythm as well as the vocabulary of Sir Thomas Browne.

Shortly after publication of the novel Hardy made the note: 'November 28 (1878). Woke before it was light. Felt that I had not enough staying power to hold my own in the world.' This sounds more like physical weakness than spiritual distress, and may have been an early symptom of the illness that was to overtake him in the following year. But that all was not well at The Larches between him and Emma is suggested by the short poem 'A January Night (1879)', a night of rain and snarling wind when he felt that 'There is some hid dread afoot/That we cannot trace.' And in the *Life* he wrote how 'they seemed to begin to feel that "there had past away a glory from the earth".'

At Christmas his father had written to say that his mother was unwell, and that he hoped they would soon come to see them at Bockhampton. So, on a freezing day at the beginning of February Hardy took the train to Dorchester, where he was met by his brother, who drove him in a wagonette through rain and sleet to his old home. He stayed a fortnight: a working holiday, for he was beginning to write a novel about the Napoleonic Wars and the threatened landing of the French in Dorset at the beginning of the century, and he wanted to study the coast carefully, as well as collect information from the Dorchester Museum. He went, therefore, to Portland and Weymouth, where George III used to spend his summer holidays, sketched the English Channel from the chalk downs, and walked about the country below them in the neighbourhood of Preston and Ringstead Bay.

When he returned to London he gave Leslie Stephen an outline of the story, to be called *The Trumpet-Major*, but Stephen had doubts about the popularity of a historical novel, so Hardy arranged for its serialisation in *Good Words* in the following year. Meanwhile, the *New Quarterly*, which had published *An Indiscretion in the Life of an Heiress*, asked for another short story, and Hardy, fresh from his visit to south Dorset, sent them *The Distracted Young Preacher*, which appeared in April. The scene is the downland between the village of Owermoigne and the coast, from Ringstead Bay to Lulworth Cove; the story a delightful comedy of a Methodist curate who falls in love with his young widowed landlady, and finds himself helping her to hide smuggled brandy in the church tower, an enterprise that is viewed with some misgiving by the other smugglers: 'If the pa'son should see him a trespassing here in his tower, 'twould be none the better for we, seeing how 'a do hate chapel-members. He'd never buy a tub of us again.' So Hardy, who might almost be called 'The Distracted Poet', found himself a writer of short stories as well as of long serials, and in the next fifteen years or so wrote about 40 of them.

He was, however, no longer the Poor Man. The proprietors of the American *Harper's Magazine* planned to publish a European edition and, to ensure its successful inauguration, asked Hardy to supply them with a serial that was to begin with their first issue in December 1880, offering him £100 for each of 13 instalments. In mid-Victorian times, when the value of money was four or five times that of today, and income tax 1d. in the £, this was a considerable sum. But before he could begin to write for *Harper's* he had to supply *Good Words* with 12 instalments of *The Trumpet-Major*, which would then be published by Smith, Elder as a novel.

In spite of all this work in hand he found time for other things during the London season. In June he attended an International Literary Congress, and in July a garden-party at the house of their neighbours, the Alexander Macmillans. There he met John Morley, whom he had not seen since he read the manuscript of *The Poor Man and the Lady*; and the New York publisher Henry Holt, who assured him that the American language, spoken by twice as many people as there were in England, must eventually supersede English. The party and thunderstorm that interrupted it were soon to supply material for a characteristic scene in *A Laodicean*. More important, since he was writing about the Napoleonic Wars and contemplating 'a grand drama' about them, was the sight of the Emperor's nephew, Prince Napoleon, at the funeral of Louis Napoleon, son of the late Napoleon III. The Prince, nicknamed 'Plon-Plon', bore a remarkable resemblance to his famous uncle, as Hardy noted: 'complexion dark, sallow, even sinister: a round projecting chin: countenance altogether extraordinarily remindful of Boney.' This glimpse of the first Napoleon's image was to be of great help to him when writing *The Dynasts*.

In August he went again to Bockhampton, where he was joined a week later by Emma. They then found rooms in Weymouth, and with his mother drove round the countryside that was the setting of his novel: to Upwey mill and Sutton Poyntz where the Lovedays and Garlands were supposed to have lived, at the foot of White Horse Hill. The English August was as wet as it is a century later, and Hardy noted the ships without passengers, pleasure-boats without customers, the anxious faces of landladies at their windows, the unusual civility of shopkeepers and remarkable fall in their prices. On returning to London they resumed the social round, and in December Hardy attended the inaugural dinner of the Rabelais Club, founded to foster virility in literature, Hardy being asked to join as 'the most virile writer of works of imagination then in London,' though it is difficult to imagine anyone less Rabelaisian than the quiet, abstemious little man, Thomas Hardy.

In January 1880 *The Trumpet-Major* started its run as a serial, and he now began to meet the most distinguished authors of his age, some of them at the house of Mrs Procter, whose acquaintance with poets went back as far as Keats, who had died 60 years before; she introduced him to Browning, and with her he went to lunch with Tennyson. Then there was Matthew Arnold, who seemed to have 'made up his mind upon everything years ago,' and Lord Houghton, who introduced him to James Russell Lowell, whose dialect poems, such as the delightful 'The Courtin',' are the New England equivalent of the Wessex poems of Barnes and Hardy himself. Lord Houghton, formerly Richard Monckton Milnes, then a man of seventy, a minor poet and patron of literature, took to Hardy and invited him to his Yorkshire home later in the year, a visit that was to be prevented by illness. Meanwhile he dined with his new friends at clubs, and even went to see the Derby; he knew and cared nothing about racing, but such sights were all parts of a novelist's work. It was just ten years since his second novel had been rejected as 'far too sensational', the ten years in which he had risen from obscurity to celebrity; just ten years since he had met Emma at St Juliot.

In April the *New Quarterly* published another of his short stories, 'Fellow Townsmen'. The town was Bridport in west Dorset, a place that rarely appears in his work, and his recent exploration of the coast may have prompted the setting. It is a sad little story of a man who marries a woman of higher social standing than himself instead of the girl he ought to have married: 'I suppose it was destiny—accident—I don't know what, that separated us, dear Lucy. Anyhow you were the woman I ought to have made my wife—and I let you slip, like the foolish man that I was!' It is a curious anticipation of 'my lost prize' in 'Thoughts of Phena', written in the house in which Hardy tells us 'their troubles began,' and by this time he may have begun to think of himself as the foolish man. Mrs Procter called him cruel: 'Why not let him come home again and marry his first love? But I see you are right. He should not have deserted her.' Perhaps Mrs Procter, all unintentionally, was the cruel one.

What Emma did while her husband dined at clubs and went on expeditions alone we do not know, but at the end of August, having finished *The Trumpet-Major*, he took her to Normandy again, and again in search of material for a novel. From Boulogne they went to Amiens and as far west as Caen, but spent some time at coastal resorts: Trouville, Honfleur, Étretât, where he indulged, probably over-indulged, his passion for swimming. On their return he went again to Dorset, and then with Emma for a week's visit to Cambridge. They were back in London on 23 October, the day of publication of *The Trumpet-Major*.

It is a singular novel for a man who had just left Dorset to have written in Upper Tooting: a Dorset romance of the time of Trafalgar. It had entailed several visits to Dorchester and Weymouth in search of information only to be found in local newspapers, periodicals and pamphlets, about such things as the organisation of the militia, and the doings of George III when on holiday by the sea. On the other hand, the British Museum was useful for more general research, and much of the material had been in his mind since childhood, stories told by his grandmother and other elderly people—there is one of them in his poem 'The Alarm'—and sights of decaying relics of the time: old uniforms, weapons, trenches on the downs, and remains of the beacon-keeper's hut. He took immense pains over detail, and made sketches of the uniforms of regiments sent to defend the Wessex coast. So we have the York Hussars with white pantaloons, scarlet shakos, blue jackets and pelisse, the gaily plumed Dragoons, black-gaitered Infantry, and drilling of the local Volunteers: 'At the word *Prime*, shake the powder into the priming-pan, three last fingers behind the rammer. . . .' There is a visit to the Weymouth theatre, managed by Elliston, to see a Colman play with Bannister in the lead, a full description of the *Victory* and of Captain Hardy at his Po'sham home, and glimpses of the King himself, first as a profile reminiscent of the current coinage, then as reviewer of his troops, as occupant of the royal bathing-machine, and finally as 'George What! What!', butt of the scurrilous Peter Pindar. Hardy makes no mention of

Wordsworth's brother John, who at that critical time, February 1805, went down with his ship when it was wrecked off Portland Bill, where Anne watched the *Victory* sail past. It would have made another touch of local colour, and he mentioned it in the first scene of *The Dynasts*.

Like *Under the Greenwood Tree*, which in many ways it resembles, *The Trumpet-Major* is a charming lightweight among the novels. The characters are simple, conventional types, most of whom can be described by a single epithet: jovial Miller Loveday, the counterpart of Tranter Reuben; tractable Mrs Garland; sentimental Anne; weathercock Bob. John is too good to be true, Festus too cowardly, and Uncle Benjy, though amusing, too fantastic. There is no great tension in the story, which is little more than a sequence of episodes—an expedition to see the review, the arrival and departure of Matilda, the press-gang raid—having little bearing on the pathos of the last scene, in which the undeserving Bob is left to marry Anne and her money, while John, selfless almost to masochism, marches into the night and death on a battlefield in Spain. Most of the scenes take place by day, there is nothing evil, and neither church nor churchyard, the nearest approach to Hardyan grotesquerie being Uncle Benjy's antics with his box and Corporal Tullidge's crunching of his bones. The writing is correspondingly simple and natural: placid narrative and dialogue, without forced allusions and with few extended descriptions of nature. Such descriptions, indeed, are curiously perfunctory, and one of them, at the beginning of Chapter 23, is taken almost word-for-word from Chapter 12 of *Desperate Remedies*. Hardy, of course, intended the book to be no more than it is: an unpretentious, entertaining, eminently readable reconstruction of country life at a critical time in English history, and he classed it with *A Pair of Blue Eyes* among his Romances and Fantasies. But there is something more than the story—Hardy himself. We hear the poet in the imagery: 'an aged form of the same colour as the road'; the Isle of Portland 'like a great crouching animal tethered to the mainland'; Casterbridge ale 'brisk as a volcano'; Uncle Benjy's carcass 'little more than a light empty husk, dry and fleshless as that of a dead heron found on a moor in January.'

And we hear the man in such observations as: 'the paving was worn into a gutter by the ebb and flow of feet that had been going on there ever since Tudor times', and 'a world where there are few good things.'

When Hardy was in Cambridge in October he had begun to feel unwell, and by the time he returned to London felt so ill that he consulted a doctor, who diagnosed an internal bleeding, which meant either an operation or lying in bed for several months. The first instalment of his new serial, *A Laodicean*, was already printed for the December issue of *Harper's Magazine*, which would appear in November, and as he had written only about a quarter of the story an operation meant that he would be unable to keep up to date with copy, and would forfeit his first really lucrative contract. Moreover, this was the first English number of the American periodical, and its successful launching depended largely on his contribution. For nearly five months, therefore, he lay on his back with his body sloping down from his feet to his head, and dictated the remainder of the book to Emma.

The opening chapters written before his illness were promising, though the choice of scene was disappointing: Dunster, a small town on the coast of Somerset, a lovely place, but one that Hardy knew little about, and with which, therefore, he could not identify himself as he could with his native Dorset. The theme was to be the impact of the new on the old, of nineteenth-century invention on relics of medievalism; the contrast between ancient isolation with its leisurely pleasures, and modern communication with its feverish fret, symbolised by the castle and the railway, the arrow-slit and telegraph-wire that entered it, by the Norman family of de Stancy and upstart family of John Power, who built the railway, bought the castle, died, and left it to his daughter Paula, the Laodicean, lukewarm in her allegiances; the contest for her hand between Captain de Stancy with his 'animal ancestry' and inherited physical characteristics, and George Somerset with a pedigree derived from the architect of the Parthenon, and a face of the man of the future.

The first chapter is almost pure autobiography. George Somerset is a young draughtsman who has returned to architecture after two unprofitable years of writing verse. He hears the hymn 'New Sabbath' sung, which reminds him of his childhood and the west-gallery period of church music, and he disputes with a Baptist minister about paedobaptism, as Hardy had argued with the good Perkins of Dorchester. In the following chapters of Book One the love affair of Somerset and Paula Power slowly unfolds, but then comes the change; William Dare, illegitimate son of Captain de Stancy, takes over, and the story plunges into the melodrama of *Desperate Remedies*.

Dare's object is to marry his father to Paula, and to do this he blackmails the architect who is Somerset's rival for the restoration of the castle, and takes him by night to make tracings of Somerset's designs; makes his father slightly drunk and gives him a peep of Paula undulating in pink flannel in her gymnasium; sends a telegram to Paula, signed 'G. Somerset' saying that he has lost all at Monte Carlo, and asking for £100; shows her a faked photograph of Somerset apparently 'advanced in intoxication'; and when his machinations are discovered he sets fire to the castle. But the most grotesque scenes take place in the church vestry; in one, Dare gambles with and fleeces his 'illegitimate father'; in the other he and Paula's uncle blackmail one another at pistol point. Apart from this melodrama, the last half of the book is an interminable conversation between Paula and de Stancy—'My sedulous avoidance hitherto of all relating to our family vicissitudes has been . . .'—relieved by Baedeker-like extracts from Hardy's travels: Strassburg—Kleber Platz—statue of General Kleber—cathedral spire—Goethe's house—the popular clock-work of Schwilgué; and in the same manner to Baden, Karlsruhe, Heidelberg, Scheveningen again, and finally to Étretât.

It must be remembered how Hardy wrote, or rather, dictated most of the last five Books of the novel, lying in an unnatural position, and often in pain and perturbation of spirit. The wonder is that he was able to concentrate as he did, for the story is at least ingenious, and if it were only half the length would be, as a thriller, entertaining. We can almost follow the course of its composition; in December he made the note, 'There is mercy in troubles coming in battalions—they neutralise each other,' and on page 226 of *A Laodicean* we read of how 'Troubles had apparently come in battalions.' And again, the note, 'Romanticism will exist in human nature as long as human nature itself exists,' is repeated verbatim in the novel 90 pages later.

In his helplessness, and as Emma was his nurse as well as amanuensis, Hardy could not give all his waking hours to his serial, even if he wished to, and he thought much about his projected drama of the Napoleonic Wars—'action mostly automatic'—but mainly about his own predicament and the predicament of man. After endless hours of 'trying to reconcile a scientific view of life with the emotional and spiritual, so that they may not be interdestructive'—the eternal conflict in Hardy's mind—he came to the conclusion:

Law has produced in man a child who cannot but constantly reproach its parent for doing much and yet not all, and constantly say to such parent that it would have been better never to have begun doing than to have *over*done so indecisively; that is, than to have created so far beyond all apparent first intention (on the emotional side), without mending matters by a second intent and execution, to eliminate the evils of the blunder of overdoing. The emotions have no place in a world of defect, and it is a cruel injustice that they should have developed in it.

If Law itself had consciousness, how the aspect of its creatures would terrify it, fill it with remorse!

Man, 'slighted and enduring', was at the mercy of unconscious natural forces, 'Law', which 20 years later was to become 'It' of *The Dynasts*, which 'works unconsciously, as heretofore.'

By the end of March 1881 Hardy was allowed to leave his bed, and in April went for a drive with Emma and his doctor, his first outing since October. Although very weak, he was able to finish the writing of *A Laodicean* himself, in pencil, and early in May went out for the first time alone, for a walk on Wandsworth Common. It was like a rebirth. He was now almost 41, and his long illness divided the first half of his life from the second much as a revolution cuts across the course of history. As a young man, five years in London had affected his health, and he had returned to Dorset; now after another three years and a severe illness, he decided to return again. They had been years of growing estrangement from his wife, an estrangement that may have begun with no more than a snub when he used a dialect word, such as Elizabeth-Jane's 'leery' which so infuriated Henchard. She was his social superior, and a deeply religious woman; any talk of an 'unconscious Law' would widen the rift, and there was no child to symbolise their union and hold them together. They had been happy at Sturminster Newton three years before; perhaps they would be happy again somewhere in Dorset, so in June they went to look for a house, and found one in Wimborne.

CHAPTER TEN

Wimborne
1881–83

Like Sturminster, Wimborne Minster is on the north bank of the Stour, though nearly 20 miles farther down the river, in the heathland not far from Bournemouth. On his first house-hunting expedition, five years before, Hardy had stayed in Wimborne, where he had entered the Minster at night and listened to the organist practising by candlelight, a characteristic incident that may have affected his choice, and his taking a two-year lease of 'Llanherne' in The Avenue, a Victorian villa with a garden full of old-fashioned flowers and ripening fruits, and a conservatory from which on the first night of their occupation, 25 June, they saw Tebbutt's comet.

The main attraction of Wimborne is its Minster, Saxon in origin, destroyed by the Danes, rebuilt by the Normans, and altered in various styles of Gothic during the Middle Ages: the kind of visual record of history that was so dear to Hardy's heart. Inside, the record is even more moving, one of people rather than of periods: a brass tablet in memory of King Ethelred

of Wessex, said to be buried here; the fifteenth-century alabaster
effigies of a Duke of Beaufort and his Duchess; the altar-tomb
of Gertrude, mother of Edward Courtenay, last Earl of Devonshire; the Jacobean monument of Sir Edmund Uvedale; and
high on the wall of the west tower a medieval clock connected
to the Jackman outside, once the figure of a monk but since the
Napoleonic Wars a grenadier who appears to strike the quarter-
hours. Such was the scene that moved Hardy to write 'Copying
Architecture in an old Minster':

> How smartly the quarters of the hour march by
>   That the jack-o'-clock never forgets;
> Ding-dong; and before I have traced a cusp's eye,
> Or got the true twist of the ogee over,
>   A double ding-dong ricochetts . . .
>
> I grow to conceive it a call to ghosts,
>   Whose mould lies below and around.
> Yes; the next 'Come, come,' draws them out from their posts,
> And they gather, and one shade appears, and another,
>   As the eve-damps creep from the ground.
>
> See—a Courtenay stands by his quatre-foiled tomb,
>   And a Duke and a Duchess near;
> And one Sir Edmund in columned gloom,
> And a Saxon king by the presbytery chamber;
>   And shapes unknown in the rear . . .
>
> Or perhaps they speak to the yet unborn,
>   And caution them not to come
> To a world so ancient and trouble-torn,
> Of foiled intents, vain lovingkindness
>   And ardours chilled and numb . . .

According to *Black's Guide,* Wimborne at this time was a
'clean, neat and healthy' little town of some 2300 inhabitants,
'but despite its manufactories of coaches and knitted hose, by
no means lively.' The Hardys, however, made friends, being
much in demand for Shakespeare readings, when they had to be
careful to omit the Bard's improprieties, and at the end of the
year they attended a ball given by Lord Wimborne at Canford

29. 'The vast tract of unenclosed wild known as Egdon Heath.' Photo. by Hermann Lea, *c.* 1900.

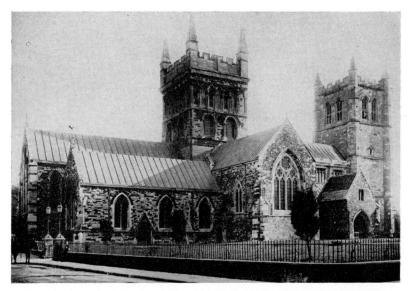

30. Wimborne Minster. (The Quarter Jack can be seen in the lower half of the tower window on the right.) The Hardys lived in Wimborne June 1881–June 1883, and here Hardy wrote *Two on a Tower*.

31. Max Gate when the Hardys moved in, June 1885: 'An unpretentious red-brick structure of moderate size, somewhat quaintly built.'

Manor, an early-nineteenth-century 'Gothick' mansion on the other side of the river, now a public school.

There were other activities. In August they went to Scotland, returning by way of the Lake District, and in September Hardy was revising *A Laodicean* for its publication in volumes. In November it was published in America without these revisions, and in England in December. Reviewers were agreed that this was Hardy's poorest novel, and *Harper's Magazine* apologised to its readers for their disappointing serial: 'its movement is languid, its actors tame and colourless, and its plot and incidents hackneyed.' Two months later, in February 1882, the unsold copies were remaindered, and Hardy destroyed the manuscript.

It was a discouraging start to the new year, but by this time he was engaged on another novel. He had been approached by the *Atlantic Monthly*, an American magazine, for a serial 'to run through six or more numbers,' and in December went to London to see their agents and to inspect Greenwich Observatory. He had always been interested in astronomy, as is clear from his description of the December sky as seen from the chalk downs in the second chapter of *Far from the Madding Crowd*:

the twinkling of all the stars seemed to be but throbs of one body, timed by a common pulse. . . . A difference of colour in the stars . . . was really perceptible here. The sovereign brilliancy of Sirius pierced the eye with a steely glitter, the star called Capella was yellow, Aldebaran and Betelgueux shone with a fiery red.

The comet that he had seen when moving into their Wimborne house had quickened his interest, and suggested the writing of a story in which 'the emotional history of two infinitesimal lives' are set against, not the Dorset landscape, but 'the stupendous background of the stellar universe.' To gain admission to Greenwich Observatory he had to write a formal letter to the Astronomer Royal stating the reason for his request, so with his tongue in his cheek he wrote a pseudo-scientific letter asking if it would be possible 'to adapt an old tower, built in a plantation in the West of England for other objects, to the requirements of a telescopic study of the stars by a young man very ardent in that pursuit.' It was true enough, though the ardent young man had only just been conceived. The old tower was a late-eighteenth-century hollow column in the park of Charborough House, some six miles west of Wimborne, and by the beginning of 1882 he was writing the opening chapters of *Two on a Tower*.

His work was interrupted in March when he and Emma went to Liverpool to see a performance of *The Mistress of the Farm*, his dramatisation of *Far from the Madding Crowd* in collaboration with J. Comyns Carr, a dramatic critic. Hardy wished to keep as close to the novel as possible, and did not approve of all Carr's alterations, particularly the reported drowning of Fanny Robin: 'Why not died in workhouse, or hung herself in workhouse?' he asked. However, the play was quite successful, and when it moved to London ran through May and June at the Globe. Unfortunately it led to controversy, for two months before the Liverpool production Pinero's *The Squire* was staged in London, with a plot resembling *Far from the Madding Crowd*. It was not Pinero's fault, for he had not read the novel, but had heard an outline of the plot of the Hardy–Carr adaptation, apparently from the actress Mrs Kendal to whom it had first been submitted. Hardy wrote a letter of protest to the *Times*, and misunderstanding led to bitterness and petty countercharges of plagiarism in *The Trumpet-Major* (his humorous drill-scene was based on a description in a book of 1817) and *A Laodicean* (some 20 lines about racing taken from an article in the *Quarterly Review* of 1833) before the matter was forgotten.

Hardy had neither taste nor time for controversy. He had to write hurriedly to supply the *Atlantic Monthly* with his serial, which began its run in the May number. He worked hard in Wimborne throughout the summer, and finished the story by September; when he took Emma on a coach-tour round Wessex: north to Salisbury, the Melchester of his novels and city of his favourite cathedral, then west across the Devonshire border to Axminster, and back through Lyme Regis, Dorchester and Winterborne Came, where they called on William Barnes. They did not stay long in Wimborne, but early in October sailed from Weymouth to Cherbourg on their way to Paris, where they took a small flat on the left bank of the river, from which they explored the city and studied old pictures in the Louvre and new ones in the Luxembourg. If they had been a little earlier they could have seen Manet's 'Bar aux Folies Bergères', and paintings by Cézanne Degas, Monet and Gauguin at the Seventh Impressionist Exhibition. But Hardy was more interested in Versailles and the French Revolution than in the revolution in French art.

Soon after their return to Wimborne *Two on a Tower* was published both in London and in the United States. It had a mixed reception, and Hardy wrote to Edmund Gosse, to whom he gave a copy: 'Eminent critics write and tell me in private that it is the most original thing I have done—that the affair of the Bishop is a triumph in tragi-comedy &c, &c. While other eminent critics (I wonder if they are the same) *print* the most cutting rebukes you can conceive—show me (to my amazement) that I am quite an immoral person.' He had never before been charged with immorality, but now Victorian taste was offended by the book's impropriety and so-called satire of the Church. Of course Hardy was not satirising the Church, but he was making fun of the Right Reverend Cuthbert Helmsdale, D.D.: 'When the Bishop arrived and gone into the chancel, and blown his nose. . . .' And the 'episcopal countenance' wears a very different expression in the churchyard when lecturing Swithin on the subject of women from the perpetual smile when larking with Lady Constantine on the lawn. It is true that her fathering him with Swithin's child is a little hard, but we cannot feel much sympathy for him, and he makes excellent comic relief. As for Viviette and impropriety: she is an ill-treated, childless, lonely, 'slightly voluptuous' young woman, whose interest in the beautiful boy whom she finds on her tower develops from patronage of promising genius into maternal affection and passionate love. Swithin St Cleeve is another Stephen Smith, an ingenuous youth of 20 devoted to astronomy, and the ripening love between the two, until it bursts 'like a spring bud', is movingly described against the background of infinity. Through his telescope he shows her the planets, then the stars, remote and ever more remote, plunging down abysses of which she has never dreamed, from the distance at which dignity begins, to those of grandeur, solemnity, awfulness, and finally ghastliness. But there is beauty as well as ghastliness in the night sky—

'Saturn is lovely; Jupiter is simply sublime'—until, a third of the way through the book, the heavens fade, and mundane melodrama begins with the entry of Louis, the horsey cigar-smoking brother of Viviette. Hardy forgets the stupendous background of the stellar universe, and we are left with two infinitesimal lives and the cobwebby machinations of brother Louis to separate them and marry Viviette to the Bishop. There is a short description of the Aurora Borealis, an allusion to the eclipse of the moon, some talk of Greenwich Observatory, and on one occasion Swithin 'remembered with interest that Venus was in a favourable aspect for observation that afternoon.'

Only in the pathos of the last few pages is the poetry of the opening scenes recaptured. Swithin returns from the Cape an experienced young man of 25, to find Viviette on top of their tower. At first glance she knows that he no longer loves her with her faded beauty, but 'Viviette!' he says, 'I have come to marry you!' and she dies of joy in his arms. He looks down from the tower for help, but 'Nobody appeared in sight but Tabitha Lark,' only a girl when he left but now a beautiful young woman. Despite, or perhaps because of, its reputation for impropriety, *Two on a Tower* was soon reprinted, pirated in America, published on the Continent by Tauchnitz, adding to Hardy's popularity; deservedly so, for despite inequality, it is one of the most poetically conceived and written of the novels.

Not long after its publication came news of Cadell Holder's death, and the living link with St Juliot was severed. Hardy remembered Emma's brother-in-law with affection, and his stories, 'rather well-found than well-founded', with amusement. And he recalled how, ten years before, he had sometimes read the lessons for him in church, and watched for Emma's smile when they sat there together. Now, at the end of 1882, they were taking lessons in First Aid, and sat facing a dangling skeleton in front of a window through which they could see the little figures of children at play.

During the winter Hardy wrote a short novel for the *Graphic*, the very *Romantic Adventures of a Milkmaid*, in which a mysterious foreign gentleman clumsily plays the part of fairy godfather, and this he followed with an article for *Longman's*

Magazine on 'The Dorsetshire Labourer'. It was a period of severe agricultural depression, when cheap corn poured into England after the railway had linked the Middle-West wheatlands of America with its eastern ports, and Hardy noted with regret the rapid depopulation of the countryside. And he compared nostalgically the picturesque costumes of countryfolk before 1870, the humorous simplicity of the men and unsophisticated modesty of the women about which he had written in *Far from the Madding Crowd*, with the shabby imitations of city clothes and manners of ten years later. All was in a state of flux; no longer did families settle in a village for life, and for lives, but migrated annually, so losing their individuality. On the other hand, they were widening the range of their ideas and gaining in freedom. 'It is too much to expect them to remain stagnant and old-fashioned for the pleasure of romantic spectators.'

Yet, it is among comparatively poor and ignorant settled communities 'that happiness will find her last refuge on earth, since it is among them that a perfect insight into the conditions of existence will be longest postponed.' For Hardy, knowledge of the true nature of the physical world meant unhappiness, as he had recently written in *Two on a Tower*: 'It is better—far better—for men to forget the universe than to bear it clearly in mind.' He had read Pascal, but it was not so much that 'Le silence éternel de ces espaces m'effraie,' as that its infinite unconsciousness was horrifying; and 'There is something in the inexorably simple logic of such men [scientists] which partakes of the cruelty of the natural laws that are their study.' In addition to the unhappiness brought about by scientific revelation was his own discovery, of which he made a note while in Paris, that he was 'living in a world where nothing bears out in practice what it promises incipiently.' It was with thoughts such as these that he visited London with Emma during the season, before leaving Wimborne in June and moving to Dorchester, into a house that they rented in Shirehall Lane at the top of the town.

CHAPTER ELEVEN

Dorchester

1883–85

It was a dark old house of which a fellow townsman remarked, 'He have but one window, and she do look into Gaol Lane.' But it was only a stopgap, for after nine years of wandering and living in other people's houses Hardy wanted one of his own, and for the last half of 1883 he was mainly engaged in buying a site and preparing to build. The site chosen was a plot of more than an acre about a mile west of Dorchester on the north side of the road to Wareham. He then had to design the house, and must have smiled wryly when he remembered his first short story of 20 years before, the prophetic-unprophetic 'How I Built myself a House': 'This notion was to build a house of our own a little further out of town . . . to fitly inaugurate the new happiness.' It was to be called Max Gate, a variation of Mack's Gate, the name given to a nearby tollgate, in the adjoining cottage of which the keeper, one Mack, had formerly lived.

There was no water-main in those days, no bathroom was planned, and in October workmen began to sink a well in the garden. Although the prehistoric barrow of Conquer Down was only 300 yds to the east, for Hardy the one drawback to his chosen site was its 'newness', its lack of history; but when they had dug three feet into the chalk they found three skeletons, each in an oval grave with knees drawn up to the chin, like a chicken in its shell. So far from having no history, the site had been a small burial-ground, perhaps of a family, when Dorchester had been Durnovaria, one of the last western outposts of Roman civilisation 1500 years before. At the end of November the house was begun, its builders, Hardy & Son of Bockhampton, and a month later, on the last day of the year, Hardy planted trees to screen it from the road.

In March 1884 he made a note: 'Write a novel entitled "Two against Time",' but what in fact he did was to begin a novel called *The Mayor of Casterbridge*: 'One evening of late summer, before the nineteenth century had reached one-third of its span, a young man and woman, the latter carrying a child . . .' It was commissioned by the *Graphic*, but as serialisation was not to begin until January 1886, he had nearly two years to finish the book and, for the first time in his career as novelist, could write at leisure. On 2 June he celebrated his forty-fourth birthday at Bockhampton, next day watered the ground at Max Gate, and then took Emma to London, where he met, among others, Burne-Jones (at a party given by Alma-Tadema) and Henry James, who was then writing *The Bostonians*, a very different novel from the one Hardy was working on. In August he went to Jersey, original home of the Dorset Hardys, in search of material, not this time with his wife, but with his brother, and by the end of the year he had almost finished the book.

In London they had met Lady Portsmouth, 'a woman of talent, part of whose talent consists in concealing that she has any,' and she invited them to spend a few days with her and her husband, a fox-hunting earl, at their home, Eggesford House, in north Devon. Unfortunately, Emma was not well enough to go, so Hardy went to his first aristocratic house-party alone, but soon after his arrival wrote her a brief account of his reception. As this is the first of his surviving letters to his wife, and written after their troubles had begun, it is worth quoting:

Friday March 13, 85

My dearest Em,

I arrived at Eggesford Station a little after 4, and found there Lord Portsmouth's brougham waiting to take me up to the house, so there was no trouble at all. The scenery here is lovely and the house very handsome—not an enormous one—on account of its position, which is on a hill in the park. I have had tea with Lady Portsmouth and the ladies—the only members of the family at home—Lord

Portsmouth not having returned from hunting yet (6 p.m.). The young ladies are very attentive, and interested in what I tell them—Lady Portsmouth charges them to take care of me—and goes away to her parish people etc.—altogether a delightful household. There are ladies here too, visiting, but of course I have only had a glimpse as yet. They sympathise with you—and Lady Portsmouth says you *must* come when you are well. I am now in the library writing this. I should say that a married daughter, Lady Rosamond Christie, I think she is, who is here, strikes me as a particularly sensible woman. If Lady Portsmouth's orders are to be carried out my room will be like a furnace—she is so particularly anxious that I should not take cold, etc. The drawing room is lined with oak panels from a monastery. When I arrived the schoolchildren were practising singing in the hall, for Sunday in Church.

In haste (as you will believe)

Yours ever

Tom.[13]

It is mainly factual, certainly not 'literary', but not without affection: 'My dearest Em,' and 'Lady Portsmouth says you *must* come when you are well.' But he does not add that he hopes she already feels better, nor does he send his love. And there are too many ladies. He spent most of the time driving round the villages and walking in the park with the Portsmouths, and did little writing, although the library was reserved for him so that he could continue his novel. However, a month after his return to Dorchester he made the note: 'Friday, April 17. Wrote the last page of *The Mayor of Casterbridge*, begun at least a year ago.'

Hardy wrote his novel of Casterbridge-Dorchester, then, while he was living in the town between the summers of 1883 and 1885, when the places he describes were only a few yards from his door—The King's Arms, Henchard's house, Maumbury Rings, Grey's Bridge—and no other small town in England has been more lovingly and faithfully depicted. It was not the Dorchester of the eighteen-eighties, however, but of the eighteen-forties when as a boy he had threaded his way up High Street between vans, horses, pig-pens, and past 'The Three Mariners' where John Standish, called Stannidge in the novel, was landlord. With the exception of *The Return of the Native* it is the most localised of the novels, all the action taking place within this square of huddled houses—apart from the opening and closing scenes. For Henchard is not a native of Dorchester, and in this lies part of the pathos. We first see him at Weydon-Priors (Weyhill), 50 miles north-east of the town, coming from we know not where, and he goes as an outcast to die in the desolation of the Dorset heath.

If not unique among the novels in unity of place, it is unique in another way. In all the others save *Jude*, where hero and heroine form what may be called a binary system, the principal character is a woman, from Bathsheba to Tess, but the *Mayor of Casterbridge* is the story of a man, Michael Henchard, a blazing sun about whom the other characters revolve as lesser luminaries. His first wife Susan is so faint as to be almost invisible; Lucetta twinkles uncertainly for a time; Elizabeth-Jane shines with simple constancy until her light is dimmed by the cold star that eclipses Henchard. 'There are, then, some Scotch people who stay at home,' Hardy had remarked when in a crowded Edinburgh he recalled Johnson's annihilating retort on hearing that Boswell 'came from' Scotland: 'That, Sir, I find is what a very great many of your countrymen cannot help.' Farfrae was one of them, and enthralled his Wessex audiences with his song of 'Hame, hame fain would I be ... hame to my own countree!' All but Christopher Coney who asked, but got no reply: 'What did you come away from yer own country for, young maister, if ye be so wownded about it?' If he had not come away, there would have been no tragedy of Michael Henchard.

There is nothing vicious about Farfrae; indeed, he is a model of virtue: kind, generous, honest, a better man than Henchard; yet he never laughs, has no sense of humour, and he is cold, or rather, he is composed of two distinct elements, a warm romanticism and a cold calculating commercialism, 'like the colours of a variegated cord ... intertwisted, yet not mingling.' He is the very antithesis of Henchard, even physically; the one is fair, slight, agile, soft-spoken, the other dark, huge, loud-voiced, 'moving like a great tree in a wind'; and he is all of a piece: fiery, impetuous, tigerish, volcanic, superstitious, loving and hating in extremes. Music moves Farfrae to sentimentalism, but for Henchard it is of regal power, and 'high harmonies transubstantiated him.' He belongs to the past or passing way of life, Farfrae to the future: happy-go-lucky emotional man, and the machine. Hardy's heart was with Henchard, but he knew that Farfrae must prevail.

He gave his novel the sub-title, 'A Story of a Man of Character,' and quoted the dictum of Novalis, 'Character is Fate.' Farfrae's good fortune is the result less of extraneous luck than of innate prudence: he would have done well for himself anywhere; and ultimately it is Henchard's character also that determines his fate. The nearest parallel to Henchard in our literature is King Lear, whose fiery temper and rash renunciation of Cordelia are the cause of his tragedy, much as young Henchard's sale of his wife was to be, 20 years later, the cause of his. Lear should have been aware of the lurking evil, but there is no evil, or very little, in *The Mayor of Casterbridge*, and it is circumstance that is the immediate cause of Henchard's wreck: the convergence of the twain, of the liner and the iceberg, his meeting with Farfrae. There is no collision, only friction, but it is Farfrae who, without malice, without percipience, acting always with the best intentions, takes from him Lucetta, his business, his mayoralty, his money, his house, his furniture, his pride, and Elizabeth-Jane. The final irony, however, has nothing to do with Farfrae; Henchard leaves Elizabeth-Jane to free her and die on the heath, Newson leaves her because he prefers a sea-view in Weymouth. Like Lear, Henchard dies a better man than he lived, but unlike Lear he has no Kent to comfort him at the end, only the Fool, the bullied but faithful Abel Whittle:

He was kind-like to mother when she wer here below, sending her the best ship-coal, and hardly any ashes from it at all. . . . I thought he looked low and faltering. And I followed en. . . . We walked on like that all night; and in the blue o' the morning, when 'twas hardly day, I looked ahead o' me, and I zeed that he wambled, and could hardly drag along. . . . But he didn't gain strength, for you see, ma'am, he couldn't eat—no, no appetite at all—and he got weaker; and to-day he died.

This is great tragic prose, though it does not mean that *The Mayor of Casterbridge* is the prose equivalent of *King Lear*; but it is one of the few works in literature that can bear comparison with Shakespeare's greatest tragedy.

Of course there are improbabilities in the plot. As usual, too much depends on overhearing conversations, and the last person to whom Henchard should have entrusted Lucetta's letters was Jopp, but it was necessary to find an occasion for the skimmity-ride and her death. The sale of a wife in nineteenth-century England may seem improbable, yet such things happened. They happened in Dorchester, and even if they had not Hardy could have heard of such a transaction when he visited the Giffords at Lanivet, near Bodmin:

A man named Walter, of the parish of Lanivet, led forward his wife by a halter, which was fastened round her waist, and publicly offered her for sale. A person called Sobey, who has lately been discharged from the 28th regiment, bid sixpence for her, and was immediately declared the purchaser. He led off his bargain in triumph, amidst the shouts of the crowd, and to the great apparent satisfaction of her former owner.[14]

Hardy himself defended the improbable, or at least the uncommon, as a main source of interest: 'The real, if unavowed, purpose of fiction is to give pleasure by gratifying the love of the uncommon.' But, 'The uncommonness must be in the events, not in the characters; and the writer's art lies in shaping that uncommonness while disguising its unlikelihood, if it be unlikely.' It is no more unlikely that Mother Cuxsom, alewife of Mixen Lane, should speak a lyrical valediction about Susan Henchard than that Mistress Quickly, alewife of Eastcheap, should speak one about Falstaff:

Well, poor soul, she's helpless to hinder that or anything now. And all her shining keys will be took from her, and her cupboards opened; and little things 'a didn't wish seen, anybody will see, and her wishes and ways will all be as nothing.

At least it is to be hoped that those really were the words of that plump Dorchester baggage. In 'Friends Beyond' the whispering shade of another Susan, Lady Susan O'Brien of Stinsford, speaks for herself in verse:

You may have my rich brocades, my laces; take each
    household key;

> Ransack coffer, desk, bureau;
> Quiz the few poor treasures hid there, con the letters kept
>   by me.

It is strange to think that the tragedy of Henchard was being played out in Casterbridge at the same time as that of the Yeobrights on the heath a few miles away. They probably never met, however, for as the background to the characters in *The Return of the Native* is always Egdon, so is the background to those in *The Mayor of Casterbridge* almost always Dorchester: Casterbridge 'shut in by a square wall of trees, like a plot of garden-ground by a box-edging.' Casterbridge, 'the complement of the rural life around,' so that butterflies flutter down High Street from the cornfields at the top to the two bridges and Frome meadows at the bottom. But for Hardy its streets and buildings, however attractive, were unimportant in comparison with the people who lived there, or rather, had lived there:

These bridges had speaking countenances. Every projection in each was worn down to obtuseness, partly by weather, more by friction from generations of loungers, whose toes and heels had from year to year made restless movements against these parapets, as they stood there meditating on the aspect of affairs.

And:

Mrs Henchard's dust mingled with the dust of women who lay ornamented with glass hair-pins and amber necklaces, and men who held in their mouths coins of Hadrian, Posthumus. and the Constantines.

He described Dorchester, present and past, with such affection and feeling for its history that it comes as something of a shock to read the note he made as he was finishing the book, at the time of his visit to the Portsmouths: 'Lady P . . . wants us to come to Devonshire. She says she would find a house for us. Cannot think why we live in benighted Dorset. Em would go willingly, for it is her native county; but, alas, my house at Dorchester is nearly finished.'

It was finished a few weeks later, and on 29 June 1885 they moved into Max Gate.

CHAPTER TWELVE

Max Gate

1885–89

How Hardy, architect, neighbour of Portland and lover of stone, could have designed such a house is something of a mystery: a cheerless, red-brick Victorian villa, with meaningless turret, fancy projections and windows of uncertain size. The inside was better, though conventional: an entrance hall, dining-room to the left, drawing-room to the right, above which, 20 years before, he would have planned a nursery, but now it was to be his first study. Emma found the house bleak and cold,[15] and he himself wondered if it was a mistake; reasons, perhaps, why they were so often away, and for many years to come went to London in spring and early summer for the 'season'.

They were there shortly before the move to Max Gate, but as Emma returned to Dorchester to make arrangements, Hardy wrote to tell her of his doings. His letter was mainly about a party given by Lady Carnarvon, at which were Lady Winifred Herbert (in blue), Lady Margaret (in black lace), Lady Dorothea, and Mrs Jeune, soon to become Lady Jeune and then Lady St Helier. It may be that Emma was interested in Lady Margaret's dull red fan, and Lady Winifred's complaint about the heaviness of the teapot, or it may be that she felt a twinge of jealousy. Ladies found Hardy attractive, or at least they took a maternal interest in him, and he was attracted by ladies; but Emma was no longer attractive: a plain middle-aged woman of nearly 45. When Robert Louis Stevenson, who was convalescing in Bournemouth, called at Max Gate in August, his wife described their visit in a letter: 'Did I tell you that we saw Hardy the novelist at Dorchester? A pale, gentle, frightened little man, that one felt an instinctive tenderness for, with a wife—ugly is no word for it!—who said "Whatever shall we do?" I had never heard a human being say it before.'

Hardy had now begun to write *The Woodlanders*, a story that he had abandoned ten years before in favour of *The Hand of Ethelberta*, to show critics that his art was not confined to the lives of Dorset tranters and shepherds. He was working too hard, more than ten hours a day, and in November was depressed, and defining tragedy as the catastrophe that follows the carrying out of some natural aim or desire. He had greeted the year 1885 with the bell-ringers in St Peter's church, only a few yards from his Shirehall-Lane house, but this time he wrote: 'This evening, the end of the old year 1885 finds me sadder than many previous New Year's Eves have done. Whether building this house at Max Gate was a wise expenditure of energy is one doubt, which, if resolved in the negative, is depressing enough.' 'And there are others,' he added.

At least he was not, or should not have been, worried about money. Weekly serialisation of *The Mayor of Casterbridge* began in the *Graphic* in January 1886, and at the same time in the American *Harper's Weekly*. Then, he was writing *The Woodlanders* for Macmillan's, the distinguished firm that had declined his first novel, but had now asked for a serial story that they would later publish in volumes. In May the first four chapters appeared in *Macmillan's Magazine*, and Smith, Elder published *The Mayor of Casterbridge*, though with some misgiving, as their reader had reported that 'the lack of gentry among the characters makes it uninteresting.' It was to be some years before the Victorians realised that it was the presence of gentry that made Hardy's novels uninteresting. Reviews were lukewarm. *Far from the Madding Crowd* was now the touchstone, and in comparison with that the *Saturday Review* found Henchard's story as disappointing as it was impossible, and though the rustics were as good as ever, there was not a single character capable of rousing a reader's interest in his or her welfare. With some qualifications, the *Spectator* praised the portrayal of Henchard, but disliked the 'fashionable pessimism' of the book. There were, however, more percipient critics: Gosse hailed Hardy as 'our greatest novelist', and Stevenson wrote to say how much he admired the book: 'Henchard is a great fellow, and Dorchester is touched in with the hand of a master.'

The Hardys were in London when the novel was published, in rooms near the British Museum, 'dining and lunching out almost every day' with hostesses such as Mrs Procter, Lady Carnarvon and Mrs Jeune. Among the many people whom Hardy met at this time were the Americans Oliver Wendell Holmes, whose *Autocrat* essays he had not read, and Henry James again, 'who has a ponderously warm manner of saying nothing in infinite sentences.' The two men had little in common, and each under-estimated the other's work. One tends to think of Hardy as a simple countryman living the year round in the depths of Wessex, and to forget that he spent almost as much time in London as in Dorset. Novel-writing had become a routine, and after the London season he returned to Max Gate to get on with *The Woodlanders*, almost half of which had already been serialised.

While he was thus engaged William Barnes died, aged 85. For the past 20 years he had been rector of Winterborne Came, a hamlet just to the south of Dorchester, and a bare mile from Max Gate. Hardy walked across the fields to attend his funeral, as described in 'The Last Signal', when a flash of the sun reflected by the coffin seemed to be a farewell wave of his old friend's hand. He also wrote an obituary for the *Athenaeum*, introduced by a characteristic portrait of the old schoolmaster-parson-poet, almost a relic of the eighteenth century, as on market days he would walk to the centre of Dorchester, a little grey dog at his heels, and carefully set his watch by the town clock. Hardy had already written an appreciation of his 'sweet rustic poems', and was later to edit a selection, with a Preface sadly describing the decay of the Dorset dialect.

For the first few weeks of 1887 he worked at *The Woodlanders*, which he finished early in February. It was a relief, as its last serial instalment was due in March, yet he was almost sorry to finish, for he had enjoyed the writing and in later years liked it, 'as a story', best of all his novels. However, its conclusion meant that he could take a holiday, and on 14 March he and Emma left Max Gate for London on their way to Italy. On the next day Macmillan's published *The Woodlanders* in three volumes.

Hardy never chose the same place twice as the centre for the action of his novels. So far he had written about Bockhampton, Stinsford, St Juliot, Puddletown, Swanage, Egdon Heath, Weymouth, Dunster, Wimborne, Dorchester, and now he moved to a part of Dorset of which he was especially fond, the woodlands and cider country of Blackmore Vale; more precisely, to the area where the Dorchester–Sherborne road falls steeply from the chalk plateau between High Stoy and Dogbury Hill to the fertile loam of 'gardens and orchards sunk in a concave': the village of Hermitage, approximately the original of Little Hintock where the Melburys lived. Hardy's descriptive writing is almost a physical transportation of the reader from the central heaths and chalklands to a region of leafy, flickering sunlight and shadow, and a more languorous air. But characteristically his imagination traces the rising stems of smoke from the cottage chimneys down to their roots in the hearths, and so to the people who inhabit them. It is, or was 100 years ago, in such isolated places that, 'from time to time, dramas of a grandeur and unity truly Sophoclean are enacted in the real, by virtue of the concentrated passions and closely knit interdependence of the lives therein.' And such a drama is *The Woodlanders*.

Not altogether, however. Shortly before its serialisation began, Hardy offered Macmillan's the choice of two titles: 'The Woodlanders', or 'Fitzpiers at Hintock', and they very wisely chose the former. Edred Fitzpiers and Mrs Charmond have nothing in common with the woodlanders; they are intruders from an urban world of wealth and fashion, and their drama is mere melodrama. The very name 'Edred Fitzpiers' symbolises the conventional cigar-smoking Victorian libertine, and Felice Charmond is a lady who reclines on a sofa, daringly puffing cigarettes and idly watching the smoke that rises from her delicately curled lips. Yet this melodrama of Fitzpiers, his seduction of Suke Damson and Felice, and Felice's murder by a hot-blooded southern-American lover, occupies the middle half of the book, while the Sophoclean drama is played by the woodlanders.

Grace Melbury is a weak vacillating girl, spoiled by her infatuated father and half-hypnotised by the fascinating Edred. She really loves Giles Winterborne, but he is the Poor Man, she the genteel educated lady, and she marries Fitzpiers. Melbury is a more interesting character. He had tricked Giles's father of the girl he loved, and to atone for his offence decided that Giles must marry his daughter, the girl he loves. When Fitzpiers shows an interest, however, he encourages his suit, persuading himself that his former plan was a mere sacrifice of Grace. Then, broken by his discovery of Fitzpiers's infidelity, he does all he can to annul the marriage and unite her with Giles. But eventually Grace is reunited with Fitzpiers, ironically enough after she has called him to save the dying Giles, and Melbury is left to mutter prophetically: 'But let her bear in mind that the woman walks and laughs somewhere at this very moment whose neck he'll be colling next year as he does hers to-night . . . It's a forlorn hope for her.'

But the real splendour of the book lies in the pages—only about half of them—in which Giles Winterborne appears. Simple, devoted, chivalrous, heroic, he is one of those men who inspire legends: 'He looked and smelt like Autumn's very brother, his face being sunburnt to wheat-colour, his eyes blue as cornflowers, his sleeves and leggings dyed with fruit-stains, his hands clammy with the sweet juice of apples.' For Grace he is 'the fruit-god and the wood-god in alternation,' but the true complement of Giles is Marty South, simple, devoted, heroic as he:

The casual glimpses which the ordinary population bestowed upon that wondrous world of sap and leaves called the Hintock woods had been with these two, Giles and Marty, a clear gaze. They had been possessed of its finer mysteries as of commonplace knowledge; had been able to read its hieroglyphs as ordinary writing; to them the sights and sounds of night, winter, wind, storm, amid those dense boughs, which had to Grace a touch of the uncanny, and even of the supernatural, were simply occurrences, whose origin, continuance, and laws they foreknew. They had planted together, and together they had felled. . . . They knew by a glance at a trunk if its heart were sound, or tainted with incipient decay; and by the state of its upper twigs the stratum that had been reached by its roots.

'They had planted together:'

'How they sigh directly we put 'em upright, though while they are lying down they don't sigh at all,' said Marty.

'Do they?' said Giles. 'I've never noticed it.'

She erected one of the young pines into its hole, and held up her finger; the soft musical breathing instantly set in, which was not to cease night or day till the grown tree should be felled—probably long after the two planters had been felled themselves.

Giles is the first to be felled, and when Grace has deserted his grave for the bed of Fitzpiers, Marty has her reward:

'Now, my own, own love,' she whispered, 'you are mine, and only mine; for she has forgot 'ee at last, although for her you died! But I—whenever I get up I'll think of 'ee, and whenever I lie down I'll think of 'ee again. Whenever I plant the young larches I'll think that none can plant as you planted; and whenever I split a gad, and whenever I turn the cider wring, I'll say none could do it like you. If ever I forget your name let me forget home and heaven! . . . But no, no, my love, I never can forget 'ee; for you was a good man, and did good things!

When Hardy laid down his pen after writing those words on the evening of 4 February 1887, did he still think that 'Fitzpiers at Hintock' might be an alternative title to 'The Woodlanders'?

The *Spectator*, at least, took Fitzpiers seriously, and took Hardy to task for showing sympathy rather than indignation for the 'sensual and selfish liar' whom he rewarded with the prize of Grace. It was a powerful but disagreeable book. Others found some of the incidents needlessly coarse and repulsive—Macmillan's had warned Hardy to be careful in his treatment of the Suke Damson episode—but reviews on the whole were favourable, and the novel was so successful that it stimulated sales of his other books.

While reviewers were airing their opinions on the merits and demerits of *The Woodlanders* Hardy was in Italy. His first glimpse of the Mediterranean, 'god-haunted Central Sea', was

a prosaic one—through washing-hung gaps between Genoese
housebacks. It was from Genoa that Garibaldi had sailed with
his Thousand on the expedition that had led to the newly united
Italy of Hardy's visit, but his thoughts were with the English
poets who had lived there early in the century rather than with
Italian history, recent or remote. In Pisa he thought of Shelley,
and the country near Leghorn inspired the writing of 'Shelley's
Skylark':

> Maybe it rests in the loam I view,
> Maybe it throbs in a myrtle's green,
> Maybe it sleeps in the coming hue
> Of a grape on the slopes of yon inland scene.

This concept of the transmigration of life, its renewal and
continuation in humbler forms, was one that always haunted
Hardy. In Florence he thought of Browning and 'The Statue
and the Bust', in Rome of Keats, who had died in the house near
which they were staying, and he visited his and Shelley's graves
in the cemetery beside the Pyramid of Cestius. So sensitive to
the past, Rome had too much history, its measureless layers
oppressed him, and it was a relief to reach Venice—where he
thought of Byron. St Mark's was his first encounter with Byzan-
tine building, and the Wessex architect found it barbaric: too
many mosaics, too much gilding. Yet it was not altogether alien:
the bell that struck the hour in the campanile had exactly the
'tin-tray *timbre*' of the one in Longpuddle belfry. And then,
there was the floor, 'worn into undulations by the infinite
multitudes of feet that have trodden it, and *what* feet there have
been among the rest!' In Milan his thoughts turned to Napoleon,
and he made an expedition to Lodi, where Napoleon's seizure of
the bridge from the Austrians marked the beginning of his career
of conquest.

They returned to England in April, and as 1887 was Jubilee
Year, the fiftieth anniversary of Queen Victoria's accession,
they stayed in London for the long and brilliant season, and on
21 June watched the royal procession from the Savile Club in
Piccadilly. The celebrations continued throughout the summer,
with receptions, luncheons and dinners, but in August, after an

absence of five months, they returned to Max Gate. It was probably now that Hardy wrote 'The Withered Arm', a gruesome story of witchcraft and the healing power of a newly-hanged man's neck, for it was published in *Blackwood's* in the following January. He was always fascinated by old superstitions. At Sturminster, for example, he heard how an old man, 'a wizard', used to bring toads' legs in small bags to the river bridge and sell them as charms to hang round the neck as a cure for scrofula. A touch of the Sovereign's hand was once supposed to cure this 'King's Evil', now it was the twitch of a toad's leg that gave the blood a 'turn', as the touch of a hanged-man's neck healed a withered limb.

Although the year went out quietly at Max Gate, Hardy was in better spirits than he had been at its beginning. It had been 'a fairly friendly one' to him, he noted: Italy had been a revelation, and *The Woodlanders* was a success. Just 20 years earlier his first novel had been rejected largely because of its radicalism and satirical portrayal of the upper classes, but his recent intimate acquaintance with the nobility had modified his views, and in January 1888 he analysed them. He was, he decided, neither Tory nor Radical, but what he called an Intrinsicalist, opposed to unearned privilege of any kind, whether aristocratic or democratic: that is, opposed to support of the idle by taxing the workers. There should be equal opportunity for all, but those who did not avail themselves of it should not be allowed to become a burden on the others. A note that he made a few weeks later is relevant: 'A short story of a young man—"who could not go to Oxford"—His struggles and ultimate failure. Suicide. There is something in this the world ought to be shown, and I am the one to show it to them.' He added that he could easily have gone 'at least to Cambridge' when he was 25 and thinking of combining poetry and the Church, until he realised that he could not conscientiously take Orders.

They went to London again in March, and early in May Macmillan's published his first collection of short stories as *Wessex Tales*. The first of these, 'The Three Strangers', written at Wimborne some six years before, is perhaps the best of all his short stories. For one thing, it *is* a short story, not a short novel: the action being confined to a single evening in the living-room of a shepherd's cottage high on Grimstone Down, a few miles north-east of Dorchester. First, the snugness of the room where the christening revels are taking place is contrasted with the wildness of the March weather outside, where 'the tails of little birds trying to roost on some scraggy thorn were blown inside out like umbrellas.' There follows the scene in which the first stranger, coming from Casterbridge, gradually realises that the second stranger, going to Casterbridge, is the man appointed to hang him in the morning, yet is obliged to drink with him and sing the chorus of his gruesome song. Then comes the search for the third stranger, and the Dorchester Dogberry's challenge: 'Your money or your life! . . . Prisoner at the bar, surrender, in the name of the Father—the Crown, I mane!' Nature, melo-drama, humorous rustic dialogue: characteristic Hardy.

At the end of May they went to Paris again, where there was shopping 'with Em', a trip to Longchamps to see the races, and the usual visits to picture galleries. Like most Englishmen, Hardy was still unaware of the revolution in French painting, though in Paris he could have seen the work of Cézanne, Gauguin, Van Gogh, and even of young Georges Seurat, whose 'Poseuses' was exhibited at the Salon des Indépendants in 1888. Had he seen some of their paintings he might have admired them, for he felt that 'Nature is played out as a Beauty, but not as a Mystery.' Mere photographic reproduction of a subject meant no more than it depicted; a work of art is the artist's interpretation, the revelation of a deeper reality. That is what he found in the late paintings of Turner, which he so much admired, and it was the mystery rather than the beauty of nature that he himself tried to reveal both in his prose and in his verse.

'To find beauty in ugliness is the province of the poet,' he wrote soon after their return to Max Gate in July; but he had little time for poetry in these months. First he had to write a story for the *Universal Review*, which he finished and sent off in August. This was 'A Tragedy of Two Ambitions', a variation on the theme of his recent note about the young man who could not go to Oxford, and a brief anticipation of *Jude the Obscure*. It is a sombre little story of two ambitious young men whose drunken

father has dissipated the money saved by their mother to send
them to the university. They struggle on as humble clergymen
without degrees, and manage to marry their sister to a wealthy
squire, but only by allowing their father to drown in a stream
into which they have seen him fall. The story ends with the
brothers standing beside the stream, and wondering if they will
ever put an end to themselves and their troubles there.

He had more important work on hand than short stories,
however. The Bolton firm of Tillotson had asked him for a novel
for serialisation in their Lancashire weekly newspapers, and in
September he made the note: ' "The Valley of the Great
Dairies"—Froom. "The Valley of the Little Dairies"—Black-
moor.' He had taken the train to Evershot, a village on the edge
of the chalk downs north of Maiden Newton, and then walked to
Woolcombe and Bubb Down overlooking the green Vale of
Blackmore. Woolcombe and other manors in the neighbourhood had belonged to the Hardys before their 'decline and fall';
and 'So we go down, down, down,' he mused. His novel was to
be about a dairymaid, descendant of a once distinguished family
that had declined like the Hardys, and in the autumn he began
to write *Too Late Beloved,* the story that was to become *Tess of
the d'Urbervilles.*

The couple spent most of the first half of 1889 in London,
taking part in the now familiar social round, Hardy, despite
his agnosticism, attending services at various churches 'with
Em.' It was August before they returned to Max Gate and he
resumed the daily routine of writing his novel, the serial publication of which was due to begin before the end of the year.
When, however, in September he sent Tillotson's the first half
of his manuscript they were shocked at what they had unwittingly agreed to publish. Episodes such as the heroine's
seduction and her baptism of her illegitimate child were no
fit matter for their readers, and they asked him to delete such
indelicacies and rewrite. In his early days, when his ambition
had been to be considered a good hand at a serial, he had meekly
agreed to such suggestions, but now he refused, and as Tillotson's
refused to publish, though offering to pay as arranged, he asked
them to cancel their contract, which they did, and returned his

manuscript. He then offered it to *Murray's Magazine*, who declined it as too explicitly improper, as for similar reasons did *Macmillan's*. He now considered abandoning serial publication and issuing the book in volume-form alone, but feeling that he could not afford to do this he began to extract the offensive passages with a view to their separate publication as little more than harmless anecdotes, and to patch the rents they had made and revise the remainder.

While he was thus engaged towards the end of the year, the *New Review* asked him for an article on 'Candour in English Fiction'. The request came at the right moment, and Hardy was able to release some of his accumulated exasperation in an outspoken attack on Victorian Grundyism. The greater part of English fiction, he maintained, was 'a literature of quackery' characterised by its insincerity. This was largely because the usual, more profitable, way of introducing a novel was as a serial in a magazine for family reading, which meant mainly for adolescents, from whom their prudish parents thought it their duty to conceal the realities of life. But 'The crash of broken commandments is as necessary an accompaniment to the catastrophe of a tragedy as the noise of drums and cymbals to a triumphal march. . . . If the true artist ever weeps it probably is then, when he first discovers the fearful price he has to pay for the privilege of writing in the English language.' Imagine what would happen if a Victorian Shakespeare were to submit *Othello* or *Hamlet* in the form of a novel for serialisation in a magazine! The novelist must be free to write for adults about 'things which everybody is thinking but nobody is saying.'

The year closed with news of the death of Browning in Venice. He was buried in Westminster Abbey on 31 December.

CHAPTER THIRTEEN

Tess

1890–91

Hardy's article on 'Candour in English Fiction' was published
in January 1890, while he was writing six stories, to be called
A Group of Noble Dames, for a special number of the *Graphic*.
Then, on 5 March he made the entry in his notebook:

In the train on the way to London. Wrote the first four or six lines
of 'Not a line of her writing have I'. It was a curious instance of
sympathetic telepathy. The woman whom I was thinking of—a
cousin—was dying at the time, and I quite in ignorance of it. She
died six days later. The remainder of the piece was not written till
after her death.

The woman was Tryphena Sparks, and the first six lines of the
poem were:

> Not a line of her writing have I,
>   Not a thread of her hair,
> No mark of her late time as dame in her dwelling, whereby
>   I may picture her there;
> And in vain do I urge my unsight
>   To conceive my lost prize

In his manuscript he called the poem 'T—A. At News of her
Death (Died 1890)', but later changed the title to 'Thoughts of
Phena. At News of her Death', and the remaining lines of the
first verse read:

> At her close, whom I knew when her dreams were upbrimming
>   with light,
> And with laughter her eyes.

32. Woolbridge ('Wellbridge') House, and bridge over the Frome: 'once portion of a fine manorial residence, and the property and seat of a d'Urberville.' (*Tess.*)

33. Looking east from Bulbarrow. The northern chalk escarpment and Blackmore Vale below, scene of *The Woodlanders*, the first novel to be written at Max Gate.

34. Emma Hardy, *c.* 1892.

Photo by Wh---ley, W---worth.   MR. THOMAS HARDY, THE NOVELIST.

35. Hardy in 1892, shortly after shaving his beard.

36. Bere Regis Church and the
    d'Urberville Window, beneath
    which Tess and the Durbeyfield
    family camped for the night.

Hardy had probably not seen Tryphena for nearly 20 years. Since her marriage with Charles Gale in 1877 she had lived at Topsham, near Exeter, and had four children, the eldest being the only girl, Eleanor Tryphena, born in 1878. After the birth of her last child in 1886 she ruptured herself, an injury from which she never fully recovered, and on 17 March 1890 she died, three days before her 39th birthday. She was buried in Topsham cemetery.

We do not know how deep had been Hardy's affection for Tryphena. He was a great treasurer of relics, yet in 1890 he had no letters of hers, no lock of her hair, though, if ever he had possessed them, he may have destroyed them after his marriage and forgotten, or half-forgotten his cousin. But he was a man who lived largely in the past, who idealised the past, like Jocelyn Pearston in *The Pursuit of the Well-Beloved,* the story that he wrote a year after Tryphena's death, when he had got over his difficulties with *Tess* and *A Group of Noble Dames.* In this serial version of *The Well-Beloved* Pearston is a young Dorset country-man living in London where he is making his name as a sculptor. We first meet him when he is burning old love-letters and a lock of hair before setting off for his native Isle of Portland, which he has not seen for nearly three years. There he is greeted and impulsively kissed by his childhood companion and cousin—for all the islanders are related—Avice Caro, who had been a mere girl when he last saw her, but is now almost a young woman of seventeen. Although 'his feeling for her now was rather one of friendship than love,' he asks her to marry him, and she agrees. But she breaks an appointment, and instead he marries a lady, Marcia Bencomb. They quarrel, and she goes to America, leaving him free to marry again if he wishes. Twenty years later he hears that Avice is dead, and he returns to Portland to visit her grave. There he meets her daughter, a second Avice, who tells him how her mother hurt her side while wringing sheets, an accident that presumably hastened her end. Back in London, Pearston looks at a photograph of his Avice which had been taken one afternoon when they were at Weymouth together 20 years before, and he muses:

He loved the woman dead and inaccessible as he had never loved her in life. He had unceremoniously forsaken her on the eve of what

would have become an irrevocable engagement, because he did not
love her; and it had been, in one view, the kindest thing he could
have done, though the harshest, no spark of passion existing. He had
thought of her but at distant intervals during the whole nineteen
years since that parting occurred, and only as somebody he could
have wedded. Yet now the years of youthful friendship with her, in
which he had learnt every fibre of her innocent nature, flamed up
into a yearning and passionate attachment, embittered by regret
beyond words. ... She had been another man's wife almost the
whole time since he was estranged from her, and now she was a
corpse.[16]

The first part of *The Pursuit of the Well-Beloved* reads like
autobiography, a thinly disguised account of his love affair
with Tryphena, as the first part of *A Pair of Blue Eyes* had been
an account of his love affair with Emma. If the characters are
not portraits, the incidents are close to what we know of Hardy's
life, and it looks as though when he met Emma his feeling for
Tryphena was 'rather one of friendship than love', 'no spark of
passion existing.' But how much of Hardy, idealiser of the past,
is summed up in three words from Browning's 'A Toccata of
Galuppi's': 'Dear dead women'! 'He loved the woman dead as
he had never loved her in life,' and youthful friendship 'flamed
up into a yearning and passionate attachment, embittered by
regret beyond words.' He must have been thinking of Tryphena,
or rather Tryphena idealised, when he wrote that shortly after
her death, thinking of the 'lost prize' whom 'he could have
wedded' instead of the childless woman who was now merely his
wife, no longer the well-beloved. Yet he was to feel the same
regret beyond words when she died. 'Dear *dead* women—with
such hair, too.'

Tryphena died, ironically enough, on the twentieth anniversary of his first visit to St Juliot, and it may well have been
now that he wrote the first draft of a poem, later 'rewritten from
an old copy' and published after Emma's death as 'The Wind's
Prophecy':

> I travel on by barren farms,
> And gulls glint out like silver flecks
> Against a cloud that speaks of wrecks,
> And bellies down with black alarms.

I say: 'Thus from my lady's arms
I go; those arms I love the best!'
The wind replies from dip and rise,
'Nay; toward her arms thou journeyest.'

A distant verge morosely gray
Appears, while clots of flying foam
Break from its muddy monochrome,
And a light blinks up far away.
I sigh: 'My eyes now as all day
Behold her ebon loops of hair!'
Like bursting bonds the wind responds,
'Nay, wait for tresses flashing fair!'

From tides the lofty coastlands screen
Come smitings like the slam of doors,
Or hammerings on hollow floors,
As the swell cleaves through caves unseen.
Say I: 'Though broad this wild terrene,
Her city home is matched of none!'
From the hoarse skies the wind replies:
'Thou shouldst have said her sea-bord one.'

The all-prevailing clouds exclude
The one quick timorous transient star;
The waves outside where breakers are
Huzza like a mad multitude.
'Where the sun ups it, mist-imbued,'
I cry, 'there reigns the star for me!'
The wind outshrieks from points and peaks:
'Here, westward, where it downs, mean ye!'

Yonder the headland, vulturine,
Snores like old Skrymer in his sleep,
And every chasm and every steep
Blackens as wakes each pharos-shine.
'I roam, but one is safely mine,'
I say, 'God grant she stay my own!'
Low laughs the wind as if it grinned:
'Thy love is one thou'st not yet known.'

This is a very different account of his journey to St Juliot from
that given in 'When I set out for Lyonnesse' and *A Pair of Blue*

Eyes. Here it is a sinister coast of predatory headlands, slamming seas and wrecks that he approaches, while the grinning wind shrieks its ominous prophecy that he will leave his old love in the east for one in the west. Yet the reticent secretive Hardy had nothing to say about this emotional upheaval when he came to write his *Life*, this sudden, full realisation of what might have been, though he casually mentioned that in June 1891, for no apparent reason, he visited Stockwell Training College, the 'city home' of Tryphena when he first set out for Lyonnesse. And if we are to believe the memory of Tryphena's daughter Eleanor, a child of eleven at the time, he visited Topsham four months after her mother's death, which could have been soon after his hearing of it. On a day in July, according to her account, he and his brother Henry cycled from Dorchester and called at Gale's house to say that they had laid a wreath on Tryphena's grave. Eleanor gave them lunch, then, 'As they were saying goodbye Henry said she was exactly like her mother, and kissed her. Thomas did not kiss her, but drew away with what Nellie [Eleanor] called a wry expression.' The card on the wreath said: 'In loving memory, Tom Hardy.'[17]

That this is substantially a true account seems to be supported by one of the *Wessex Poems* published in 1898 and called 'To an Orphan Child', but in later editions 'To a Motherless Child':

> Ah, child, thou art but half thy darling mother's;
> Hers couldst thou wholly be,
> My light in thee would outglow all in others;
> She would relive to me.
> But niggard Nature's trick of birth
> Bars, lest she overjoy,
> Renewal of the loved on earth
> Save with alloy.
>
> The Dame has no regard, alas, my maiden,
> For love and loss like mine—
> No sympathy with mindsight memory-laden; . . .

'Mindsight memory-laden.' It is a development of Pearston's regret that Avice's bright mind has been dimmed in her daughter by 'admixture with the mediocrity of her father's'.

We do not *know*, there is no definite proof, that Hardy was thinking of Tryphena when he wrote the passage from *The Pursuit of the Well-Beloved*; that she is the ebon-haired girl of 'The Wind's Prophecy'; that 'The Motherless Child' is her daughter, that Hardy visited her grave soon after her death; but we do know that he wrote 'Thoughts of Phena', called her 'my lost prize', in his serial echoed the first words of the poem, 'not a line of her',[18] and illustrated it when published with a drawing that resembles the figure on a tomb a few feet away from hers in Topsham cemetery.[19] Then, Hardy himself tells us in the Preface to *Jude* that 'some of the circumstances' in the novel were 'suggested by the death of a woman' in 1890, and as niggard Nature barred for him renewal of the loved on earth save with alloy, so Jude could find no consolation in thinking of Sue's children by another man as a continuation of her identity, for 'by the wilfulness of Nature ... Every desired renewal of an existence is debased by being half alloy.' Whatever Hardy's feeling for the living Tryphena had been in 1870, and it seems probable that it was no more than a cousinly affection, 'no spark of passion existing', there can be little doubt that in 1890 he loved the woman dead, the idealised woman, with an embittered retrospective love that would leave him with little affection for the living woman for whom he had left her and chosen as his wife.

If he visited Topsham in July, it must have been at the very end of the month, for he was in London—'getting tired of investigating life at music-halls and police courts'—until at least the 26th. Emma had had to leave him to go to her dying father, and on the 24th he wrote from the Savile Club to say that he expected to return to Dorchester on either the 26th or 28th. 'I think it is all right with the *Graphic*,' he added. He had been having trouble with the directors of the firm about the too-great candour of his *Noble Dames*, particularly the story of 'Squire Petrick's Lady' as related by the Crimson Maltster. He blue-pencilled a number of passages in his manuscript and added a note: 'The above lines were deleted against author's wish, by compulsion of Mrs Grundy.'

Now that *A Group of Noble Dames* was out of the way, Hardy

took his brother to see the sights of Paris, and spent the autumn at Max Gate finishing *Tess* and preparing a bowdlerised version for the *Graphic*. In this, Tess is not seduced by Alec, but tells her mother she has been through a form of marriage service that has proved to be false. There is no illegitimate child, and there-fore no baptism scene; and instead of Angel's carrying the dairymaids across the flooded lane in his arms, he more decorously transports them in a wheelbarrow. In the course of writing, Hardy changed his heroine's name several times. Her original surname was Woodrow, but when her father was conceived as a descendant of the Turbervilles of Bere Regis, it became Trouble-field before the final Durbeyfield. Then, her first name was successively Love, Cis, Sue and Rose Mary before he finally chose Tess, perhaps as a tribute to Tryphena, Teresa being a near-rhyme, as he called one of the birds she looked after Phena. The title of the novel went through similar changes: from 'Too Late Beloved' to 'A Daughter of the D'Urbervilles' before becoming 'Tess of the d'Urbervilles'.

At the beginning of December he was in London again, staying with the Jeunes in Wimpole Street. He wrote to 'Dearest Em' to tell her of his safe arrival in the city of smog, and to ask her to send a copy of the *Graphic* to Mrs Childs of Weymouth, wife of a distant cousin. This was the Christmas number in which the bowdlerised versions of his *Noble Dames* appeared. He wrote dutifully and frequently, telling her how he had breakfasted with Mr Goschen, Chancellor of the Exchequer, and that the publisher James Osgood assured him that the United States Senate would pass the Copyright Bill: 'Probably I shall just save the Copyright of *Tess* in America—owing to delay. If all goes well how for-tunate.' And he added that if she had to come to London about the lameness in her knee, Mrs Jeune said she was to stay with her. He was back at Max Gate for Christmas, and the New Year came in as he looked at the young snow-covered pines in their garden, which seemed to breathe: ' 'Tis no better with us than with the rest of creation, you see!'

Although he was fond of Mrs Jeune and other hostesses who entertained him while in London, he was still critical of fashion-able society, its artificiality and selfishness. Thinking of Tess, he wrote: 'These women! If put into rough wrappers in a turnip-field, where would their beauty be?' And again, at a dinner where the talk was all of politics, it was about everything 'except the people ... Their welfare is never once thought of.' Nevertheless, he had come to enjoy these social occasions, and he and Emma were in London for the 1891 season as usual. In April he was elected to the Athenaeum Club, and in May the episode of the baptism extracted from *Tess* was published as an independent sketch in the *Fortnightly Review* as 'The Midnight Baptism: A Study in Christianity.' This was followed at the end of the month by the volume edition of *A Group of Noble Dames*, now ten stories instead of the six issued in the *Graphic*.

Hardy had a passion for genealogy, and the source of some of his tales was Hutchins's *History and Antiquities of Dorset*, the pedigrees in which, with their—often irreconcilable—dates of marriages, births and deaths, sometimes illuminated by traditions, encouraged him to make dramatic reconstructions of these buried lives. To link the tales he borrowed the Chaucerian device: not Canterbury pilgrims, but members of a Wessex Antiquarian Club who are rain-bound and, instead of their projected expedition, spend an afternoon and evening telling tales of vanished Wessex ladies: tales of ladies told by men. They did not add to his reputation, for Hardy the poet is not there, only the ingenious weaver of melodramatic fantasies. Thus, according to the Old Surgeon, Lord Uplandtowers cured his wife's love for her former handsome husband by forcing her, night after night, to look at his horribly mutilated statue: ' "Ho-ho-ho!" says he. "Frightened, dear one, hey? What a baby 'tis! Only a joke! ... ho-ho-ho!" ' In the Rural Dean's tale the Lady Caroline secretly marries the parish-clerk's son, who drops dead in his lady's chamber. She lugs the corpse to his parents' cottage, and persuades his first love Milly to say that she was his secret wife: 'Then this noble lady took from her bosom the ring she had never been able openly to exhibit, and, grasping the young girl's hand, slipped it upon her finger as she stood upon her lover's grave.' She also slipped her unwanted baby upon Milly, and married the Marquis of Stonehenge. Years later, left a childless widow, she tried to win back her handsome son, but he rejected her, and 'That day was the beginning of death to the unfortunate Marchioness of Stonehenge.'

A Group of Noble Dames is not to be taken seriously, nor was the bowdlerised and almost incomprehensible version of *Tess* that began its weekly run in the *Graphic* in July, not made any more lucid by the illustrations of four different artists. Its serialisation began at the same time in America, a fortnight after the passing of the International Copyright Bill, which prevented piracy of the works of English authors in America, ensured the proper payment of royalties, and meant, therefore, a substantial increase in Hardy's income. After a September visit to Scotland and return journey by way of Durham, York and Peterborough— Hardy made a point of seeing all the English cathedrals—he returned to Max Gate to complete the restoration of the mutilated manuscript of *Tess* for its publication in volumes. Meanwhile, in mid-November the expurgated seduction scene was printed in the Edinburgh *National Observer* as 'Saturday Night in Arcady.' Then, at the end of the month Osgood, McIlvaine, published the three volumes of *Tess of the d'Urbervilles: A Pure Woman Faithfully Presented.*

Six months later, in his Preface to the fifth edition, Hardy acknowledged the generous welcome given to the novel by most reviewers. It was 'a work of genius', 'truly tragic and dramatic', 'second to no work of its time', 'its author's masterpiece'. There were reservations, however, and some reviews were downright hostile: 'All [the characters] are stagey, and some are farcical'; 'the terrible dreariness of this tale, which, except during the few hours spent with cows, has not a gleam of sunshine anywhere'; 'this clumsy sordid tale of boorish brutality and lust.' From America came: 'a pretty kettle of fish for pure people to eat . . . this sad story of sin and shame.' And American-born Henry James wrote to R. L. Stevenson: 'The good little Thomas Hardy has scored a great success with *Tess of the d'Urbervilles*, which is chock-full of faults and falsity and yet has a singular beauty and charm.' And a year later: '. . . she is vile. The pretence of "sexuality" is only equalled by the absence of it, and the abomination of the language by the author's reputation for style. There are indeed some pretty smells and sights and sounds.'

London society was divided into those who defended Tess as 'a poor wronged innocent', and those who condemned her as 'a little harlot'.

Although opinion was divided about Tess, it could scarcely be divided about her seducer, Alec d'Urberville. He belongs to the world of Aeneas Manston, Edred Fitzpiers and Louis Glanville, a cigar-smoking 'horsey young buck' with a 'bold rolling eye', who later reappears as a fanatical preacher before reverting to animalism when he meets Tess again. After this he haunts and frightens her in various guises: twirling a gay walking-cane, in a smockfrock, in a white mackintosh, on horseback, as an effigy on a d'Urberville tomb. At least he made splendid material for the *Punch* of the day : 'Even the very, very strong ejaculations wherein this bold bad man indulges on the slightest provocation belong to the most antiquated vocabulary of theatrical ruffianism.' But bad joke though he is, the irony should not be missed that it is Angel's father, old Mr Clare, who frightens him into a ferocious Christianity, and not only Tess's beauty but also her recital of Angel's philosophy that paves his way back to her.

Tess forgives Angel for his desertion, but it is not easy for the reader to forgive him. Afraid of endangering his chance of winning her, he waits until they are married before confessing to once having had two days and nights of dissipation' 'with a stranger'. Tess had tried time and again to make her confession, but he would not listen, and when, after forgiving him, she tells of her affair with Alec, he accuses her of self-preservation, despises her as 'an unapprehending peasant woman', and goes off to Brazil with his umbrella, and almost with Izz Huett as his mistress. It may be said in his extenuation that he is the antithesis of Alec : fastidious, devoid of animalism ; that his love was ethereal ; that he had made a social sacrifice in marrying Tess, and when he found she was not the woman he had idealised she appeared to him quite another woman. If only she had treated him as she treated Alec : with a flash of her ancestral spirit slapped him across his little mouth with her heavy glove, she might have made him realise that she was still Tess of the d'Urbervilles.

The most complete portrait of Tess is drawn, strangely enough, by the ascetic evangelical Mrs Clare, though she is merely repeating Angel's description: 'fine in figure; roundly built; had deep red lips like Cupid's bow; dark eyelashes and brows, an immense rope of hair like a ship's cable; and large eyes violety-bluey-blackish.' If she had seen and heard her, she might have added the distracting lift in the middle of that deep-red upper lip, and the 'stopt-diapason note' of her speech when deeply moved—a note, Hardy added, 'which will never be forgotten by those who knew her.' He admitted that most of his characters were drawn from life, but said he only once saw Tess —as a beautiful girl driving a cart one evening, and urging her horse 'with rather unnecessary violence of language'.[20] That scarcely suggests flute-like organ music, but Angel's description does suggest Tryphena's photograph, and it may well be that in the course of revision Hardy made Tess resemble his lost prize in appearance and voice. Certainly the words, 'which will never be forgotten by those who knew her' were added at the last moment, for they do not occur in the manuscript.[21]

Tess was a young woman when Angel met her as a dairymaid in the Frome meadows, but when Alec met her she was only a girl of 16, though even then she had 'a luxuriance of aspect, a fulness of growth, which made her appear more of a woman than she really was'—a description that some critics found disagreeable. This beautiful inexperienced girl, one of the first products of the board schools, is sent by a drunken father and childish mother to claim acquaintance with a bogus d'Urberville family of a blind mother and her dissolute son Alec. One evening, when she is desperately tired, he rescues her from a brawl and takes her on his horse far into the woods, where she falls asleep. (In a cancelled paragraph in the manuscript he makes her unknowingly drink brandy.) There follows the so-called seduction; but it is not seduction, it is rape. Tess goes home, has her baby, buries it, and finds work as a dairymaid at Talbothays. There Angel falls in love with her, marries her, and leaves her after her confession. While she is working on an unfriendly upland farm her father dies and, pestered by Alec whom she regards as her natural husband but is unable to marry, for the sake of her mother, young sisters and brothers, she at length agrees to become his mistress. When Angel returns—'Too late! too late!' —with another flash of ancestral fire she stabs the man who has ruined her life to show the man she adores how much she loves him.

When Hardy added the sub-title 'A Pure Woman' to *Tess* it was a challenge. Tess was innocent in spite of what she did, and he described his own position in the musings of Angel, who had mentally aged a dozen years after his experiences in Brazil:

Having long discredited the old systems of mysticism, he now began to discredit the old appraisments of morality. He thought they wanted readjusting. Who was the moral man? Still more pertinently, who was the moral woman? The beauty or ugliness of a character lay not only in its achievements, but in its aims and impulses; its true history lay, not among things done, but among things willed.

How then about Tess?

Angel did not answer, but Hardy did, in his interview with Raymond Blathwayt:

I still maintain that her innate purity remained intact to the very last; though I frankly own that a certain outward purity left her on her last fall. I regarded her then as being in the hands of circumstances, not morally responsible, a mere corpse drifting with the current to her end.

There is no absolute measure of guilt. Its degree depends on circumstance and motive, and Tess was the helpless prey of circumstance, which Hardy personified in the last paragraph of his book as the President of the Immortals. And there can be few readers today who would maintain that there was ever any evil motive behind her actions. She had to suffer, of course, although the last years of her short life, save for one brief interlude, had been a period of unrelieved suffering. And therein lies the tragedy.

For *Tess* is a great tragic novel, the greatest in the English language, in which the reader experiences the true catharsis and is left with a feeling of exaltation. It is the tragedy of a beautiful, passionate, devoted, heroic girl who belongs more to the world of nature than to the world of men: 'On these lonely hills and dales her quiescent glide was of a piece with the element she moved in. Her flexuous and stealthy figure became an integral part of the scene.' We see her decked like Maia, with 'roses at her breast; roses in her hat; roses and strawberries in her basket to the brim.' We see her milking the cows—Dumpling, Fancy, Lofty, Mist—at Talbothays dairy, tying and stooking the autumn sheaves of corn, threshing and hoeing, and weeping as she puts an end to the suffering of birds that have been wounded by sportsmen. She had a soul that could feel for kindred sufferers as much as for herself, a soul that left her body at the sound of music, or when she lay on the grass at night looking up at the stars. The tragedy is that this innocent child of nature should have to be judged and made to suffer according to the arbitrary code of man-made laws.

As poetry, great verse, is not so much the thing said as the way of saying it, so great tragedy is not so much the story as the way of telling it. Into a commonplace tale of jealousy and murder Shakespeare infused his poetry and created *Othello*, and the telling of *Tess* is a comparable achievement in prose. The novelist has the advantage over the dramatist of being able to describe the scene of his action in detail, and this is the main reason why a dramatised form of a Hardy novel can never equal the original. An essential element is missing, and even in a film there can be no more than a reproduction, a photograph, of the background, not Hardy's interpretation of it. The background of *Tess*, so much more than a background, is more varied than that of the earlier novels, and with Tess we travel through most of the natural regions of Dorset: from the small fields and orchards of Blackmore Vale to the sylvan antiquity of Cranborne Chase, the water meadows of the Frome, the bleak chalk downs of Flintcomb-Ash, and the heathland of her ancestral home at Bere Regis. There are set descriptions, but it is the succession of minor touches, often in the form of images, that keeps the scene ever before the reader, or rather, immerses him in its atmosphere: 'Herons came, with a great bold noise as of opening doors and shutters'; 'the rush of juices could almost be heard below the hiss of fertilization'; 'winter . . . came on in stealthy and measured glides, like the moves of a chess-player';

'strange birds from behind the North Pole began to arrive silently on the upland of Flintcomb-Ash.' It is details such as these that make us feel that we, too, have been there.

Then, the telling of *Tess* is a sequence of unforgettable episodes: the baptism of Sorrow; Angel's carrying the dairy-maids, whom he finds 'clinging to the roadside bank like pigeons on a roof-slope'; Dairyman Crick's story of how old William Dewy escaped from a bull by fiddling the 'Tivity hymn' and making it kneel in its ignorance, Hardy's last piece of comedy as novelist; the long lyrical interlude in the Valley of the Great Dairies, like the slow movement of some great symphony; Tess's heartbroken, heart-breaking cry when Angel returns, 'Too late! too late!'; the brief ecstasy of the flight that ends at Stonehenge. Parson Maybold's advice to Fancy Day had been, 'Tell him everything'; 'Don't tell,' Tess's mother advised. Tess told too late, and was too late beloved.

The story comes full circle, ending, in a sense, where it had begun. Angel is left with Tess's sister 'Liza-Lu, whom she had implored him to marry: 'She has all the best of me without the bad of me; and if she were to become yours it would almost seem as if death had not divided us.' 'Liza-Lu, her spiritualised image, is the same age as Tess was when Angel first saw her at the May Day club-walking at Marlott.

CHAPTER FOURTEEN

Jude

1892–95

It was probably less for its excellence than for its notoriety that *Tess* was so eagerly bought. By the end of 1892 some 20,000 copies had been sold in England, and in America it had a similar success. Moreover, it was translated into numerous languages, including Russian and Japanese, so that Hardy was now on the way to becoming a wealthy man with a world-wide reputation. With fame came devotees such as Rebekah Owen from America,[22] and interviewing journalists such as Raymond Blathwayt, both of whom called at Max Gate in 1892. Now aged 52, and without the beard that he had worn for more than 20 years, Blathwayt found Hardy 'a gentle and a singularly pleasing personality. Of middle height, with a very thoughtful face and rather melancholy eyes, he is nevertheless an interesting and amusing companion,' by no means the Dorset rustic of popular conception. His wife looked younger, and was 'so particularly bright, so evidently a citizen of the wide world,' that the traces of Anglican ecclesiasticism were puzzling 'until the information is vouchsafed that she is intimately and closely connected with what the late Lord Shaftesbury would term "the higher order of the clergy".' It was she, Hardy said, who suggested that Tess should make her confession wearing the jewels that Angel gave her. And, Emma confided when her husband was out of the room, it was she who once overheard a labourer, who was always called 'Sir John' by an antiquarian clergyman, boasting of the 'skelingtons' in his family vault at Bere Regis.

'I am only a learner in the art of novel writing,' Hardy told Blathwayt, 'Still I do feel very strongly that the position of man and woman in nature, things which everyone is thinking and nobody saying, may be taken up and treated frankly.' But when he read the review in the *Quarterly* about his 'coarse and disagreeable story,' he wrote, 'If this sort of thing continues, no more novel writing for me. A man must be a fool to deliberately stand up to be shot at.' Yet he was already writing another novel. When Tillotson's cancelled their contract for *Tess* they had no wish to break with Hardy, and they soon asked him for another serial more suitable for family reading. He agreed, and by the end of 1891 was busily writing *The Pursuit of the Well-Beloved*, in which, he assured Tillotson's, there would not be a word or scene to offend the most fastidious taste. The theme of a face that goes through a number of generations had been in his mind for a year or two, and as the scene was to shift between fashionable London and the Isle of Portland he spent some time revisiting that 'Gibraltar of Wessex'.

His father, aged 80, was now failing, and in May he made the note that he 'went upstairs for the last time.' He died two months later, and was buried in Stinsford churchyard. Hardy had a great affection and admiration for the old master-mason, unambitious, 'wealth-wantless', whom he compared to Hamlet's stoical friend Horatio, and he commemorated him in the poem 'On One who Lived and Died where he was Born.' His mother and unmarried brother and sisters were still left in their Bockhampton home where they and he himself had been born, and a few weeks later, when Stinsford House was burned, he met Mary in the churchyard 'laying flowers on Father's grave, on which the firelight now flickered.' A churchyard, a grave, a fire—it might be a scene from one of his novels.

Soon after this, at the beginning of October, he was in London, and on the 12th wrote from the Athenaeum to tell 'My dearest Em' that he had just attended Tennyson's funeral in Westminster Abbey. He had liked Tennyson, and always regretted that he had never accepted his invitation to visit him in the Isle of Wight. A fine photograph of the late Laureate appeared in the *Illustrated London News* of 8 October, a week after the issue that included the first instalment of *The Pursuit of the Well-Beloved*, preceded by a photograph of 'Mr Thomas Hardy, the Novelist'.

In the revised version of the novel, published nearly five years later, Jocelyn Pearston falls in love with the three Avices at intervals of twenty years, but finally marries Marcia when they are both over sixty. In the serial, however, Pearston marries Marcia when Avice I fails to keep her appointment. They quarrel and part, and assuming that she is dead he marries Avice III when he is sixty. As she, aged twenty, pines for her young lover from Jersey, he plans to drown himself, but is rescued and recovers to find himself being nursed by the 'parchment-covered skull' that is his returned wife Marcia. The story ends with his uncontrollable agonised laughter at this conclusion to his 'would-be romantic history'.

The main interest in this fantasy is autobiographical: his

desertion of Avice I for Marcia, and his love of the woman dead 20 years later. That there is autobiography in the story is clear. In the *Life*, for example, when lightly describing his adolescent loves, he wrote:

One day at this time Hardy, then a boy of fourteen, fell madly in love with a pretty girl who passed him on horseback near the South Walk, Dorchester, as he came out of school hard by, and for some unaccountable reason smiled at him. She was a total stranger. Next day he saw her with an old gentleman, probably her father. He wandered about miserably, looking for her through several days, and caught sight of her once again—this time riding with a young man.

Thirty years earlier than the writing of the *Life* he made Pearston tell his friend Somers about the early incarnations of the Well-Beloved:

I was standing on the kerbstone of the pavement in Budmouth-Regis, outside the Preparatory School, looking across towards the sea, when a middle-aged gentleman on horseback, and beside him a young lady, also mounted, passed down the street. The girl turned her head, and—possibly because I was gaping at her in awkward admiration, or smiling myself—smiled at me. . . .

I could not see which way they had gone. In the greatest misery I turned down a side street, but was soon elevated to a state of excitement by seeing the same pair galloping towards me. . . . She smiled again, but, alas! upon my Love's cheek there was no blush of passion for me.

That, with slight variations, is obvious autobiography. And so does Pearston's musing appear to be:

One thing it passed him to understand: on what field of observation the poets and philosophers based their assumption that the passion of love was intensest in youth and burnt lower as maturity advanced. It was possibly because of his utter domestic loneliness. . . .

Compare this with the poem 'I Look into My Glass':

> I look into my glass,
> And view my wasting skin,
> And say, 'Would God it came to pass
> My heart had shrunk as thin!'

He leaned back to the church wall, warm from the afternoon sun, and sat down upon a window-sill facing the grave.

37. 'He loved the woman dead and inaccessible as he had never loved her in life.' Illustration for the serial, *The Pursuit of the Well-Beloved*, 1892.

38. Hardy's drawing to illustrate 'Thoughts of Phena' in *Wessex Poems*, 1898.

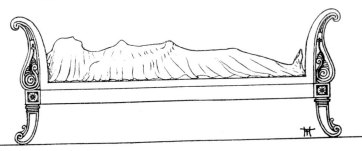

39. 'One who lived and died where he was born.' Hardy's father (1811–1892), a painting (from a photograph) by his sister Mary.

41. (*opposite*) 'I have seen the loveliest "Byke" for myself – £20!' Hardy *c.* 1899.

40. 'A face of dignity and judgment.' Hardy's mother (1813 – 1904), a painting from life by Mary Hardy.

42. 'Jude at the Milestone.' Illustration by W. Hatherell for the serial in *Harper's New Monthly Magazine*, 1895: 'A tragedy in itself; and I do not remember ever before having an artist who grasped a situation so thoroughly.' Hardy framed the set of 12 illustrations and hung them in his study.

For then, I, undistrest
By hearts grown cold to me,
Could lonely wait my endless rest
With equanimity.

But Time, to make me grieve,
Part steals, lets part abide;
And shakes this fragile frame at eve
With throbbings of noontide.

This was published in 1898, and may have been written at about the time he was writing *The Pursuit of the Well-Beloved* in 1891. It looks as though Tryphena's death had reawakened in Hardy, so quiet and seemingly self-controlled, what he now called 'the strongest passion known to humanity'. He was soon to find another incarnation of the Well-Beloved.

While *The Pursuit* was being serialised towards the end of 1892, he was already engaged on yet another novel. The germ of it was in the note he had made five years before: 'A short story of a young man who could not go to Oxford.' By 1890 it was to be a long story, 'some of the circumstances being suggested by the death of a woman' in that year. Then, while he was in London in October 1892 he revisited the scene, the village of Great Fawley on the Berkshire Downs, 20 miles south-west of Oxford. He had first visited it in 1864 when, as Blomfield's architectural assistant, he had made a sketch of the old hump-backed church, about to be replaced by one of 'German-Gothic design'. He was interested in the place because it was the native village of his grandmother Mary Head, who had lived with his parents at Bockhampton until her death when he was 17. He celebrated her in his new novel by calling the village Mary-green, his heroine Bride-head, while his hero was given its real name, Fawley.

On his return from London he spent the rest of the year and the spring of 1893 writing an outline of the narrative of 'The Simpletons', as he first called *Jude the Obscure*; then, for the first time, took a London house for the season instead of renting rooms. In May, however, they left it for a week to go to Dublin as guests of the second Lord Houghton, whose sister, Mrs Arthur

Henniker, acted as hostess. Like her father, who had made a point of meeting Hardy, she was a writer, having just finished her third novel, and Hardy found her 'a charming *intuitive* woman' of 38. They became friends at once, and on his return to England began to correspond, and in October to collaborate in the writing of 'The Spectre of the Real', a Hardyan short story of a Poor Man and a Lady. 'All the wickedness (if it has any),' he wrote, 'will be laid on my unfortunate head, while all the tender and proper parts will be attributed to you.' They met frequently in London and elsewhere, and according to the second Mrs Hardy 'A Thunderstorm in Town (*A Reminiscence: 1893*)' refers to one of these meetings :[23]

> She wore a new 'terra-cotta' dress,
> And we stayed, because of the pelting storm,
> Within the hansom's dry recess,
> Though the horse had stopped; yea, motionless
>   We sat on, snug and warm.
>
> Then the downpour ceased, to my sharp sad pain
> And the glass that had screened our forms before
> Flew up, and out she sprang to her door:
> I should have kissed her if the rain
>   Had lasted a minute more.

Perhaps. Yet it was only a reminiscence and, fond as he was of her, there is no reason to think that his relations with Florence Henniker ever strayed beyond the bounds of friendship, a friendship that lasted until her death 30 years later.

Emma, however, had some reason for jealousy, and her husband's letters at this time would scarcely mend matters. He often slipped up to London alone and, though he did not mention Mrs Henniker, daughter and daughter-in-law of peers and a viceroys's sister, they were full of the names of aristocratic, and even royal, ladies: Lady Jeune with whom he stayed, the Duchess of Teck, Princess Christian, Lady Bantry 'a widowed young Countess', Lady Londonderry, the Duchess of Manchester, Lady Pembroke 'a woman I rather like', Princess Mary. . . . 'You know,' Emma remarked to one of his lady admirers, 'he's very vain and very selfish. And these women that he meets in London society only increase these things. They are the poison; I am the antidote.' These are the incautious words of a jealous woman, but they may have had some truth in them; if she, the Lady, could boast of her uncle the Archdeacon of London, the Poor Man could now boast of far grander friends and acquaintances. There were faults on both sides. According to T. P. O'Connor, her 'whole bitter purpose seemed to be to discourage and belittle and irritate him,'[24] and though Hardy was not vain and selfish—though parsimonious—he was proud and sensitive, and the roll-call of noble dames in his letters may have been his riposte, conscious or unconscious, to her belittlement. In any event, relations at Max Gate were strained while he was writing *Jude* in the autumn and winter of 1893, even though the New Year came in peacefully as they stood together outside the door 'listening to the muffled peal from the tower of Fordington St George.'

The hero of the novel he was then writing at full length from the outline he had made, Jude Fawley, was a stone-mason who by night rambled under the walls of medieval Oxford colleges, 'feeling with his fingers the contours of their mouldings and carving.' It might be Hardy himself, the architect, and it probably was, for he was at this time engaged in restoring the church at West Knighton, about two miles from Max Gate. Ironically, the last church he had restored had been St Juliot. The *Builder* of 26 May 1894 reported his activities:

The ancient church at West Knighton, which was closed for repairs in August last, has just been re-opened. The chancel roof, which was decayed, has been removed and a new roof with stone tiles erected. The inner walls have all had the old plaster cleaned off and been cemented throughout. Mullions and tracery have been added to the windows on the north side, and both windows have been made uniform. This restoration was carried out under the direction of Mr Thomas Hardy. ... The gallery has been removed, and a new gallery has been put in its place. ... The floor has been laid throughout with encaustic tiles.[25]

Although well done in its Victorian way, Hardy did not mention this return to church restoration after 20 years when he came to write his repentant paper, 'Memories of Church Restoration', for the Society for the Protection of Ancient Buildings in 1906.

Despite this architectural venture and the writing of *Jude*, he found time to collect a number of his short stories for republication in a volume which appeared in February 1894 as *Life's Little Ironies*. The best was the most recently written, 'The Fiddler of the Reels', a tale of a fiddler who could draw souls out of bodies like spiders' threads, and by his enchantment wrecked the lives of an over-sensitive girl and her lover. The book came out too late for mention by the young poet and critic Lionel Johnson, whose *Art of Thomas Hardy* appeared in 1894, the first book to be written about his work. Johnson especially admired Hardy's power of design, the memorable architectural quality of the novels, the best of which he considered to be *The Return of the Native*, and he concluded:

By the severity of thought and of style, which he rarely deserts, he takes his place among those writers, who from the early stages of literature have expressed in art a reasonable sadness. That deep solemnity of the earth in its woods, and fields, and lonely places, has passed into his work: and when he takes it in hand to deal with the passions of men, that spirit directs and guides him. I do not find his books quite free of all offence, of anything that can hurt or distress; but I never find them merely painful: their occasional offences are light enough, and unessential; the pain, they sometimes give, is often salutary.

He could not altogether approve of *Tess*, however, in which 'the passion of revolt has led the writer to renounce his impassive temper.' He must have had even greater reservations about *Jude*, with its still more passionate revolt, when he read it.

The first of twelve monthly instalments appeared in November 1894 in *Harper's Magazine*, published in both London and New York. It was still called 'The Simpletons', an apt and attractive title, but as it might lead to confusion with Charles Reade's recent *A Simpleton*, it was changed to 'Hearts Insurgent' in the second instalment. When making the contract Harper's had asked for an assurance that the serial would in every way be suitable for family reading, and Hardy had replied that it would be 'a tale that could not offend the most fastidious maiden.' As he wrote, however, he found that 'the development of the story was carrying him into unexpected fields' and, as he could not be sure where it would lead him, suggested cancellation of the contract. However, a compromise was arranged, and the serial abridged and bowdlerised, as *Tess* had been, to make it suitable for the family circle. Even the pig-killing was modified, and as there were no unmarried mothers in Victorian England, readers were puzzled by the unaccountable appearance of a child.

While the novel was running its course as a serial throughout 1895, Osgood, McIlvaine were publishing at monthly intervals the first uniform edition of Hardy's works in 16 volumes, beginning with *Tess*. In April he was in London making arrangements about this, revising, correcting proofs, and at the same time looking for, and finally renting, a flat in Westminster for the season. Then, at Whitsuntide he went to stay with his friend Edward Clodd at Aldeburgh, George Crabbe's birthplace, where he met Edward Whymper, the first man to climb the Matterhorn, (in 1865) when four of his companions were killed: a tragedy that Hardy vividly remembered and, after visiting Zermatt a few years later, commemorated in a curiously old-fashioned sonnet 'To the Matterhorn.' By the end of the summer he was back at Max Gate restoring 'Hearts Insurgent' to its original state for publication in book-form with the title *Jude the Obscure*, while Emma, shocked by its coarseness and contempt for the laws of marriage, did her best to prevent it, apparently going to London to see Richard Garnett, Director of the British Museum, to beg him to use his influence in persuading her husband not to publish it. Nevertheless, *Jude the Obscure* was published on 1 November 1895.

In his Preface Hardy wrote that the novel dealt with the 'derision and disaster' that may result from 'the strongest passion known to humanity'; with a deadly war between flesh and spirit; and with 'the tragedy of unfulfilled aims'. The first section of the book is partly autobiographical, though Jude Fawley is by no means entirely Thomas Hardy. Young Jude comes from Mellstock, is crazy for books, lies on the grass, pulling his straw hat over his face and wishing not to grow up. He teaches himself Latin and Greek, abandons Homer for the New Testament, but fails to enter either University or Church.

Then, according to the original scheme, he should have committed suicide; and he does half-heartedly try to drown himself before going to Christminster, but gets drunk instead. It is here that the theme unsuitable for family reading enters the story: that of the war between flesh and spirit, between sexual passion and ideals. Yet flesh in the person of Arabella causes only a preliminary stumbling, a delay in Jude's move to Christminster, though the marriage into which she has trapped him prevents his wooing of Sue. And with Sue autobiography returns, or an element of autobiography.

'Sue is a type of woman which has always had an attraction for me,' Hardy wrote to Gosse, 'but the difficulty of drawing the type has kept me from attempting it till now,' and his second wife told Professor Purdy that she was in part drawn from Mrs Henniker.[26] He had met her shortly before writing *Jude* at full length and, like Sue, she was a small woman: 'My dear little friend,' he called her in his letters. On the other hand, he was just finishing the outline of the story when he met her, and it is improbable that he would make a prominent society woman the recognisable original of such a controversial character. Lois Deacon, Terry Coleman and F. R. Southerington argue that Sue was drawn largely from Tryphena. Hardy himself tells us that 'some of the circumstances' in the book were 'suggested by the death of a woman' in 1890; Sue Bridehead came from Marygreen (Fawley), Jude Fawley from Mellstock (Stinsford), and they were cousins; Mary Head of Fawley was Hardy's grandmother, and he and Tryphena Sparks were cousins. That Sue was drawn to some extent from life seems certain from two charming descriptions, the first when she is taking her pupils to see the model of Jerusalem in Christminster (for she like Tryphena was a schoolmistress), the second when she and Jude visit the Agricultural Show at Stoke Barehills:

They marched along the road two and two, she beside her class with her simple cotton sunshade, her little thumb cocked up against its stem.

Sue in her new summer clothes, flexible and light as a bird, her little thumb stuck up by the stem of her white cotton sunshade.

140

Then, 20 years after the writing of *Jude*, Hardy wrote 'The Sunshade':

> Where is the woman who carried that sunshade
> Up and down this seaside place?—
> Little thumb standing against its stem. . . .

The memory was obviously so vivid as to be unforgettable, one of those rare visions indelibly printed on the mind's retina, and if we knew who was the woman who carried that sunshade we should have a clue to the original of Sue. She may have been Tryphena, the woman Hardy 'could have wedded', or rather, Tryphena idealised, perhaps a composite portrait, at least in appearance and mannerisms, of his two Avices, his 'lost prize' and his recently found 'dear little friend'. But it seems improbable that either of these two women, the one who married Charles Gale or the other long-married when he met her, greatly resembled Sue in character, 'a phantasmal, bodiless creature almost devoid of animal passion.'

There was such a complete understanding between Jude and Sue that they seemed almost to be two parts of a single whole, able to communicate without speech, merely by glance and movement. Yet, when they met they were very different in some of their ideas. Jude was a devout Christian, with a reverence for medievalism, Gothic cathedrals, and all that Christminster stood for; but Sue would rather sit in a railway station than in a cathedral: 'The Cathedral was a very good place four or five centuries ago; but it is played out now . . . I am not modern, either. I am more ancient than medievalism.' She was pre-Christian, a pagan who bought and hid statues of Venus and Apollo from the eyes of her ecclesiastical employers, a non-conformer, and she quoted J. S. Mill: 'She or he "who lets the world, or his own portion of it, choose his plan of life for him, has no need of any other faculty than the ape-like one of imitation." '

And this is what *Jude* really is about. 'The letter killeth' is the epigraph on the novel's title-page: 'Thou shalt not do this! Thou shalt not do that! Thou shalt conform!' and *Jude* is the tragedy of two simpletons who think they can defy society by their refusal to conform: above all, to conform to the accepted view of marriage. 'To live on intimate terms when one feels as I do is adultery, in any circumstances, however legal,' Sue says to Phillotson; and to Jude, 'the moment you had contracted to cherish me under a Government stamp, and I was licensed to be loved on the premises by you—Ugh, how horrible and sordid.' Shortly before his own marriage Hardy had written *Far from the Madding Crowd* with its key-words 'Marry me': ten years later, on going to live at Max Gate, he had written *The Woodlanders*, in which an indissoluble marriage is the cause of the hero's death; and now, after another ten years, he added his comment on the marriage of Jude and Arabella:

And so, standing before the aforesaid officiator, the two swore that at every other time of their lives they would assuredly believe, feel, and desire precisely as they had believed, felt, and desired during the few preceding weeks. What was as remarkable as the undertaking itself was the fact that nobody seemed at all surprised at what they swore.

And more bitterly: 'the antipathetic, recriminatory mood of the average husband and wife of Christendom.' He and Emma were among the average ones in marriage.

It is as though all Hardy's accumulated resentment at the sorry state of affairs in the world were precipitated by Tryphena's death, his impossible love for Florence Henniker, and thoughts of what might have been. There was the apparent failure of the impercipient First Cause to realise the development of mankind's capacity for suffering. There was the cruelty of nature and of man in the constant struggle for survival and superiority: 'Every successful man is more or less a selfish man. The devoted fail.' For the heart-halt and spirit-lame there is no comfort to be found in a wood, for

> . . . having entered in,
>   Great growths and small
> Show them to men akin—
>   Combatants all!
> Sycamore shoulders oak,
> Bines the slim sapling yoke,
> Ivy-spun halters choke
>   Elms stout and tall.

'O why should Nature's law be mutual butchery!' Sue exclaims; and Phillotson: 'Cruelty is the law pervading all nature and society.' It was the cruelty of society that reserved for the rich and powerful the universities that had been founded for the poor; that thwarted natural instincts by insisting on conformity, ostracising and punishing those who rebelled.

It is Sue's refusal to conform that brings disaster, and the disaster breaks her. 'Arabella's child killing mine was a judgment —the right slaying the wrong.' 'We must conform,' she sobs, and she leaves Jude to be re-married to Phillotson. But Jude, taught by Sue, has come to despise convention as much as she once did, and adversity only strengthens his resistance. Although desperately ill, he goes from Christminster to see her at Marygreen, where he pleads with her in the church: 'Sue, Sue! we are acting by the letter; and "the letter killeth!" ' But she maintains that she is right to re-marry Phillotson, Jude right to re-marry Arabella. 'God above!' he exclaims,

If there is anything more degrading, immoral, unnatural, than another in my life, it is this meretricious contract with Arabella, which has been called the right thing! . . . O you darling little fool; where is your reason? . . . Where is your scorn of convention gone? I *would* have died game!

'My darling love,' she calls him, and kisses him passionately, and he makes his last appeal:

We've both re-married out of our senses . . . I was gin-drunk; you were creed-drunk. Either form of intoxication takes away the nobler vision. Let us then shake off our mistakes, and run away together!

No; again no!—Why do you tempt me so far, Jude! It is too merciless!—But I've got over myself now. Don't follow me—don't look at me. Leave me, for pity's sake!

Jude returns to Christminster to die, having deliberately killed himself by making the long journey in cold wet weather. And Sue returns to Phillotson to make her conscience right by doing penance—'the ultimate thing': giving herself to him in what she had once called adultery.

The last meeting of Jude and Sue is too near despair to rouse the feeling of exaltation that is a quality of the greatest tragedy, but Hardy himself was near despair when he wrote, and this parting of the cousins is the most unforgettably searing scene in any of his novels. He had travelled a long way since writing *Desperate Remedies,* and now professed that it was no business of the chronicler of moods and deeds to express his personal view. Yet he did, making the unrepentant Sue his mouthpiece: 'When people of a later age look back upon the barbarous customs and superstitions of the times that we have the unhappiness to live in, what *will* they say!'

The new novel from the celebrated author was eagerly awaited and bought, but *Jude,* like *Tess,* had a mixed reception. Some critics were enthusiastic: 'powerful and moving'; 'a masterpiece'; 'a work of genius'; 'a book that alone would make 1895 a memorable year.' 'The greatest novel written in England for many years,' wrote Hardy's young admirer Havelock Ellis; 'Irresistible . . . splendid success,' wrote his old friend Edmund Gosse, though he hoped Hardy would soon return to the rural beauty of the Hintocks, Egdon and 'the singing of the heather'; and he asked, 'What has Providence done to Mr Hardy that he should rise up in the arable land of Wessex and shake his fist at his Creator?' Hardy wrote to thank him for his discriminating review, but did not answer his question. He was evasive; the book, he said, was primarily about a poor man's failure to get a university degree; secondarily about two bad marriages, owing to a doom of hereditary temperament, the *general* marriage question comprising only half-a-dozen pages in five hundred. But he added a revealing postscript about 'the contrast between the ideal life a man wished to lead, and the squalid real life he was fated to lead.'

Other critics were less enthusiastic: 'Jude the Obscene'; 'Hardy the Degenerate'; 'dirt, drivel and damnation'; 'hoggishness and hysteria'; 'farrago of miscellaneous miseries'; 'A Novel of Lubricity . . . speculating in smut'; 'coarsely indecent'; 'a great many insulting things are said about marriage, religion, and all the obligations and relations of life which most people hold sacred.' The Bishop of Wakefield wrote an open letter to the *Yorkshire Post* saying he was so disgusted with the book's insolence that he threw it into the fire: 'It is a disgrace to our great public libraries to admit such garbage.' He also wrote privately to one large circulating library, and *Jude* was quietly withdrawn from its shelves.

'If this sort of thing continues, no more novel-writing for me,' Hardy had written after reading the abusive reviews of *Tess*. It *had* continued, and *Jude* was the last of his novels.

CHAPTER FIFTEEN

Wessex Poems

1896–1900

It was not abusive reviews alone, however, that led to Hardy' 'no more novel-writing'. He had always regarded the craft as mere journey-work, the profession he had chosen in order to make a living, though it became, of course, something very much more than that. But after the publication of *Jude* he could afford to retire. Twenty thousand copies were sold within three months, it was translated, added to the uniform edition of the 'Wessex Novels' then being issued, and its success stimulated sales of all his earlier works. Then, five years before, on Christmas Day 1890, he had written: 'While thinking of resuming "the viewless wings of poesy" before dawn this morning, new horizons seemed to open, and worrying pettiness to disappear.' Poetry had been his first love which, apart from occasional pieces, he had been obliged to abandon for prose; but now, when even the originally remaindered *Desperate Remedies* was in its fourth edition, he could return to verse and begin a new, less profitable, literary career.

His achievement had been a remarkable one. The Poor Man with no initial advantages, he had left school at 16, worked as an architect's assistant until he was 30, and in the preceding 25 years published 14 novels and three volumes of short stories. Now at the age of 55 he was one of the most celebrated writers of his day, a comparatively rich man moving in the highest London society. His work was uneven, however: inevitably so when he had to write against time within the conventions of the serial story, to please young ladies who were, or were supposed to be, ignorant of the facts of life. But this was not the only reason. The purpose of fiction, he maintained, was 'to give pleasure by gratifying the love of the uncommon,' by which he meant strangeness of event, not of character. He was a born romantic, delighting in sunsets, the lurid light of fires, superstitions, gruesome stories, medieval church interiors, their ritual, organ music and, despite his acquired rationalism, the mysterious and supernatural. He always regretted that he had never seen a ghost. This love of the uncommon inspired many of his most memorable scenes—Troy's exhibition of sword-play, Venn's gambling by glow-worm-light, Tess's baptism of her baby—but when inspiration failed, the uncommon declined into the common melodrama of Manston's and Dare's machinations, of Alec d'Urberville's and Fitzpiers's philanderings.

Then, there are the persistent clumsinesses: 'he was enabled to perceive'; 'he found himself precipitated downwards to a distance of several feet'; 'months subsequent to the time of the Duke's death'; the strange preference for colourless poly-syllabic latinisms instead of simple Wessex English: 'commence-ment', 'discern', 'anterior to'; the pedantic allusions that obscure rather than intensify: 'The green lea was speckled with them [cows] as a canvas by Van Alsloot or Sallaert with burghers'; 'He had seen the virtual Faustina in the literal Cornelia, a spiritual Lucretia in a corporeal Phryne.' Hardy thought a living style should be, or seem to be, a little careless, but these pedantic ponderosities are deliberate: they helped to swell a three-decker novel. They are only minor and occasional blemishes, however, and his major relapses were ultimately owing to his inability, or refusal, to recognise the limitation of his range. Thackeray was at his best with London high-life, Dickens with its low-life; neither could write convincingly about the country and country-folk, and Henry James, like Gwendolen in *The Importance of*

Being Earnest, might well have been happy to say that he had never seen a spade. But neither could Hardy write convincingly about urban life and the upper classes: when he did so he produced *Desperate Remedies, The Hand of Ethelberta, A Laodicean* and *A Group of Noble Dames.* In the Wessex edition the first three of these were called 'Novels of Ingenuity', and all are comparative failures. *A Pair of Blue Eyes, The Trumpet-Major, Two on a Tower,* and *The Well-Beloved* were 'Romances and Fantasies', by no means failures, but below the standard of the chief category, 'Novels of Character and Environment.'

It is a revealing phrase, though perhaps 'Novels of Environment and Character' would be even better. For the characters, like the trees and heather, are products of their environment: Bathsheba and Gabriel Oak of the chalklands; Mrs Yeobright and Clym of Egdon Heath; Giles Winterborne and Marty South of the orchards and woodlands of Blackmore Vale; Tess of its dairies; Henchard of Dorchester and its surrounding cornlands; and Joseph Poorgrass, Christian Cantle, Abel Whittle, Dairyman Crick and the rest of the humble countryfolk all spring from their native soil. The basic quality of Hardy's genius as a novelist is his poet's ability to recreate his environment in words, the sights and sounds of the Wessex countryside in description and vivid imagery: 'the poetry diffused through the prose,' as Leslie Stephen puts it. Then, within the environment appear his countryfolk whom, by his lifelong understanding of their ways and speech, by his compassion and Shakespearean self-identification, he made into people with something of a legendary grandeur, yet people whom we seem to know as well as, even better than, our most intimate friends, and with whom we, too, sympathise and identify ourselves. In one sense all Hardy's greatest novels gratify our love of the uncommon, for they reveal a world, nineteenth-century rural Dorset, of which without them we should know very little.

Although Hardy never lost his sense of humour, his later novels, from *The Mayor of Casterbridge* onwards, reflect his deepening sense of tragedy in life. There was the 'Unfulfilled Intention, which makes life what it is,' a perpetual struggle of species and creatures with an almost infinite capacity for physical suffering and mental torment. To the cruelty of Nature's laws was added the cruelty of man's, the cruelty of man to man, of man to Nature. More personal, there was the tragic gap between the real and the ideal, what is and what might be; the ever-widening gap between past and present, the more to regret with the passing of the years; the inability to find comfort in beliefs that reason rejected, for unbelief and happiness 'are mutually antagonistic'. The greater estrangement from Emma that followed the publication of *Jude* increased his distress, and out of the depths in the winter of 1895–96 he wrote the three poems of 'In Tenebris', and strengthless, friendless, heartless, he waited 'in unhope, . . . one born out of due time' into a world that is 'a welter of futile doing.'

Nevertheless, he and Emma spent the spring and early summer of 1896 in London as usual, before beginning a long tour that took them to Worcester, Stratford, Dover and Belgium. This was the decade of the safety bicycle with pneumatic tyres, when cycling began the reanimation of the roads after half a century of desertion for the railway. In February Hardy had written to Emma from London to say that he had seen 'the loveliest "Byke" ' for himself, '£20!', and Emma, always a rider rather than walker, took her bicycle to the level fields of Flanders, while Hardy walked, as he had once walked beside her while she rode on Fanny from St Juliot to Beeny and Tintagel. From Brussels he revisited the Field of Waterloo, wondered at the nearness of the French and English lines, and made the note: 'Europe in throes. Three Parts. Five Acts each. *Characters:* Burke, Pitt, Napoleon, George III, Wellington . . . and many others.' The plan of *The Dynasts* was becoming clear in his mind. Then on their return to Max Gate in October, he made the significant entry:

Poetry. Perhaps I can express more fully in verse ideas and emotions which run counter to the inert crystallized opinion—hard as a rock —which the vast body of men have vested interests in supporting. To cry out in a passionate poem that (for instance) the Supreme Mover or Movers, the Prime Force or Forces, must be either limited in power, unknowing, or cruel—which is obvious enough, and has been for centuries—will cause them merely a shake of the head;

but to put it in argumentative prose will make them sneer, or foam, and set all the literary contortionists jumping upon me, a harmless agnostic, as if I were a clamorous atheist, which in their crass illiteracy they seem to think is the same thing.

One prose work remained unpublished, however: *The Well-Beloved*, which had appeared only in serial form four years earlier. In the course of 1896 Hardy revised the story, and in March 1897 Osgood, McIlvaine, issued it as Volume XVII of the Wessex Novels. The revised version makes pleasanter reading than the original. Although 60-year-old Pearston pursues 20-year-old Avice III, he does not marry her, and there is no hysterical ending to his would-be romantic history. The artistic sense deserts him, as well as visions of the Well-Beloved; he marries the aged Marcia, and busies himself with pulling down Elizabethan cottages in Portland and replacing them with damp-proof Victorian ones, full of ventilators. The book sold well, but after *Tess* and *Jude* was something of an anti-climax, though there are one or two memorable descriptive passages, notably of the imaginary shape or essence of those drowned off Portland, 'who had rolled each other to oneness on that restless sea-bed. There could almost be felt the brush of their huge composite ghost as it ran a shapeless figure over the isle, shrieking for some good god who would disunite it again.' The theme of *The Well-Beloved* is one for verse rather than prose: the pursuit of the ideal, the unattainable Platonic 'Idea' to which all transient earthly things can only approximate, and had Hardy written in verse he might have avoided the sneers of literary contortionists who found in the novel the most unpleasant of all forms of sex-mania, 'Wessex-mania', and read 'unmentionable moral atrocities' into its innocent pages. And he did, in fact, at about this time write a poem of 'The Well-Beloved', in which the lover riding towards his beloved is joined by the 'shape' of a woman who says:

> 'O fatuous man, this truth infer,
>   Brides are not what they seem;
> Thou lovest what thou dreamest her;
>   I am thy very dream!' ...

> When I arrived and met my bride
> Her look was pinched and thin,
> As if her soul had shrunk and died,
> And left a waste within.

Rather than moral atrocities, critics might more legitimately have found a brief description of the author's home-life in the novel: 'that kind of domestic reconciliation which is so calm and durable, having as its chief ingredient neither hate nor love, but an all-embracing indifference.' It was to escape from the oppressive atmosphere of Max Gate that the Hardys spent so much time in London, but as 1897 was the year of Queen Victoria's Diamond Jubilee, to avoid the crowds they spent the spring in Basingstoke, the 'Stoke-Barehills' of *Jude*, some 50 miles west of London, to which they made expeditions every few days. Then, in the middle of June they started for Switzerland, almost devoid of British tourists, and on Jubilee Day, 20 June, were in Berne. A week later they were in Lausanne, where Hardy sat until midnight in the garden where, between the hours of eleven and twelve on 27 June 1787, Gibbon wrote the last lines of his *Decline and Fall of the Roman Empire*. And he imagined the great historian walking to the end of the acacia alley, then turning to ask about the world at the end of the nineteenth century:

> 'How fares the Truth now?—Ill?
> —Do pens but slily further her advance?
> May not one speed her but in phrase askance?
> Do scribes aver the Comic to be Reverend still?
>
> 'Still rule those minds on earth
> At whom sage Milton's wormwood words were hurled:
> *"Truth like a bastard comes into the world*
> *Never without ill-fame to him who gives her birth"?'*

Hardy was now an enthusiastic cyclist and spent much of his spare time cycling about Dorset, sometimes with Emma, and farther afield with his brother. He also resumed the sketching that he had practised as a young architect, and made drawings for the poems that he was collecting for publication. He offered to pay the cost himself so that his publishers, Harper's, should not be out of pocket, but they refused, and in December 1898 published his first volume of verse, *Wessex Poems*.

It was courageous of the famous/notorious novelist to offer this volume to the critics, for only four of the 51 poems had previously been published, and the first sixteen had been written 30 years earlier, when he was working for Blomfield in London. Few of these are memorable, but it is interesting to see how early was his fondness for unusual, obsolete, coined and dialect words —*ostent, ghast, lewth*—and his peculiar use of the prefix *un-*: *unblooms, unknows*, for 'does not bloom', 'does not know'. The best of this group are the four remaining sonnets of a longer sequence that he destroyed, 'She to Him', for characteristically he speaks for the woman. The second is especially interesting, as it illustrates his use of old material:

> Perhaps, long hence, when I have passed away,
> Some other's feature, accent, thought like mine,
> Will carry you back to what I used to say,
> And bring some memory of your love's decline.
> Then you may pause awhile and think, 'Poor jade!'
> And yield a sigh to me—as ample due. . . .

This had been written in 1866 and, after rejection by magazine editors, became the prose of Cytherea's speech on page 291 of *Desperate Remedies*:

And perhaps, far in time to come, when I am dead and gone, some other's accent, or some other's song, or thought, like an old one of mine, will carry them back to what I used to say. . . . And they will pause just for an instant, and give a sigh to me, and think, 'Poor girl!' believing they do great justice to my memory by this.

But most moving of all is the first of the sequence, opening with lines that might have been written by Shakespeare, and were certainly inspired by him:

> When you shall see me in the toils of Time,
> My lauded beauties carried off from me,
> My eyes no longer stars as in their prime,
> My name forgot of Maiden Fair and Free;

> When, in your being, heart concedes to mind,
> And judgment, though you scarce its process know,
> Recalls the excellencies I once enshrined,
> And you are irked that they have withered so:
>
> Remembering mine the loss is, not the blame,
> That Sportsman Time but rears his brood to kill,
> Knowing me in my soul the very same—
> One who would die to spare you touch of ill!—
> Will you not grant to old affection's claim
> The hand of friendship down Life's sunless hill?

That sonnet, one of the finest in our language, was also written in 1866, four years before Hardy met Emma Lavinia Gifford, and if read in the light of 1898 the pathos of She's appeal to Him is heightened by the 'Ditty' that follows, the lyric written in 1870 to 'E.L.G.', the 'Sweet' who makes her dwelling at St Juliot the most precious place on earth. Surely Hardy paused awhile and thought, 'Poor jade!', yielding a thought to Emma, sport of Time, as he put these poems together.

Among those that follow this early work, however, is the one about an earlier, yet in a sense later, love: 'Thoughts of Phena', the girl he had known 'when her dreams were upbrimming with light,/And with laughter her eyes'; and it may be, as Lois Deacon suggests, that the dead woman of 'Her Immortality' is also Tryphena. If so, the poem was written in 1897. Hardy, if the 'I' of the poem really is Hardy, imagines he meets in the pasture where they parted the shade of his Love who had died seven years before. He tells her he is so lonely that he will join her that night, but she cries: 'Think, I am but a Shade!'

> 'A Shade but in its mindful ones
>   Has immortality;
> By living, me you keep alive,
>   By dying you slay me.'

He promises to live for her sake, but his grief grows with the realisation that his inevitable end will also mean her spirit's end, 'Never again to be.' In the Preface to his next volume Hardy was to warn his readers not to assume that his poems were autobiographical, that they were 'in a large degree dramatic or personative ... even where they are not obviously so.' This is true; yet he admitted that there was more autobiography in his verse than in his prose. If so, there is a great deal, for there is much autobiography in the Wessex novels.

Many of the remaining poems are clearly dramatic, some of them tales of the Napoleonic Wars, possibly written as part of his earlier projected 'Iliad of Europe'. Others are just as clearly personal, the 'passionate poems' he wished to write, expressing ideas that a conventional public found unacceptable in prose. In 'Nature's Questioning' he imagines the fields and sheep and trees, like children chastened by a schoolmaster, wondering why they are there. Has some Vast Imbecility framed them in jest? or some Automaton unaware of pain? or are they the vanguard, the forlorn hope of Good storming the citadel of Evil? Hardy has no answer, 'And earth's old glooms and pains/are still the same.' The next poem, 'The Impercipient' was probably composed after, even during, a service in the cathedral that he loved so well, Salisbury, visited with Emma in 1897. It is written, ironically enough, in the verse-form of a hymn, and he wonders why the faith of others seems fantasy to him, why he should thus be 'consigned to infelicity.'

> Since heart of mine knows not that ease
>   Which they know; since it be
> That he who breathes All's Well to these
>   Breathes no All's Well to me, ...
>
> O, doth a bird deprived of wings
>   Go earth-bound wilfully!

Nowhere, perhaps, is the conflict between wish and inability to believe more clearly or more movingly expressed than here. Hardy was a reluctant agnostic, but he was saved from the depths by a capacity for happiness and his buoyant sense of humour, and one of the best things in *Wessex Poems* is the racy 'Bride-Night Fire', a modified version of 'The Fire at Tranter Sweatley's', written 30 years before. To his amusement, some critics without his sense of fun took the poem seriously, deploring the tranter's painful end in the fire that reduced him to a single bone.

However, the poems were favourably received on the whole,

though there were some who treated his verse condescendingly as the work of an elderly novelist experimenting in a medium that he did not really understand. Nothing, of course, could be further from the truth. Hardy had begun by writing verse, and though he had had little time to practise it during his 25 years as novelist, he had constantly experimented with metrical forms, without necessarily fitting words to them. And when criticised for irregularity, he replied that he liked it that way. A Gothic architect by training, he loved the spontaneity, un-expectedness, irregularity—rule-breaking—of medieval build-ings, and architecture and verse, both functional arts, were close allied. Stress was more important than a pedantic counting of syllables, content, texture, than superficial ornament and veneer, a rough surface, like a worn threshold, preferable to smoothness and exactness.

The year 1899 brought another tragic subject for his verse, when in October the Boer War began. He was proud of being an Englishman, a West Saxon, and in that sense a patriot; but there was nothing of the jingoist in him, and his war poems, like those of Wilfred Owen 15 years later, were concerned not with glory, might, dominion, but with 'the pity of War'. He saw troops embarking at Southampton, and wrote:

> When shall the saner softer polities
> Whereof we dream, have sway in each proud land,
> And patriotism, grown Godlike, scorn to stand
> Bondslave to realms, but circle earth and seas?

Then, after watching the going of the Battery from Dorchester Barracks on a wild November night, he thought of those they were leaving behind, and wrote a 'Wives' Lament'. A month later he imagined the souls of the slain returning to listen to talk of their glory, but it was not of their recent deeds of war but of their former deeds of home that their widows were thinking:

> 'Alas! then it seems that our glory
>   Weighs less in their thought
>   Than our old homely acts,
> And the long-ago commonplace facts
> Of our lives—held by us as scarce part of our story,
>   And rated as nought!'

He foresaw the time when foes should be friends, and 'The Battle-god is god no more,' and the year and the century went out on a note of hope, an old thrush's 'full-hearted evensong of joy':

> So little cause for carolings
>   Of such ecstatic sound
> Was written on terrestrial things
>   Afar or nigh around,
> That I could think there trembled through
>   His happy good-night air
> Some blessed Hope, whereof he knew
>   And I was unaware.[27]

A year later, in January 1901, the old Queen died, and the Victorian Age, like the nineteenth century, was over.

CHAPTER SIXTEEN

The Dynasts

1901–08

The age of the Wessex Novels which, from *The Trumpet-Major* to *Tess*, covered most of the nineteenth century, was also over. Hardy had been born three years after Queen Victoria's accession, and now at 60 found himself an elderly Edwardian at the beginning of a revolutionary century of electricity, telephone, motor-car and aeroplane. He still enjoyed cycling, however, as when in September 1900 he rode up to Bulbarrow with Mrs Wood Homer of Bardolf Manor, Puddletown, and his niece Lilian Gifford, while his young admirer Hermann Lea drove Emma in a trap. They took field-glasses, for their object was to identify from that central height of Dorset the towns, villages and natural features mentioned in the novels.[28] Lea was a photographer, who eventually managed to interest Hardy in an illustrated guide-book to his work, which he published in 1913 as *Thomas Hardy's Wessex.*

Lilian Gifford and her brother Gordon were the children of Emma's youngest brother, who had recently died, and they had come to live for a time at Max Gate, adding a touch of gaiety to life there. Gordon, however, had gone to London, where Hardy had been able to place him as a pupil in the office of Arthur Blomfield, an architect like his father Sir Arthur, Hardy's former employer, who had died in 1899. In November 1903 Emma took Lilian to France, and Hardy wrote regularly to 'Dear Em', in Dover, Calais and Paris. It seems probable that one reason for the strained relations between them was her lack of humour. We can imagine what amusing letters he might have written had she been able to appreciate them, but all are flat, lifeless as withered leaves: the butcher's bill, the cats, the weather, the cats, don't run out of money, London rain and influenza, take care, the cats, 'Love to Lilian' (but not to Em), 'Yours T.'

Meanwhile he cycled and visited old friends such as Swinburne and Meredith, and there was his new acquaintance A. E. Housman, whose recent *Shropshire Lad* he must have read with uncommon interest and pleasure. And the devotees descended on Max Gate, not only single spies like Rebekah Owen, but in battalions like the Whitefriars Club. His mother, now nearly 90, was unable to attend tea in the tent on the lawn, but his sisters Mary and Kate pushed her in her wheel-chair from their Bockhampton home to the highroad, where she could see and wave to the carriages of the literary society that had come to pay homage to her celebrated son, made even more celebrated by the publication of his *Poems of the Past and the Present* in November 1901.

Few of the poems are dated, but most of them appear to be of the present rather than of the past, in the sense that they were recently written, though 'The Ruined Maid' is a *jeu d'esprit* of 1866, and the grotesquely humorous 'Levelled Churchyard', in which the 'late-lamented . . . are mixed to human jam,' was written in 1882 when they were living in

Wimborne, where the Minster had recently and ruthlessly been restored. After the poems of war and Italian travel follows a group in which Nature is personified as the Mother, in one of them mourning that quick-witted man has aped her own slaughters and is destroying the beauty of her creation—an early appeal for the conservation of a threatened world; in others she is sightless, and 'How her hussif'ry succeeds/She unknows and unheeds,' while God only dimly remembers, when reminded, that he once made the earth which he assumed had long since perished. How, Hardy wonders in the sonnet 'At a Lunar Eclipse', how can the placid shadowed profile on the moon be that of troubled earth? There are half-a-dozen short narrative poems, reminiscent of the melodramatic stories of *A Group of Noble Dames* or medieval ballads, the most macabre being that of the man who hanged himself on the rood-screen of the church he had built 'To glorify the Lord'; the best, the medieval legend of 'The Lost Pyx'. Among the more personal poems those about birds illustrate Hardy's compassion and humanity, and he repeated the theme of 'Her Immortality' in 'His Immortality' and 'The To-be Forgotten', the final oblivion that follows the death of the last who remember the dead. Two poems of the past are recollections of his early years. In one he celebrated his calf-love for 'Dear Lizbie Browne, Sweet Lizbie Browne', the red-haired gamekeeper's daughter, one of the girls whom, like Tryphena and Louisa Hardinge, he had 'let slip'; and in 'The Self-Unseeing' he recalled his ecstatic dancing as a very small boy to his father's playing of the fiddle, while his grandmother gazed into the embers:

> Here is the ancient floor,
> Footworn and hollowed and thin,
> Here was the former door
> Where the dead feet walked in.

> She sat here in her chair,
> Smiling into the fire;
> He who played stood there,
> Bowing it higher and higher.

> Childlike I danced in a dream;
> Blessings emblazoned that day;
> Everything glowed with a gleam;
> Yet we were looking away!

It is very essence of Hardy: fiddle, dance, the floor worn by dead feet; a poem of the past—and one of his best.

He had been right: it was possible to express in verse, as it was not in prose, an unorthodox view of the Prime Force without antagonising his readers, and the new volume was received without any of the abuse that accompanied *Jude*. The main criticism was of manner rather than matter, of prosody and diction rather than content. It lacked the music and smoothness of Tennyson; it was harsh, bristling with strange words: 'Mr Hardy is a master of fiction, but not a master of music.' Yet even if he was sometimes coarse and lacked a singing voice, it had to be admitted that his verse was interesting.

Sensitive as he was to criticism, Hardy at this time was too deeply absorbed in another work to take much notice. It is almost true to say that he had been composing *The Dynasts* all his life, at least since as a boy he had found and read the periodical taken by his grandfather, who had served in the militia during the Napoleonic Wars. His interest was nourished by his surroundings: Gloucester Lodge, George III's summer residence at Weymouth, was only a few miles away, as was Portisham, home of Captain Hardy of the *Victory*; his grandmother had told him tales of the invasion scare of 1805, and on Rainbarrow behind his birthplace were remains of the beacon-keeper's hut. By 1875 he had conceived 'An Iliad of Europe from 1789 to 1815.' In the next year, when he visited Waterloo, it became 'a grand drama' that might be called 'Napoleon' or 'Josephine'. Then, after writing *The Trumpet-Major*, and while brooding in bed during his long illness of 1880–81, it was to be 'a historical drama. Action mostly automatic.' In 1889 he added, 'A spectral tone must be adopted . . . Title: "A Drama of Kings",' and a few months later, 'View the Prime Cause . . . as "It".' After revisiting Waterloo in 1896, it was to be called 'Europe in Throes', featuring Burke, Pitt, George III, Napoleon, Wellington and others; and by 1902, having published poems that had been rejected

35 years before, he was ready to begin the concentrated writing of the work that he thought of as the culmination of his career. In September 1903 he sent his manuscript to Macmillan's, who had already published *The Woodlanders* and *Wessex Tales*, and in January 1904 they published *The Dynasts . . . Part First.*

It was Part I of a trilogy that was to cover the decade 1805–15, from Trafalgar to Waterloo, and only because of a sudden feeling that he might not finish the whole did he publish it before writing the other two parts. The scale of his epic-drama, as he called it, was a tremendous one, and may have owed something to Tolstoy's correspondingly huge *War and Peace*, which dealt with Russia's struggle against Napoleon from 1805 to 1812. It has been said that Hardy had not read *War and Peace* before writing The *Dynasts*,[29] but this seems improbable. The first English translation appeared in 1886, and in 1893 Hardy attended a lecture on Tolstoy; while Tolstoy's conception of man's will becoming less and less free the more it is concerned with the activities of others has much in common with Hardy's portrayal of Napoleon as one who only dreams his motions free. *War and Peace* contained some of the material of his theme, but it was a novel, whereas he conceived the struggle in terms of epic and poetic drama; and the manner, as distinct from the matter, of *The Dynasts* owes most to the blank verse and lyrics of Shelley's *Prometheus Unbound,* a drama of Overworld and Underworld, of Gods and Spirits and Choruses of the Earth and Moon and Hours. Another possible model was Shakespeare's historical trilogy of *Henry IV Parts I and II* and *Henry V*, particularly *Henry V,* which is almost as much an epic as a play, the narrative being related by a few of the subordinate characters and the Chorus, who also describes the scene, combining the functions of Hardy's Recording Angel, Dumb Show, and 'stage' directions.

Homer introduced the gods of Greek mythology into his epics, Olympians such as Apollo, Athene and Poseidon, who had much to do with the Trojan War and fortunes of Odysseus, but Hardy created his own mythology of Phantom Intelligences of the Overworld, not as influencers of events, however, but as a supernatural Chorus, spectators of and commentators on the earthly action, and expounders of its principle. For they are powerless, no more able than men to influence the course of history, which is predetermined by 'It', the First Cause or Immanent Will that works blindly and unconsciously, Its 'Will-webs' interpenetrating all matter, as occasionally revealed by the showman, the Spirit of the Years:

The scene becomes anatomised and the living masses of humanity transparent. The controlling Immanent Will appears therein, as a brain-like network of currents and ejections, twitching, inter-penetrating, entangling, and thrusting hither and thither the human forms.

'It' is the voiceless, unseeing and unseen ruler of all things; Its minister and mouthpiece is the Spirit of the Years, the dis-interested chairman of the other Spirits, reminding them that 'The ruling was that we should witness things/And not dispute them.' Chief among the others are the Shade of the Earth, travailler and thrall of It, and the Spirit of the Pities, which speaks for humanity: 'a mere juvenile,' sneers the Spirit Ironic, 'who only came into being in what the earthlings call their Tertiary Age!' Although Hardy disclaimed any systematised philosophy in the doctrines of his Spirits, it is approximately the one he had evolved over the years, and the Spirit of the Pities and its Chrous might equally well be called 'The Spirit of Hardy':

> *We would establish those of kindlier build,*
> *In fair Compassions skilled,*
> *Men of deep art in life-development;*
> *Watchers and warders of thy varied lands,*
> *Men surfeited of laying heavy hands*
> *Upon the innocent,*
> *The mild, the fragile, the obscure content*
> *Among the myriads of thy family.*
> *Those, too, who love the true, the excellent,*
> *And make their daily moves a melody.*

And when the Spirit of the Years explains that the ceremony of Napoleon's crowning in Milan Cathedral is according to the rites

of 'A local cult called Christianity', the comment of the Spirit
of the Pities is as deeply personal as it is dramatic:

> *I did not recognise it here, forsooth;*
> *Though in its early, lovingkindly days*
> *Of gracious purpose it was much to me.*

In *Antony and Cleopatra* Shakespeare had exploited to the full
his cinema-like technique of a rapid succession of short scenes,
of which there are 42 in the play; but the audience within his
wooden O had to supply imaginary scenery as well as puissance,
and Hardy in his closet epic-drama of 35 scenes was able still
further to develop the method, not only shifting at will from
Wessex to Paris, London to Milan, but also from the Overworld giving an astronaut's view of the earth beneath—'The
nether sky opens, and Europe is disclosed as a prone and
emaciated figure'—and, as with a telescopic lens, altering the
range: 'The point of view then sinks downward through space.'
'The point of sight is withdrawn high into the air, till the huge
procession on the brown road looks no more than a file of
ants crawling along a strip of garden-matting.' When Hardy
wrote, the cinema was in its infancy, and his descriptions are a
remarkable anticipation of its developed technique.

To this variety of presentation he added variety of style, for
the Spirits of the Overworld had to speak in a way somehow
different from that of the earthlings. The Choruses, therefore,
speak in rhyming verse of varying forms, from the couplets and
triplets of those of the Years and Pities to the limericks of the
Chorus of Spirits Ironic. At the other extreme is the prose of
ordinary mortals such as the Weymouth boatmen who discuss
the bringing home of Nelson's body in a cask of spirits: 'They
were a long time coming . . . and grog ran short, because they'd
used near all they had to peckle his body in. So—they broached
the Adm'l.' This is the dialogue of Hardy the novelist, and he
took the opportunity to introduce characters from his novels;
the boatman had the story from Bob Loveday of Overcombe, and
Private Cantle of the Bang-up-Locals appears on Rainbarrow,
where he had already appeared as Granfer Cantle, 'a old ancient
man', in *The Return of the Native*. And from the beacon the

young militiaman looks down to the Frome valley and the lantern at Mack's Turnpike, where Max Gate was to be built just 80 years later, and where Hardy was then writing the scene.

Hardy the novelist was in his element when writing the prose of peasants and rhyming verse of Spirit Choruses, but there remained the speech of the principal characters, of the Spirits in the Overworld, and of the Emperors, Queens and Ministers of the world below. As the only alternative to prose and rhyme is unrhymed verse, and the only acceptable form of rhymeless-verse dialogue in English is the blank verse evolved by the Elizabethan dramatists, both Spirits and the more exalted mortals had to speak it. To distinguish the two, therefore, Hardy gave the Spirits a language full of strange words and abstractions:

> You cannot swerve the pulsion of the Byss.—
>   For the large potencies
> Distilled into his idiosyncracy.—
> And Life's impulsion by Incognizance.—
> But see the intolerable antilogy.

Such writing invites parody—such as Max Beerbohm's 'confirm'd misogyn'—rather than immortality, and Hardy modified his Spirits' speech as he went on. Before embarking on *The Dynasts* he had probably written little blank verse, for he had published none, and was a comparative novice at this most difficult of all verse-forms; and in spite of his delight in irregularity in architecture and poetry, his verse is strangely over-regular, lacking in variety, often wooden and monotonous. Here is the 'Voice of Napoleon' towards the end of Part I:

> Now let us up and ride the bivouacs round,
> And note positions ere the soldiers sleep.
> —Omit not from to-morrow's home dispatch
> Direction that this blow of Trafalgár
> Be hushed in all the news-sheets sold in France,
> Or, if reported, let it be portrayed
> As a rash fight whereout we came not worst,
> But were so broken by the boisterous eve
> That England claims to be the conqueror.

The rhythm is little more than a succession of regular beats—
te-tum te-tum te-tum te-tum te-tum—ten syllables followed by a
pause at the end of the line, almost the only irregularities being
the initial reversed beats of 'Now let' and 'As a'. There is no
exploitation of the run-on line, mid-line pause and redundant
syllable, above all no counter-rhythm set up by trochaic words
emphasised by assonance, as in Shakespeare. In the early plays
these half-rhyming disyllables are confined to the line:

> To watch the coming of my punished duchess.
> Cheated of feature by dissembling nature.

Then the device is extended beyond the line:

> 'Tis beauty truly blent, whose red and white
> Nature's own sweet and cunning hand laid on:
> Lady, you are the cruellest she alive
> If you will lead these graces to the grave,
> And leave the world no copy.

Finally, in the later plays, this falling rhythm distinguished by
assonance and woven into the basic rising one forms a counter-
point that harmonises the longest speeches.

Only occasionally does Hardy achieve a comparable music,
sometimes in a single line:

> 'To rocking cities casemented with guns,'

which may be an unconscious memory of the Chorus's description of the English fleet in *Henry V*:

> 'A city on the inconstant billows dancing';

sometimes, when deeply moved by things he loved, in a more
extended passage, as when Captain Hardy tells the dying Nelson
his childhood memories of his Wessex home:

> The tumbling stream, the garden,
> The placid look of the grey dial there,
> Marking unconsciously this bloody hour,
> And the red apples on my father's trees,
> Just now full ripe.

But Hardy was not a master of blank verse, and in long speeches, such as those of the opening debate in the House of Commons, the over-regular beat soon becomes monotonous.

Another weakness in Part I, judged by itself, as it had to be when first published, is its lack of a hero. Nelson is a failure, idealised, and so full of proper sentiments that he can say of the dead man who had mortally wounded him:

> He was, no doubt, a man
> Who in simplicity and sheer good faith
> Strove but to serve his country. Rest be to him!
> And may his wife, his friends, his little ones,
> If such he had, be tided through their loss,
> And soothed amid the sorrow brought by me.

Napoleon unifies *The Dynasts* as a whole, but here he is little more prominent than Nelson and Pitt, and the reader's attention is so divided that he has little chance to become greatly interested in any of the scores of characters who flit through the scenes, except perhaps in Villeneuve, whose tragedy is movingly described. Even more important is the lack of a heroine, for Hardy without a heroine is almost like *Hamlet* without the Prince. However, he introduced the Empress Josephine, who was later to play a more prominent role.

It is, and was when published, easy to pick out the weaknesses in Part I: to ridicule such pedestrian verse as Pitt's 'Could I have/A little brandy, sir, quick brought to me?', and by concentrating on detail to miss the grandeur. Like *Paradise Lost*, *The Dynasts* pursued 'Things unattempted yet in prose or ryhme,' and partly for this reason, because it was not fully understood, partly because it was only a fragment, the first act of the drama, its reception was generally unfavourable. Wilfrid Blunt could find nothing in it 'which has any business to be called poetry,' and from America came 'a failure in the colossal style,' and 'so ridiculous that the second part would never be heard of.' And there were those who objected to Hardy's tentative philosophy, his concept of a world directed by an unconscious Immanent Will. 'If . . . I had constructed a theory of a world directed by fairies, nobody would have objected,' he wrote ironically.

While he was reading and occasionally replying to reviews in the early spring of 1904 his mother died, aged 90. When at Max Gate, he used to walk or cycle to Bockhampton to see her every Sunday, and the loss of his old companion, teller of tales of pre-Victorian times, was a sad one. It was she who had inspired him with a love of literature as a small boy, and encouraged him as a young man. She was beautiful in old age, and her portrait painted by his sister Mary reminded him of Whistler's famous painting of his own mother. He commemorated 'Our well-beloved' in the elegy 'After the Last Breath', and they buried her in Stinsford churchyard in the grave of her husband, who had died twelve years before.

Hardy was nearly 64 when he lost his mother, but soon after her death another woman entered his life, when Mrs Henniker called at Max Gate with a friend whom she introduced as a distant relation of his. She was Florence Emily Dugdale, a shy young woman of 25, a schoolmaster's daughter, an admirer of Hardy's work and herself a modest writer of children's books; and when she heard that he often went to London in search of material in the British Museum she offered to help him. This was relatively easy for her as she lived at Enfield on the northern outskirts of London, and so, with some help from her, Hardy continued the writing of *The Dynasts*. There was an interruption in April 1905, when he went to Scotland to receive the honorary degree of LL.D. from Aberdeen University, but by the end of September he had finished Part Two. It was published in February 1906, and Part Three followed just two years later, in February 1908.

Part One had been confined to the events of 1805 and mainly English affairs, but now the scene exhibited by Showman Years to the spectators in the Overworld broadens, shifting to Europe, where the drama of Napoleon's triumph, decline and fall is played over a period of ten years. Like some great symphony—one thinks inevitably in terms of orchestration—it develops irresistibly from the victories of Jena and Friedland to the disaster of the retreat from Moscow and catastrophe of Waterloo; and, like a symphony, *The Dynasts* must be judged as a whole, not by parts or movements only. For the subject is now

Napoleon, who is seen directing battles, laughing at the ridiculous loss of the Grand Army he deserted, cajoling and bullying emperors and kings and, more important dramatically, cajoling and bullying empresses and queens. There is the weeping Queen Louisa of defeated Prussia, who almost persuades him to return Magdeburg with a rose; the childless Empress Josephine pleading against divorce and dying broken-hearted:

> Tell him—these things I have said—bear him my love—
> Tell him—I could not write!

There is the Archduchess Maria of Austria, 'the river-flower the current drags,' who succeeds Josephine as Empress. 'Disasters mostly have to do with me,' she murmurs, 'And yet/It matters little. Nothing matters much.' Hardy was at his best when writing of suffering women, and spoke as Chorus of the Pities when mothers held their children aloft as they drowned in the river Beresina: 'Yea, motherhood, sheerly sublime in her last despairing, and lighting her darkest declension with limitless love.'

Then, there is another Maria: 'She's always doing it. Whenever I hear of some lady fainting about upon the furniture at my presence, and sending for a glass of water, I say to myself, There's Maria at it again, by God!' But that is Prinny speaking of his Mrs Fitzherbert. When Hardy was a boy, Weymouth looked much as it did when George III and his Court frequented it, and in imagination he always peopled it with bucks and belles of late-Georgian and Regency times, so that when he came to write *The Dynasts* some of his English characters and scenes are almost as convincing as those of Jane Austen, more real than those of contemporary Victorian society in *The Hand of Ethelberta* and *A Laodicean*, for they were almost as much part of his early life as the Wessex countryside and its workfolk. The Prince Regent's remarks about his discarded mistress are made at the heartless Carlton House revels that follow the pathetic scene of his crazy father the King in his padded room in Windsor Castle, mourning for his lost daughter. And there is the memorable remark of Uxbridge at Waterloo as a cannon-shot hisses past: 'I have lost my leg, by God!', and Wellington's 'By God, and have you!'

Like the public hangings he witnessed as a boy, war had a strange fascination for Hardy: 'Few persons like better to write of war in prose or rhyme,' he wrote to Florence Henniker at the beginning of the Boer War.[30] But if it was grand and romantic as a snow-storm to begin with, it became dreary and tedious in its disappearance; and it has to be admitted that sometimes this tedium is communicated both to prose description of battle and epic verse:

> *Now Blücher has arrived; and now falls to!*
> *Marmont withdraws before him. Bernadotte*
> *Touching Bennigsen, joins attack with him,*
> *And Ney must needs recede. . . .*

It is not for this sort of thing that we read *The Dynasts*, and it is with relief that we reach the lyric verse of the Wessex poet and novelist who, in the guise of the Chorus of the Years, thought of the small wild creatures that suffered at Waterloo, for he was a man who used to think of such things:

> *Yea, the coneys are scared by the thud of hoofs,*
> *And their white scuts flash at their vanishing heels,*
> *And swallows abandon the hamlet-roofs.*
>
> *The mole's tunnelled chambers are crushed by wheels,*
> *The lark's eggs scattered, their owners fled;*
> *And the hedgehog's household the sapper unseals.*
>
> *The snail draws in at the terrible tread,*
> *But in vain; he is crushed by the felloe-rim;*
> *The worm asks what can be overhead. . . .*

The cruelties and horrors of war sickened him, and with the Pities he grieved at the cries of wounded men and horses, wondered at the barbaric splendour 'That would persuade us war has beauty in it,' rejoiced when exhausted French and British soldiers gripped hands across the stream from which they drank, and with the Spirit Ironic finally summed up war as

> *Plied by the Managed for the Managers;*
> *To wit: by frenzied folks who profit nought*
> *For those who profit all!*

When Hardy wrote, the Boer War was over, Britain had enjoyed an unprecedented century of comparative peace, and he finished Part Two on a modest note of hope: that ' "It" may wake and understand.' The conclusion of the whole matter was even more optimistic:

> *But—a stirring thrills the air*
> *Like to sounds of joyance there*
> > *That the rages*
> > *Of the ages*
> *Shall be cancelled, and deliverance offered from the darts that were,*
> *Consciousness the Will informing, till It fashion all things fair.*

The Spirit Ironic did not tell him, or he failed to hear, that an even more fearful drama of Dynasts than the Napoleonic Wars was then in the making.

CHAPTER SEVENTEEN

St Juliot revisited

1908–13

In April 1908, soon after publication of the last part of *The Dynasts*, some of its Wessex scenes were performed by the Dorchester Debating and Dramatic Society. This, and a performance of 'The Miller's Little Entertainment' from *The Trumpet-Major*, were prelude to a series of adaptations by a local dramatist, A. H. Evans, performed annually by the Society. *The Trumpet-Major* was produced in November of this year, *Far from the Madding Crowd* in the following November, 'The Mellstock Quire', adapted from *Under the Greenwood Tree* in 1910, and 'The Distracted Preacher' with Hardy's own adaptation of 'The Three Strangers' in 1911.

These were years of loss for Hardy. His old friend Swinburne died in April 1909, and he remembered the excitement with which he had read his early poetry 40 years before while walking along the crowded London streets to his imminent risk of being knocked down. On a recent visit to see him, he had quoted with amusement an extract from a Scottish newspaper: 'Swinburne planteth, Hardy watereth, and Satan giveth the increase,' and the two had laughed and sympathised with each other at having been the most abused of living writers, the one for *Poems and Ballads*, the other for *Jude the Obscure*. Swinburne was buried at Bonchurch in the Isle of Wight, and there Hardy wrote his elegy on 'A Singer Asleep'. George Meredith followed a month later, and this time Hardy remembered how,

> Forty years back, when much had place
> That since has perished out of mind
> I heard that voice and saw that face,

and how he had followed his advice to scrap *The Poor Man and the Lady* and write another novel with a more complicated plot—*Desperate Remedies*. Diffidently, because of his notorious reputation in some quarters, he accepted the invitation to succeed Meredith as President of the Society of Authors, and wrote another elegy, published in the *Times* on the day of his funeral, and in *Time's Laughingstocks* at the end of the year.

Like his last volume of verse, *Time's Laughingstocks* was also one of poems of the past and the present, mainly of the past, some of them having been written between ten and 40 years earlier, and most of the others—in spite of the Preface in which he wrote that he hoped they would take the reader forward—looked backward. There are characteristic melodramas, ballad-like stories written in the first person, such as *The Trampwoman's Tragedy*, which he considered, on the whole, his most successful poem, and *The Flirt's Tragedy*, in both of which a lover kills his rival. But the theme is that of the volume's title, the Laughingstocks of Time, of Sportsman Time who rears his brood to kill. Most of his victims are women, and in poem after poem he wrote of former beauties disfigured by 'dull defacing Time' with his 'transforming chisel'; 'faded ones' with 'faded faces', whose 'fair looks fade to a skull's grimace.' But we are all the sports of Time, and its cruelty, not only in thus disfeaturing beauty but also in leaving memories and regrets by its mere passage, is a constantly recurring theme with Hardy. 'It is the on-going —i.e. the "becoming"—of the world that produces its sadness,' he wrote, and there is a sonnet of 1871, 'The Minute before Meeting', in which he describes how the thought of anticipated happiness becoming the past robs the present of 'A full-up measure of felicity'. Presumably he was writing of a meeting with Emma in the St Juliot days of their early love; if so, 'The Division' of 20 years later, if also written of her,[31] makes tragic reading:

> Rain on the windows, creaking doors,
>   With blasts that besom the green,
> And I am here, and you are there,
>   And a hundred miles between!
>
> O were it but the weather, Dear,
>   O were it but the miles
> That summed up all our severance,
>   There might be room for smiles.
>
> But that thwart thing betwixt us twain,
>   Which nothing cleaves or clears,
> Is more than distance, Dear, or rain,
>   And longer than the years!

Many of the other personal poems are memories: of the dead Mellstock Quire, of his grandmother telling her tales of Napoleon, of his mother guiding his infant steps on the Roman road, of his old home and perished people, to whom he describes himself as 'A pale late plant of your once strong stock'. But as well as to the dead he talks to The Unborn, who ask him with eager innocence about the world they are soon to enter: 'A scene the loveliest, is it not?/Where all is gentle, true and just?' He cannot answer, and turns away in anguish as the all-immanent Will drives them out of their cave into the world they so desire.

Yet the world was not altogether without delight for Hardy in the first decade of the century. The age of motoring had begun, and though he decided to 'stick to the old bicycle', partly because it was cheaper, partly because it gave him exercise, he enjoyed being driven about Wessex by his friend Hermans, Lea in search of the scenes in his novels. When they first met in 1898 Lea found him shy and diffident, but shyness passed an friendship ripened, and he was always kind, sympathetic, compassionate, generous in his insistence on paying all expenses of their tours, and with a 'vast fund of humour', unsuspected by those who did not know him well, which meant the ability to appreciate a joke against himself. Perhaps T. P. O'Connor did not know him well enough, for he remembered him as a melancholy little man, 'shrinking, almost furtive in demeanour . . . so drab, so sad.' A younger friend of these years, Miss Wood Homer, agreed that he was shy and unassuming, but found him genial with young people, cheerful, with a quiet chuckling laugh. And his sister Kate agreed with her.[32] On the other hand, Newman Flower never heard him laugh, though he would chuckle, and 'a happy smile would flick across his face.'

A man is what his companion makes him, but all were agreed on his modesty and humanity, and most that his unhappiness was caused by his wife; 'She leads him a Hell of a life,' said Mrs Sheridan of Frampton Court. It was not altogether Emma's fault. She was one of Time's laughingstocks, a once beautiful girl transformed into a 'phenomenally plain' woman, who at the critical time when Hardy met Florence Henniker was 'got up just like "Charlie's Aunt".'[33] She had no children, and her frustrated maternal instincts had been diverted to cats. Proud of her family, she had married beneath her, and though it was she who had persuaded Hardy not to give up writing for architecture, had encouraged and helped him as amanuensis and secretary, she regretted it when the outcome was *Jude the Obscure*. For she was a religious woman; not altogether a conventional Victorian, however. She shared her husband's humanitarianism, detesting bloodsports and any form of cruelty to animals, and she so resented the inferior status of women that in 1907 she went to London to walk in a suffragette procession. She was large and defiantly jolly-looking, he was small and retiring, and she felt herself physically his equal, once telling an astonished Edmund Gosse that she beat him every morning—'with a rolled-up copy of the *Times*'. It was only the jest of a humourless woman, but gradually she came to feel herself his equal in genius as well. One way to assert herself was to belittle him, and to O'Connor this seemed to be her whole bitter purpose. Another was to suggest that the Wessex Novels, all but the last, were in the nature of a collaboration; and if he could write poetry, so could she, and her message should be a very different one:

> Beseeching man—he piteous cries,
> 'Who art Thou?'
> The Invisible replies,
> 'I am,' and none in his heart denies
> That power which rules the earth and skies.

She had apocalyptic visions: 'Calamities of all kinds . . . must be set down to the great hater—Satan . . . But the fire of Hell keeps alive in pain and wretchedness all who come into it,' and the Last Judgement is to begin 'at 4 o'clock a.m. according to western time.'[34] Self-importance was becoming megalomania, mysticism verging on religious mania, and in 'The Interloper' Hardy was to describe the figure of Madness that he came to realise had haunted her even in the happy days of St Juliot and Sturminster Newton:

> Nay: it's not the pale Form your imagings raise,
> That waits on us all at a destined time,
> It is not the Fourth Figure the Furnace showed;
> Of that it were such a shape sublime
>   In these latter days!
> It is that under which best lives corrode;
>   Would, would it could not be there!

How far, if at all, Hardy was responsible for this domestic distress is difficult to say. His fondness for the company of beautiful women cannot have helped matters; he was well known to be parsimonious, and may have neglected his wife, and is said often to have forgotten her birthday. His very meekness may have been an irritant; indeed, he says as much in 'Tolerance':

> . . . I refrained
> From masteries I might have gained,
> And for my tolerance was disdained.

According to Miss Wood Homer, even when Emma became 'very queer and talked curiously,' he was always polite to her, at least in public, looking at her 'in a rather quizzical but kindly way.' But at last the situation became unbearable, and he had a staircase built from the garden to his study, in which retreat he could live alone, cut off from the rest of the house.[35] 'I am very lonely and dull down here,' he wrote to his 'dear little friend' Florence Henniker, and to Florence Dugdale after a visit:

> Come again with the feet
> That were light on the green as a thistledown ball,
> And those mute ministrations to one and to all
> Beyond a man's saying sweet.

Despite discord the Hardys took a London flat for the season of 1910, but Emma returned to Max Gate before he received the Order of Merit from the new King, George V, on 19 July. On the 15th he wrote:

Dear E: I am glad to hear that you got home safely ... I manage very well at the flat now. ... Put 'O.M.' *only*, on the envelope after my name. T.

Lady St. Helier wires to me to dine with her to-night: so I shall.

And on the 18th:

Dear E: I send the study key herewith ... Lady St. Helier and others say I look fagged out. Miss Dugdale is coming this afternoon, or tomorrow, to see that I am all right. ... It does not rain this morning, but I think it will soon. ... T.

They were only initials to each other now: E and T, or T.H.

In November there was a more homely celebration, when he received the Freedom of Dorchester and made one of his rare public speeches. It was characteristic. First the humour. It seemed to him that he had long possessed the freedom of Dorchester, considering the liberties he had taken, the way he had made free with the town in his novels. Then, an appeal to preserve as much of old Dorchester as possible. And yet, our power to preserve is largely an illusion. The real Dorchester is not the buildings, but the people who live in them, the people who have lived in them, and, as in his novels, the narrative

178

leads to a graveyard, the cemetery on the outskirts of the town, where the Dorchester of his youth now dwelt. The presentation was followed by the first performance of Evans's comedy, 'The Mellstock Quire'.

Emma was there, as was Florence Dugdale, but instead of taking his wife to London in 1911, Hardy took two holidays with his brother: first a visit to the Lake District, where he found tourists—like those who afflicted him at Max Gate—sending off picture postcards near Wordsworth's grave at Grasmere; then a tour of cathedrals in the Midlands. He was especially interested in Gloucester Cathedral, where the exclusively English style of Perpendicular Gothic originated, by accident according to his imagining, and wrote 'The Abbey Mason' which he dedicated to his first instructor in architecture, John Hicks. He also took his younger sister Kate for a holiday in north Somerset, passing through Nether Stowey where Coleridge had once lived, and Dunster, scene of *A Laodicean*.

Much of 1912 was spent in revision for the definitive Wessex Edition of his works, which Macmillan's began to publish in that year. Towards the end of April, for example, reading ten hours a day, he finished the proofs of Volume IV, *The Return of the Native*, and came to the conclusion that Clym Yeobright was the 'nicest' of his heroes, though *as a story* he liked *The Woodlanders* best. He also wrote a General Preface—it should be remembered that it was nearly 20 years since he had written a novel—in which he answered the criticism that by restricting his scene to Wessex he restricted the delineation of human nature. This, he maintained, was quite untrue of the elementary passions. The Greek dramatists had confined their scene virtually to their own small country, and 'there was quite enough human nature in Wessex for one man's literary purpose.' Incidentally, this unity of place had an unforeseen advantage; his novels were a fairly true record of a vanished way of life: 'things were like that' in nineteenth-century Wessex. As for the pessimism with which he was charged: he had never advanced a consistent philosophy, but only impressions of the moment, conjectures that harmonised with experience and seemed likely to be true, and truth was an even higher characteristic of philosophy than optimism.

43. View of Dorchester across Maumbury Rings from the cemetery. 'There is the Dorchester that I knew best:... names on white stones.' (One of Hardy's drawings for *Wessex Poems*.)

44. The Portisham home of Captain Thomas Hardy of the *Victory*, and of *The Dynasts*.

45. 'Yes: I have re-entered your olden haunts at last.' Beeny, March 1913.

46. Hardy and Florence Emily Dugdale *c.* 1910.

On 2 June his seventy-second birthday was celebrated at Max Gate, when Henry Newbolt and W. B. Yeats came to present him with the gold medal of the Royal Society of Literature. Emma's seventy-second birthday followed on 24 November, but she spent it in bed. She had not been well for some time, and early in the morning of the 27th she died. It was the day of the Dramatic Society's performance of *The Trumpet Major*, too late for cancellation, and the news of her death was announced from the stage. She was buried in Stinsford churchyard, and Hardy sent a wreath 'From her lonely husband—with the old affection,' and designed her gravestone with the inscription, 'This for Remembrance.'

Among the letters of condolence was one from Florence Henniker, to which he replied on 17 December:

. . . I have reproached myself for not having guessed there might be some internal mischief at work, instead of blindly supposing her robust and sound and likely to live to quite old age. In spite of the differences between us, which it would be affectation to deny, and certain painful delusions she suffered from at times, my life is intensely sad to me now without her. The saddest moments of all are when I go into the garden and to that long straight walk at the top that you know, where she used to walk every evening just before dusk, the cat trotting faithfully behind her.

I think I have told you before that her *courage* in the cause of animals was truly admirable, surpassing that of any other woman I have ever known. I have nothing at all approaching it myself. . . .

He reproached himself not only for his failure to realise that she was dangerously ill, but for any failure of understanding or sympathy, for any neglect that might have widened the rift between them over the years. When going through her belongings he had found a long manuscript with the title, 'What I think of my Husband': he did not read very far, but tore up the pages and threw them into the fire.[36] He was filled with remorse, and the long unhappy years were forgotten when he recalled the early idyllic times of St Juliot and Sturminster Newton. The pattern was repeating itself: he loved the woman dead and inaccessible as he had never loved her since the early days of

Thomas Hardy

their marriage, and to the ghost of the young woman of St
Juliot he wrote some of the greatest love poems in the language:

> Woman much missed, how you call to me, call to me,
> Saying that now you are not as you were
> When you had changed from the one who was all to me,
> But as at first, when our day was fair.

After their marriage they had never revisited the scene of their
meeting, and now she was calling from St Juliot. But 'Why go
to St Juliot? What's Juliot to me?' he asked desperately in
February 1913; the past was only a dream:

> Does there even a place like St Juliot exist?
> Or a Vallency Valley
> With stream and leafed alley,
> Or Beeny, or Bos with its flounce flinging mist?

But March confirmed the tragic reality. It was no dream:

> O the opal and the sapphire of that wandering western sea,
> And the woman riding high above with bright hair flapping free—
> The woman whom I loved so, and who loyally loved me . . .
> Still in all its chasmal beauty bulks old Beeny to the sky,
> And shall she and I not go there once again now March is nigh,
> And the sweet things said in that March say anew there by and by?

Yet again, why go to St Juliot? Why go to Beeny?

> What if still in chasmal beauty looms that wild weird western shore,
> The woman now is—elsewhere—whom the ambling pony bore,
> And nor knows nor cares for Beeny, and will laugh there nevermore.

And yet, even if the woman now was—elsewhere, the ghost of
the girl he had loved there was calling, and on 6 March he set
out again for Lyonnesse. At Launceston he remembered how, on
that other March day, he had hired horse and man to drive
him to St Juliot Rectory, where he was received by the young
lady in brown, and on the 7th, exactly 43 years after his first
momentous journey, he re-entered her olden haunts at last:

> Yes: I have re-entered your olden haunts at last;
> Through the years, through the dead scenes I have tracked you;
> What have you now found to say of our past—

Scanned across the dark space wherein I have lacked you?
Summer gave us sweets, but autumn wrought division?
    Things were not lastly as firstly well
       With us twain, you tell?
But all's closed now, despite Time's derision.

But the grey-eyed ghost was voiceless that drew him to the waterfall in the Valency Valley, to Pentargon Bay and Beeny, where

    Ignorant of what there is flitting here to see,
      The waked birds preen and the seals flop lazily;
    Soon you will have, Dear, to vanish from me,
      For the stars close their shutters, and the dawn whitens hazily.
    Trust me, I mind not, though Life lours,
      The bringing me here; nay, bring me here again!
       I am just the same as when
    Our days were a joy, and our paths through flowers.

Again he recalled her words of an August day in 1870, and at Boscastle he wrote:

        'It never looks like summer here
          On Beeny by the sea.'
        But though she saw its look as drear,
          Summer it seemed to me.

Then starkly, bleakly, finally as Wordsworth's lines to another vanished woman:

        It never looks like summer now
          Whatever weather's there;
        But ah, it cannot anyhow,
          On Beeny or elsewhere!

CHAPTER EIGHTEEN

The Last Years
1913–28

'My niece and Miss Dugdale are here ministering to my wants,' Hardy wrote to Florence Henniker, 'I don't know what I should do without them.' One solution, now that Max Gate was without a mistress, would have been to join his unmarried brother and sisters, Henry, Mary and Kate, who had just left their old home at Bockhampton, which they let to Hermann Lea, and moved into a much bigger house designed by Hardy and built by Henry near West Stafford. This was Talbothays, named after an old family property near the Frome meadows, and scene of Tess's lyrical interlude as a dairymaid. But, although Hardy had not cared for Max Gate when first built, and had rarely been happy there, in his mood of remorse and memories he was reluctant to leave it and the garden, with their accumulated associations. And there was another solution. 'Florence Dugdale and I,' he wrote to the other Florence on 11 February 1914, 'were married yesterday at Enfield.' He was 73, she only 35, and it was, in a sense, a marriage of convenience; yet he loved the quiet, melancholy-eyed young woman, much the same age as Emma when he married her, who brought order and peace to Max Gate, shielding him from the sightseers and autograph-hunters who so often inconsiderately intruded. 'She is a very tender companion,' he wrote, and when he inscribed the first copy of *Moments of Vision* it was 'To the first of women, Florence Hardy.'

Six months before his second marriage he had been given an

honorary degree at Cambridge and elected an honorary Fellow
of Magdalene College. He was already an LL.D. of Aberdeen, and
other universities followed: Oxford, where he was also made a
Fellow of Queen's, St Andrews and Bristol. But between the
ceremony at Cambridge and that at Oxford came the war years
of 1914–18.

In April 1914 he had written a premonitory poem, 'Channel
Firing', in which mice, frightened by the guns, 'let fall the
altar-crumb', and coffined shapes start up, thinking it is the
Judgement Day. But 'No,' God calls,

> The world is as it used to be:
> All nations striving strong to make
> Red war yet redder.

This was published in the *Fortnightly Review* in May, and by the
time war was declared in August Macmillan's were setting it as
one of a century of poems that they published in November
with the title *Satires of Circumstance*. There were only 15 of
these satires, which Hardy called 'caustically humorous productions' that he had issued light-heartedly in a periodical in
1911. But there is little light-hearted in these anecdotes of
death-beds, coffins, graves and graveyards, and they read like
the products of a dejected author in search of a subject. So do
some of the miscellaneous poems, such as 'The Newcomer's
Wife', in which the husband is found drowned 'with crabs upon
his face'. This, too, may have been meant to be caustically
humorous, and humorous it is in a sense—as parody.

But 1912 brought fresh subjects. In April the newly-launched
liner *Titanic* struck an iceberg and sank, and Hardy wrote 'The
Convergence of the Twain', a tense poem of sinister stillness—

> And as the smart ship grew
> In stature, grace, and hue,
> In shadowy silent distance grew the iceberg too—

until the sudden and unexpected catastrophe when 'The Spinner
of the Years said "Now!"' Then, Emma's death in November
and the reawakened memories of 40 years were inexhaustible
subjects that fired a new creative energy and inspired the writing

of his retrospective love lyrics. Some 20 of these 'Poems of 1912–13' were included in a special section of the *Satires* volume, and there are others elsewhere. 'Under the Waterfall' is an incident recalled on reading Emma's 'Recollections', and it is she who speaks and describes how 'Whenever I plunge my arm like this,/In a basin of water,' she thinks of the hot August day when they lost their picnic tumbler in the little Valency river. And 'Regret Not Me', one of Hardy's best and most characteristic poems, if not spoken by Emma, must have been inspired by thoughts of her.

In 1907 he had concluded *The Dynasts* in the belief, or half-belief, or hope, 'That the rages of the ages shall be cancelled,' and even during the Boer War had written that a new light had spread, that the Battle-God was sick, a patched-up figure of painted lath. The Great War of 1914, therefore, was a severe blow which, according to *The Life*, destroyed all his belief in the gradual ennoblement of man; and to Mrs Henniker he wrote that, so far from there being any sign of improvement in the world, it appeared to be getting worse and worse. Yet the song of the soldiers in 'Men Who March Away' was 'In our heart of hearts believing/Victory crowns the just,' the kind of optimism that puzzled him in Browning: 'Never dreamed though right were worsted wrong would triumph.'

The song was one of the 'Poems of War' in his next volume of verse, *Moments of Vision*, published in November 1917. There were 159 poems, nearly all written in the last four years, but apart from a dozen or so about the war most of them again were poems of the past, even the best-known, and best, of the war poems, 'In Time of "the Breaking of Nations",' being a St Juliot memory of 1870. Haunted by these memories, in 1916 he took Florence to St Juliot, where in the church he inspected the marble tablet that he had designed in memory of Emma. He also motored to the places where they had lived before settling at Max Gate: to Swanage, where once 'we two stood, hands clasped; I and she!' Newman Flower drove him to Riverside Villa at Sturminster Newton, scene of the two years' idyll where he had written *The Return of the Native*, and a letter from a friend carried him back to the time when they had lived at Wimborne.

But most of these memories were of Emma at St Juliot: an early visit and leavetaking, a service in the church, the Rectory summerhouse, sketching on Beeny. Then there were memories of their excursions from Max Gate, south to Ridgeway or north to Cerne Abbas, while indoors her portrait reminded him of their first meeting on that March day, and of 'The Last Performance' on that November day when, after playing all her favourite old tunes, she left the piano, saying she would play no more:

> A few morns onward found her fading,
>   And, as her life outflew,
> I thought of her playing her tunes right through;
> And I felt she had known of what was coming,
>   And wondered how she knew.

There were other memories. His sister Mary died in 1915, and in 'Logs on the Hearth' he remembered how they had climbed the now burning apple-tree together, she 'Laughing, her young brown hand awave.' And in 'Looking Across' she is the fourth 'out there', the others being their father and mother and Emma, while he remains wondering why there are not five. 'The Five Students' is a similar, though more enigmatic poem about 'dark He, fair He, dark She, fair She, I' striding on through the years and falling out one by one: Horace Moule first, Tryphena perhaps the third, then Emma, while 'I still stalk the course.' Other memories were those of music, as when he recalled psalm-singing in Stinsford church as a small boy, and the sight of his father's old violin conjured up visions of his playing in the gallery there. Beauty of association meant more than beauty of appearance, and he loved old furniture because he saw there the hands of its former owners,

> Hands behind hands, growing paler and paler,
>   As in a mirror a candle-flame
> Shows images of itself, each frailer
>   As it recedes.

Much of the melancholy in Hardy's poetry derives from his spectral housekeeping with the Past, the happier the visioned event the sadder being its recall. He was a spectre talking to spectres; yet he celebrated the 'Great Things' that had given him happiness: cyder, dance and love, 'Joy-jaunts, impassioned flings,/Love, and its ecstasy.' The volume ended with a vision of the future, when, he hoped, he would be remembered, not as a writer, but as a lover of nature and protector of all innocent creatures:

When the Present has latched its postern behind my tremulous stay,
  And the May month flaps its glad green leaves like wings,
Delicate-filmed as new-spun silk, will the neighbours say,
  'He was a man who used to notice such things'?

He was nearly 74 when the war began, 78 when it was over, too old to do much to help, yet he did what he could. He was one of a committee of writers for the statement of Britain's case, wrote an appeal to America to help the Belgian refugees, gave manuscripts, including *Far from the Madding Crowd*, to be auctioned on behalf of the Red Cross, visited British hospitals and German prisoners' camps, carried on his work as a Dorchester magistrate, and was Chairman of the Anti-Profiteering Committee, which made him unpopular in the town, but that was 'a hundred times better than sitting on a Military Tribunal and sending young men to the war who did not want to go.' Then, after the war he opened a club-room in Bockhampton as the village war memorial, close to his first school and on the site of the boot-making shop of Robert Reason, original of Robert Penny of the flashing spectacles in *Under the Greenwood Tree*.

When the universities opened again, Oxford offered him a D.C.L. which, presumably with memories of Jude, he went to receive in February 1920, and in the evening attended a performance of *The Dynasts* by the Oxford University Dramatic Society. Although he had not intended his epic-drama for performance, in 1914 he had prepared a stage-version for Granville Barker, who produced it in London soon after the beginning of the war, 'a splendid failure' of 72 performances, and this was the version presented by the OUDS. Their President Charles Morgan, just back from war service, recorded his impressions of Hardy in his eightieth year. To the young man he seemed prodigiously old, with the thin neck and tight-skinned brow of great age, and eyes like those of 'some still young man who had been keeping watch at sea since the beginning of time.' Yet he was sprightly and alert, like 'a small bird with a great head'—most observers remarked on this bird-like quality. And he was modest, making no attempt to impress in any way. Morgan met him again two years later at Max Gate, when he talked sadly and bitterly of what he considered the prejudice of critics against his 'pessimism', but what impressed him most was the contrast between his quiet behaviour and 'the passionate boldness of his mind'.

Another visitor at Max Gate at this time was Robert Graves, like Morgan a young man back from the war and now at Oxford, where he had met Hardy, who then seemed to him to be suffering from aphasia and wandering attention. But now he was alert and gay in his cluttered drawing-room, imitating bishops asking for tea at the Athenaeum, talking about poetry, disparaging his novels, praising cyder as the finest medicine he knew, but complaining of autograph-hunters and critics who accused him of pessimism.[37]

Yet another, though considerably older, Oxford man, Vere H. Collins of the University Press, called at Max Gate in 1920, and wrote an account of his *Talks with Thomas Hardy*. It is an unintentionally amusing little book with its polite drawing-room conversation, for Collins was no Boswell and Hardy no Johnson, but interesting as another man's impression of Hardy: about five feet five inches tall, he looked much younger than he was; erect, brisk, bright-eyed, clear of speech with perfect hearing; a quiet easy manner, composed but alert; his face deeply lined, but not melancholy in expression. Collins paid a second visit at the end of the year:

27 December 1920. Mrs. H *and* C *in the drawing-room at Max Gate. Enter* H *from a walk, with his dog.* H *and his visitor shake hands, and sit down.* Mrs. H *serves tea. . . .*

C: I've not seen your dog before, but I have been hearing all about him, and how he made friends with Barrie, but snapped at Mrs. Granville Barker.

The dog takes a log of wood from the grate, and carries it to the hearth-rug, where he lies down gnawing it.

Mrs. H: He always does that to impress strangers.

C *asks* H *to accept a copy of the* Oxford Almanac *for* 1921 *which he has brought with him.* H *examines it with interest, asks who painted the original, and thanks* C *for it.* C *says he would like to get it framed for him.*

H: I will not trouble you to do that. I will fasten it up in my study with drawing-pins.

C: We are all very much interested in London at hearing about your local star, Miss Bugler. I am looking forward to seeing her at the Guildhall School of Music next month. . . .

H: Do you know what size the room is, and what the hearing is like?

C: I am sorry I cannot tell you. I have never been in it.

The dog was the notorious Wessex, or 'Wessie', a wire-haired terrier that Mrs Hardy had brought to Max Gate when she married, and his death exactly six years after this conversation, 27 December 1926, was a sad loss to Hardy. Gertrude Bugler was a Dorchester girl who had played Marty South in Evans's dramatisation of *The Woodlanders* in 1913, after which, apart from 'Scenes from The Dynasts', the local Dramatic Society, who changed their name to 'The Hardy Players', gave no more performances until November 1920, when Miss Bugler played Eustacia Vye in an adaptation of *The Return of the Native*, repeated in London in January 1921. 'She is exactly the physical type I had in mind when I imagined Eustacia Vye—tall and dark,' Hardy told Collins.

When writing *Jude* 30 years before, in answer to a question he had written a short article on 'Why I Don't Write Plays.' He had in fact, he said, written outlines of several, but found that novels gave more scope to the author 'for getting nearer to the heart and meaning of things,' especially in the then condition of the theatre, with its star actors and subordination of play to scenery (though Granville Barker was changing all that). On finishing *Jude* and novel-writing, however, he made a dramatic version of *Tess*, which was successfully produced in New York in 1897, and now the post-war success of the Hardy Players encouraged him to write a play for them—the theme, Tristram and Iseult, one that had been in his mind for 50 years, since his first visit to Tintagel with Emma. Yet, after going to St Juliot with Florence in 1916 and revisiting Tintagel, he had written to his friend Sydney Cockerell: 'I fear your hopes of a poem on Iseult—the English, or British, Helen—will be disappointed. I visited the place 44 years ago with an Iseult of my own, and of course she was mixed in the vision of the other.'[38] At last, however, in 1923 he wrote *The Famous Tragedy of the Queen of Cornwall*, a dark-age classical play with Chorus, conforming to the unities of time and place. The verse is undistinguished, and it is too brief for the development of great tragedy; perhaps the best things are Tristram's song to Iseult, 'Let's meet again to-night, my Fair,' and his dying words to King Mark, who has treacherously stabbed him: 'Yet you requite me thus! You might—have fought me!' The book, published a few days before the first performance in November, had as frontispiece Hardy's 'Imaginary View of Tintagel Castle', based on a water-colour long-ago painted by Emma.

Gertrude Bugler, now Mrs Bugler, having married a cousin, was unable to take part in *The Queen of Cornwall*, but agreed to play Tess in Hardy's dramatisation of the novel, which he revised for the 1924 production of the Players in the Dorchester Corn Exchange. This was seen by Frederick Harrison, who at once asked Mrs Bugler to play the part in a London production;[39] but, according to Sydney Cockerell, Florence Hardy was so distressed by her husband's 'infatuation' for his 'Tess', that she appealed to her not to accept the invitation, as he might wish to go to see her, a journey which at his age could be too much for him. So Gwen Ffrangçon-Davies played the part in the London production of 1925.

Hardy was then 85. His eightieth birthday, 2 June 1920, had been celebrated by a deputation from the Society of Authors, and his eighty-first by the presentation of a first edition of Keats's *Lamia* with an address signed by more than a hundred younger writers:

... In your novels and poems you have given us a tragic vision of life which is informed by your knowledge of character and relieved by the charity of your humour, and sweetened by your sympathy with human suffering and endurance. ...

We thank you, Sir, for all that you have written . . . but most of all, perhaps, for *The Dynasts*.

Fifty years later it is not primarily for *The Dynasts*, great work though it is, that we thank the shade of Hardy, partly perhaps because two World Wars have dwarfed an almost two-century-old European conflict, but mainly because Hardy himself is rarely there, lost among the great ones of a foreign scene. W. R. Rutland hailed *The Dynasts* as the greatest, 'most universal' of Hardy's works. But that is rather its essential defect. Hardy's genius was not for the universal, but the local, for the countryfolk among whom he had grown up in his native Wessex. For us the novels, at least, half-a-dozen of them, are more important, but more important still are the poems. Hardy himself thought that if he were to be remembered at all it would be for his poetry, and Edward Thomas told Vere Collins that it would be primarily as a poet that he would ultimately live. That was in 1918, shortly after publication of *Moments of Vision*, when there were three more volumes of verse to come.

In 1922 came *Late Lyrics and Earlier*, the first of them being one of his latest and best: 'This is the weather the cuckoo likes.' He introduced the volume with an Apology in which he returned to the charge of pessimism in his work. So far from being a pessimist, he maintained, he was a meliorist, one who thought that the world could be bettered by human effort; but, as he had written in 'In Tenebris', 'If way to the Better there be, it exacts a full look at the worst,' and his 'pessimism' was no more than the exploration of reality, the necessary first step towards improvement, as a doctor's examination of a patient is the essential preliminary to the cure of his disease. His meliorism had been shaken by the war, but he did not take a long enough view: 'People are not more humane, so far as I can see, than they were in the year of my birth,' he wrote on his eightieth birthday. He realised that there were comparatively few who, like himself, were working to reduce suffering to a minimum 'by loving-kindness, operating through scientific knowledge,' but as a disciple of Darwin and Huxley he should have known that man's moral evolution could make little progress within the pigmy span of one man's life. He took a gloomy view of the immediate future of literature and the other arts (though they were already poised for a revolutionary advance). The war had so barbarised taste, encouraged selfishness, and increased knowledge at the expense of wisdom that another Dark Age threatened, and the only hope for the world seemed to be an alliance between religion and complete rationality 'by means of the interfusing effect of poetry.' And yet, as Comte said, progress was never in a straight line, and perhaps the regression was a drawing back for a leap forward. He hoped, though forlornly, that it was so.

Another volume of verse, *Human Shows*, followed *Late Lyrics* in 1925, when he was already at work on *Winter Words*, which he hoped to publish on his 88th birthday. In these poems of his ninth decade—though some were written earlier—Emma is still a constant theme, for it was she who had opened not only the doors of the West, of Romance and of Love to him, but also the door of the Past with its magic lights. And there are memories of their early love, and the sad, revealing 'Monument-Maker' about his visit to see her memorial in St Juliot church. As he admired it, her ghost laughed over his shoulder, 'you . . . carve there your devotion;/But you felt none, my dear!'

> And then she vanished. Checkless sprang my emotion
>> And forced a tear
> At seeing I'd not been truly known by her,
> And never prized!—that my memorial here,
>> To consecrate her sepulchre,
>> Was scorned, almost,
>> By her sweet ghost:
> Yet I hoped not quite, in her very innermost!

Almost all the poems are about people, both living and dead. Their shades return at night to sit, light as air, on a garden seat, and they speak to him from their graves, and as flowers and shrubs growing out of them:

> These flowers are I, poor Fanny Hurd,
>> Sir or Madam,
> A little girl here sepultured.
> Once I flit-fluttered like a bird
> Above the grass, as now I wave
> In daisy shapes above my grave.

187

There are ballads, versified short stories, even brief one-act plays, often grim or grotesque, sometimes humorous, such as the ballad of what happened, or did not happen, on New Year's Eve when the bell-ringers 'swilled the Sacrament-wine.' The occasional satire, too, is humorous, not bitter. In 1924 Hardy was one of those who urged the erection of a memorial to Byron in Westminster Abbey, but 'the grave Dean' refused:

> 'Twill next be expected
> That I get erected
> To Shelley a tablet
> In some niche or gablet.
> Then—what makes my skin burn,
> Yea, forehead to chin burn—
> That I ensconce Swinburne!

Even his conversation with 'It' about the sad state of the world in 'A Philosophical Fantasy' is irreverently and delightfully humorous. Music and dancing, as ever, are frequent themes, and one of the most moving of the poems is 'At the Railway Station', in which a small boy plays 'This life so free' on his fiddle to comfort a handcuffed convict. In his old age Hardy returned more and more to childhood and a younger world of superstition, among his very latest poems being one about his earliest memories, and the charming:

> 'More than one cuckoo?'
> And the little boy
> Seemed to lose something
> Of his spring joy. . . .
> He'd used to think
> There was only one,
> Who came each year
> With the trees' new trim
> On purpose to please
> England and him.

Hardy loved the poetry of Browning because it was about people, as the titles of his books announced: *Men and Women, Dramatic Lyrics*; and one of his favourite poems was 'The Statue and the

Bust' in *Dramatic Romances*, the first verse of which illustrates his indebtedness:

> There's a palace in Florence, the world knows well,
> And a statue watches it from the square,
> And this story of both do our townsmen tell.

The lines might be Hardy's, but he could not understand Browning's optimism—'All's right with the world.' All was not right with the world, as he told 'It', and one reason why he so admired Shelley was because he faced the reality of an imperfect world and did his best to improve it. Swinburne was a disciple of Shelley—and then, he wrote in new intoxicating rhythms.

Hardy was largely self-taught, and much of his early reading was the literature of the eighteenth century, whose poets wrote in the standard heroic couplet. They were even-numbered men who practised the classical precepts of symmetry, balance, regularity, repose, and wrote polished lapidary lines that may be compared to the architrave of the Parthenon. But Hardy was a romantic by birth, a near-peasant brought up on country superstitions and traditional melodramatic ballads, then trained in Gothic architecture, the principles of which he almost inevitably applied to his verse. His was not the lapidary line— such a one as 'Where might have sailed this cargo of choice beauty?' is exceptional—for he was an odd-numbered craftsman like his own Abbey Mason, with a natural preference for the Gothic qualities of asymmetry, irregularity, spontaneity, restlessness, surprise, variety. The capitals of Greek columns were standardised Doric, Ionic or Corinthian, but those of Gothic were as various as their carvers, and often grotesque. Hardy's poems are full of these Gothic irregularities, crudities, grotesqueries, and there can be few poets who have experimented in so many verse forms. Consider the unusual words and usages in the twelve-line poem beginning 'When moiling seems at cease' —'roomage', 'quick-cued mumming', 'onfleeing'—and the irregularities in the opening lines of 'The Three Tall Men':

> 'O, 'tis a man who, when he has leiaure,
> Is making himself a coffin to measure.
> He's so very tall that no carpenter
> Will make it long enough, he's in faer.'

Coinages as well as dialect words are pressed into service, and Hardy told Robert Graves that one critic had complained of the line, 'his ship smalled in the distance.' 'Now, what else could I have written?' he asked.

He wrote, or rather, published too much verse. He enjoyed the writing, the fitting together of rhymes and rhythms, even when there was no compulsion to do so, much as some people enjoy solving cross-word puzzles. As a result there is no more feeling in this mechanically constructed verse than in over-wrought lines in which all feeling has been polished away; and if the feeling is subtracted from Hardy's poetry little remains but ragged verse, for his poetry is in the feeling rather than in the music of words. He never, he said, made more than three, or perhaps four, drafts of a poem. He was afraid of its losing its freshness; and the occasional roughness, even awkwardness, and apparent carelessness of his verse do seem to preserve this freshness, giving it the spontaneity of the old ballads that he so loved, and a ring of sincerity that is the image of the man. And it is this revelation of the man, unassuming, humane, understanding, compassionate, with all his inner conflicts and memories, his simple goodness, that makes his poetry so endearing, so consolatory, sometimes, notably in the poems of 1912–13, raising it to the pitch of greatness. 'The ultimate aim of the poet,' he wrote, 'should be to touch our hearts by showing his own'; and this is precisely what he does, not ostentatiously, but shyly, flitting like a shade among the words:

> I am the one whom ringdoves see
> Through chinks in boughs
> When they do not rouse
> In sudden dread,
> But stay on cooing, as if they said:
> 'Oh; it's only he!'

When revisiting Swanage he had found the skeleton of a sunshade by the sea, and wondered, 'Where is the woman who carried that sunshade?' and now, towards the end, the sight of an even more

He resolves to say no more.

O my soul, keep the rest unknown!
It is too like a sound of moan
        When the charnel-eyed
        Pale Horse has nighed:
Yea, none shall gather what I hide!

————

Why load men's minds with more to bear
That bear already ails to spare?
        From now alway
        Till my last day
What I discern I will not say.

————

Let Time roll backward if it will;
(Magians who drive the midnight quill
        With brain aglow
        Can see it so,)
What I have learnt no man shall know.

————

And if my vision range beyond
The blinkered sight of souls in bond,
        —By truth made free—
        I'll let all be,
And show to no man what I see.

————

47. The last poem in the last volume, *Winter Words*, 1928.

48. Tintagel, scene of *The Famous Tragedy of the Queen of Cornwall.* 'I visited the place forty-four years ago with an Iseult of my own.'

49. 'His ashes were buried in Poets' Corner, Westminster Abbey, but his heart in Emma's grave among the Hardys in Stinsford churchyard.'

prosaic relic of humanity, a second-hand suit, prompted a similar question:

> Where is, alas, the gentleman
>   Who wore this suit?
> And where are his ladies? Tell none can:
>   Gossip is mute.
> Some of them may forget him quite
>   Who smudged his sleeve,
> Some think of a wild and whirling night
>   With him, and grieve.

'Mais où sont les neiges d'antan?' asked Villon, and inspired by thoughts of great ladies of yester-year made great poetry; but Hardy made more moving poetry, call it great or not, out of the junk in a pawnshop: 'To find beauty in ugliness is the province of the poet.'

The decade of the nineteen-twenties was that of the debunking of eminent Victorians, and in 'An Ancient to Ancients' Hardy wrote sadly of how 'The bower we shrined to Tennyson/Is roof-wrecked', but rose in defence of his generation and, remembering the joys of his mid-Victorian days in London when he was strong and vigorous, deplored the loss of sprightlier times, defiantly revealing his own old-fashioned tastes: in dance the polka, 'Trovatore' in opera, Etty, Mulready, Maclise in painting, the throbbing romances of Scott and Dumas. And then, triumphantly:

> And yet, though ours be failing frames,
>   Gentlemen,
> So were some others' history names,
> Who trode their track light-limbed and fast
> As these youth, and not alien
> From enterprise, to their long last,
>   Gentlemen.
>
> Sophocles, Plato, Socrates,
>   Gentlemen,
> Pythagoras, Thucydides,
> Herodotus, and Homer,—yea,
> Clement, Augustin, Origen,
> Burnt brightlier towards their setting-day,
>   Gentlemen.

> And ye, red-lipped and smooth-browed; list,
>   Gentlemen;
> Much is there waits you we have missed;
> Much lore we leave you worth the knowing,
> Much, much has lain outside our ken:
> Nay, rush not: time serves: we are going,
>   Gentlemen.

Hardy was 82 when he wrote that; he was going, but as a poet he still burned brightly. Florence Henniker went in the following year: 'After a friendship of 30 years!' he entered in his notebook.

The most intimate account of life at Max Gate in his last years is given in the reminiscences of his parlour-maid.[40] There was still no bathroom, water had to be pumped from the well, lighting was that of oil-lamps, and fires were small, for Hardy though wealthy, retained the frugality of the former poor man. He was very quiet in the house, though he announced his approach by whistling softly on a single note, like 'a quiet drab little sparrow hopping around.' There was a regular routine: he spent most of the day writing in his study above the kitchen, though he generally took a short walk, always with Wessex and sometimes with Mrs Hardy, who looked after him 'like a nurse-maid', and read to him after dinner, for his eyes were failing. A kind and very compassionate man who seemed to live in the past, he sought solitude, talked little at meals, never laughed, smoked or played games, and apparently had no hobbies. It was a quiet, uneventful sort of life—very different from the discord and pestering of Emma's days—though the monotony was sometimes broken by the arrival of visitors.

Among these visitors were Leonard and Virginia Woolf, daughter of Hardy's old friend and publisher Leslie Stephen, then (May 1926), writing *To the Lighthouse*; but she found time to write several pages in her diary about this tea-party. They were received by Mrs Hardy, a woman with large melancholy eyes and a look of resignation, who talked about the dog. The door opened:

At first I thought it was Hardy, and it was the parlour-maid, a small thin girl, wearing a proper cap. ... Then again the door opened, more sprucely, and in trotted a little puffy-cheeked old man, with

an atmosphere cheerful and business-like in addressing us, rather like
an old doctor's or solicitor's, saying "Well now—" or words like
that as he shook hands. ... His nose has a joint in it and the end
curves down. A round whitish face, the eyes now faded and rather
watery, but the whole aspect cheerful and vigorous. ...

He puts his head down like some old pouter pigeon. He has a very
long head; and quizzical bright eyes, for in talk they grow bright. ...
And he smiled, in his queer way, which is fresh and yet sarcastic a
little; anyhow shrewd. Indeed, there was no trace to my thinking of
the simple peasant. ...

There was not a trace anywhere of deference to editors, or respect
for rank or extreme simplicity. What impressed me was his freedom,
ease and vitality. He seemed very 'Great Victorian' doing the whole
thing with a sweep of his hand (they are ordinary smallish, curled up
hands) and setting no great stock by literature; but immensely
interested in facts; incidents; and somehow, one could imagine,
naturally swept off into imagining and creating without a thought
of its being difficult or remarkable; becoming obsessed; and living
in imagination. ...[41]

Another, and very different visitor from the Woolfs, friends of
Lytton Strachey, arch-debunker of the Victorians, was Hardy's
new friend T. E. Lawrence, now disguised as Aircraftman Shaw
and stationed at a neighbouring R.A.F. camp. In 1923 he wrote
to Robert Graves of the 'cheerful calm' of Max Gate:

There is an unbelievable dignity and ripeness about Hardy: he is
waiting so tranquilly for death, without a desire or ambition left
in his spirit, as far as I can feel it: and yet he entertains so many
illusions, and hopes for the world. ... They used to call this man a
pessimist. While really he is full of fancy expectations.

Then he is so far away. Napoleon is a real man to him, and the
country of Dorsetshire echoes that name everywhere in Hardy's ears.
He lives in his period, and thinks of it as the great war. ...

If I were in his place I would never wish to die. ... The peace
which passeth all understanding;—but it can be felt, and is nearly
unbearable.[42]

A week after the visit of the Woolfs Hardy celebrated his eighty-
sixth birthday by writing 'He Never Expected Much', and here
again is the old endearing intimacy: he has a chat with the

World, as he chatted with It, with shades of his friends, with the
dead and unborn, with animals, birds and flowers:

> Well, World, you have kept faith with me,
> > Kept faith with me;
> Upon the whole you have proved to be
> > Much as you said you were.
> Since as a child I used to lie
> Upon the leaze and watch the sky,
> Never, I own, expected I
> > That life would all be fair. . . .
>
> 'I do not promise overmuch,
> > Child, overmuch;
> Just neutral-tinted haps and such,'
> > You said to minds like mine.
> Wise warning for your credit's sake!
> Which I for one failed not to take,
> And hence could stem such strain and ache
> > As each year might assign.

On his eighty-seventh birthday he and his wife motored into
Devonshire to have lunch with the Granville Barkers. It was a
tiring day, and on his return he seemed to be depressed, and his
wife tried to cheer him by describing her plans for celebrating
his ninetieth birthday, which would be a great occasion. 'With
a flash of gaiety he replied that he intended to spend that day
in bed.' He kept his gay promise, though his bed was not to be
at Max Gate. Towards the end of the year he wrote his last poem,
'He Resolves to Say No More', and in December his strength
began to fail. Mrs Hardy's sister Eva came to help to nurse him,
and on the morning of 11 January 1928 he seemed much stronger.
At dusk he asked his wife to read him a verse from *Omar
Khayyam*:

> Oh, Thou, who Man of baser Earth didst make,
> And ev'n with Paradise devise the Snake:
> > For all the Sin wherewith the Face of Man
> > Is blacken'd—Man's forgiveness give—and take!

Later in the evening he was heard to call, 'Eva! Eva! what is
this?' and shortly afterwards he died. His ashes were buried in
Poets' Corner, Westminster Abbey, but his heart in Emma's
grave among the Hardys in Stinsford churchyard.[43]

Notes

1. See also *Wessex Tales*, p. 57.
2. *Mayor of Casterbridge*, p. 69.
3. 'Memories of Church Restoration', 1906.
4. *Desperate Remedies*, p. 163.
5. *Life's Little Ironies:* 'A Tragedy of Two Ambitions', p. 91.
6. See Appendix.
7. F. R. Southerington: *Hardy's Vision of Man*, p. 261.
8. *Sunday Times*, 22 January 1928.
9. Published in bowdlerised form in the *Gentleman's Magazine*, Nov. 1875, and in *Wessex Poems*, 1898, as 'The Bride-Night Fire'.
10. The second Mrs Hardy told her friend Miss Irene Willis that Mrs Holder was largely responsible for the match. Miss Willis's notebook is in the Dorset County Museum.
11. The diary is in the Dorset County Museum.
12. *Early Years*, p. 163.
13. C. J. Weber, *'Dearest Emmie'*, p. 1.
14. *West Briton* newspaper, 13 November 1818.
15. See the poem, 'Everything Comes'.
16. *Illustrated London News*, October 1892, p. 515.
17. Lois Deacon & Terry Coleman, *Providence & Mr Hardy*, p. 64.
18. *Illustrated London News*, October 1892, p. 481.
19. *Providence & Mr Hardy*, p. 113. According to R. L. Purdy, *A Bibliographical Study*, p. 102, the bier was 'drawn from a sofa formerly in the dining-room at Max Gate.'
20. Raymond Blathwayt, 'A Chat with the Author of "Tess" ', in *Black and White*, 27 August 1892. Quoted in *Thomas Hardy and his Readers*, ed. L. Lerner and J. Holmstrom.
21. W. R. Rutland, *Thomas Hardy, A Study of his Writings*, p. 237.
22. See C. J. Weber, *Hardy and the Lady from Madison Square*.
23. See Purdy, *Bibliographical Study*, p. 161 and Appendix IV.

24. 'Personal Traits of Thomas Hardy', J. S. Cox *Monograph* 54.
25. C. J. P. Beatty, *The Architectural Notebook of Thomas Hardy*, p. 30.
26. Purdy, *Bibliographical Study*, p. 345.
27. 'The Darkling Thrush.' First published in the *Graphic*, 29 December 1900, with the title 'By the Century's Deathbed', but the MS. title was originally 'The Century's End, 1899.'
28. 'Thomas Hardy through the Camera's Eye,' J. S. Cox *Monograph* 20.
29. A. McDowall, *Thomas Hardy*, p. 167.
30. 11 October 1899. Hardy's letters to Mrs Henniker are in the Dorset County Museum.
31. Purdy (p. 141) suggests 'that the poem is to be associated with Mrs. Henniker.'
32. J. S. Cox *Monographs* 20, 54, 18.
33. *Hardy and the Lady from Madison Square*, pp. 83, 137.
34. 'Poems and Religious Effusions,' J. S. Cox *Monograph* 29.
35. Newman Flower, *Just As It Happened*, pp. 81–108.
36. Newman Flower, *Just As It Happened*, ibid.
37. Robert Graves, *Goodbye to All That*, pp. 268–272.
38. Sydney Cockerell, *Friends of a Lifetime*, p. 284.
39. Gertrude Bugler, 'Personal Recollections of Thomas Hardy.' (Dorset Natural History and Archaeological Society, 1964.)
40. E. E. Titterington, 'The Domestic Life of Thomas Hardy 1921–28.' J. S. Cox *Monograph* 4.
41. *A Writer's Diary*, pp. 89–94.
42. *Letters of T. E. Lawrence* (1938), p. 429.
43. How the shade of Hardy must have chuckled when it heard that, until the funeral-casket was made, his wife kept his heart in a biscuit-tin. (J. S. Cox *Monograph* 4, p. 16.)

Tryphena Sparks

Until recently little or nothing was known about Tryphena. Thus, in his splendid *Thomas Hardy, A Bibliographical Study* of 1954, Professor Purdy was unable to identify the Phena of 'Not a line of her writing have I', and could only wonder if this cousin who died in 1890 was the woman mentioned in the Preface to *Jude* as having died in that year.

For our knowledge of Tryphena we are indebted to Miss Lois Deacon, who met Tryphena's daughter Eleanor Tryphena Bromell in 1959. Mrs Bromell was then 80, and between 1959 and her death in February 1965, when she was 86, she gave Miss Deacon either verbally, and generally in the presence of witnesses, or in writing, her recollections of Hardy and her mother. She was in full possession of her faculties until shortly before her death, when she began to fail. She was only 11½ when her mother died, but said that her recollections were supplemented by her father Charles Gale and by family gossip.

Facts of Tryphena's life

1851   20 March: born at Puddletown, and registered in Dorchester as the sixth child of James Sparks and his wife Maria (Hardy).
Attends school at Athelhampton.

1866   7 November: becomes pupil-teacher at Puddletown School.

1868 16 January: reproved for 'neglect of duty', and possibly dismissed. (See F. R. Southerington, *Hardy's Vision of Man*, p. 261.)

1869 September: enters Stockwell Training College, Clapham, London.

1871 December: leaves Stockwell with first-class certificate, and is appointed Headmistress of the Girls' Department of Plymouth Public Free School.

1877 15 December: resigns from Plymouth school and marries Charles Gale, hotelier of Topsham, aged 30.

1878 13 October: Eleanor Tryphena (Mrs Bromell) born.

1880–86: three sons born.

1890 17 March: dies: buried in Topsham cemetery.

Hardy and Tryphena: Summary of Mrs Bromell's Recollections.

By the time her mother, Tryphena, was 16 she was a beautiful girl with 'dark chestnut hair, heaps of it', dark arched eyebrows, and very dark eyes. Men liked her, but she was not a flirt.

Hardy and Tryphena took long walks together, and became engaged. 'She was knocking round with him before she went to London, and he went there too.' When she left College she began to wear his ring. She often used to talk to Eleanor of the time when she was engaged to Tom Hardy.

In Plymouth Tryphena met Charles Gale, who told her she ought not to marry Hardy, as he was her cousin, 'and it was not allowed by the Church.' At length she returned the ring to Hardy, writing that she 'did not feel she could go on with it.'

[1874: Hardy married Emma Gifford.
1877: Tryphena married Charles Gale.
1878: Eleanor (Bromell) born.
1890, 17 March: Tryphena died, aged nearly 39.]

In July 1890 Eleanor, aged 11, met Hardy and his brother Henry when they cycled to Topsham to lay a wreath on Tryphena's grave. Her father did not want to see Tom Hardy. Henry kissed her and said she was just like her mother, but Tom drew away 'with a wry expression'. The card on the wreath said, 'In loving memory. Tom Hardy.'

Mrs Bromell had Tryphena's album of photographs, one of which was of a boy aged about 8, whom she identified as a little boy who used to go to see Tryphena at Plymouth [before her marriage]. Shortly before she died, she said, 'That was Hardy's boy.' ... 'Everyone knew it was Hardy's boy.'

When shown another photograph of a young man of about 20, she seemed to think he was the same boy grown up. Later, she said he was. 'He was a Sparks. He was a cousin.' He was called Randy— Randal, and had hurt his right hand. His aunt Rebecca [Tryphena's eldest sister] brought him up: she looked after both Tryphena and Randal. Then he went to live in Bristol with his uncle Nathaniel [Tryphena's youngest brother]. He became an architect, and died unmarried before his uncle Nat [who died in 1917].

Although Mrs Bromell did not say that Randal was Tryphena's son, but only that 'he was a Sparks', from this evidence, and from allusions in Hardy's poems, notably 'The Place on the Map' and 'On a Heath', Miss Deacon concluded that Tryphena and Hardy were lovers in the hot dry summer of 1867, and that she bore him a son in the following spring.

But there is no further trace of the mysterious Randal, either in official records or family gossip, and the recollections of an old lady of 85, who was only 11 when her mother died, are insufficient evidence that Hardy and Tryphena had a son. One almost wishes it were true, for a son might have made Hardy a happier man.

There can be no doubt, however, that Hardy was in love with Tryphena, may even have been engaged to her, before he met Emma Gifford, then thought of her but rarely until her death, when he realised what a prize he had lost.

For further information, see: *Providence & Mr Hardy* by Lois Deacon and Terry Coleman; *Tryphena's Portrait Album* by Lois Deacon (J. S. Cox *Monograph* 33); *Hardy's Vision of Man* by F. R. Southerington.

Select Bibliography

HARDY, FLORENCE EMILY: *The Early Life of Thomas Hardy*, 1928, *The Later Years of Thomas Hardy*, 1930, published together as *The Life of Thomas Hardy*, 1962. Ostensibly written by his second wife, but clearly written or dictated by Hardy himself, it is the book with which all biographical and critical studies must now begin.

ABERCROMBIE, LASCELLES, *Thomas Hardy, a Critical Study.* 1912

BAILEY, J. O., *The Poetry of Thomas Hardy: a Handbook and Commentary.* 1971

BEATTY, C. J. P., *The Architectural Notebook of Thomas Hardy.* Foreword by Sir John Summerson. 1966

BLUNDEN, EDMUND, *Thomas Hardy.* 1942, 1967

CECIL, LORD DAVID, *Hardy the Novelist.* 1943

COCKERELL, SYDNEY C., *Friends of a Lifetime*, ed. Viola Meynell. 1940

COLLINS, VERE H., *Talks with Thomas Hardy at Max Gate, 1920–22.* 1928

COX, J. STEVENS, General Editor, *Monographs on the Life, Times and Works of Thomas Hardy*, a series of some 70 illustrated pamphlets.
The Thomas Hardy Year Book. 1970, 1971

DEACON, LOIS & COLEMAN, TERRY, *Providence & Mr Hardy.* 1966

FLOWER, NEWMAN, *Just As It Happened*. 1950

GUERARD, A. J., *Thomas Hardy, the Novels and the Stories*. 1949

HARDY, EVELYN, *Thomas Hardy, a Critical Biography*, 1954. Ed. *Thomas Hardy's Notebooks*. 1955

HOWE, IRVING, *Thomas Hardy*. 1966

JOHNSON, LIONEL, *The Art of Thomas Hardy*. 1894, rev. 1923

LEA, HERMANN, *Thomas Hardy's Wessex*. 1913

LERNER, LAURENCE AND HOLMSTROM, JOHN, *Thomas Hardy and his Readers: a Selection of Contemporary Reviews*. 1968

LEWIS, C. DAY *The Poetry of Thomas Hardy*. A lecture published in the Proceedings of the British Academy. June 1951

MILLER, J. HILLIS, *Thomas Hardy: Distance and Desire*. 1970

MILLGATE, MICHAEL, *Thomas Hardy: His Career as a Novelist*. 1971

OREL, HAROLD, ed. *Thomas Hardy's Personal Writings*. 1966

PINION, F. B., *A Hardy Companion*. 1968

PURDY, RICHARD L., *Thomas Hardy: a Bibliographical Study*. 1954

RUTLAND, WILLIAM R., *Thomas Hardy: A Study of his Writings and their Background*. 1938, 1962

SOUTHERINGTON, F. R., *Hardy's Vision of Man*. 1970

STEWART, J. I. M., *Thomas Hardy*. 1971

WEBER, CARL J., *Hardy of Wessex: his Life and Literary Career*. 1940, rev. 1965
Hardy and the Lady from Madison Square. 1952
'*Dearest Emmie*': *Thomas Hardy's Letters to His First Wife*. 1963

Index

Stinsford ('Mellstock'), 6, 8, 9, 133, 165, 175, 194
Sturminster Newton, 75–8, 114, 180
Surbiton, 67
Swanage, 73, 74, 180, 190
Swetman, Elizabeth, 7
Swinburne, 30, 189
Switzerland, 139, 150

Talbothays, 130, 178
Tennyson, 20, 29, 63, 133, 191
Tess of the d'Urbervilles, 116, 124, 126–31, 184, 185
Thackeray, W. M., 20, 26, 64
'Three Strangers, The', 114, 168
Time's Laughingstocks, 169–70
Tinsley Brothers, 38, 43, 44, 45, 54, 55, 57, 58
Tintagel, 42, 44, 185
Tolpuddle Martyrs, 11
Tolstoy, 159
Topsham, 119, 122
'Tragedy of Two Ambitions, A', 115
Trollope, Anthony, 26
Trumpet-Major, The, 85, 88–90, 96, 168, 175
Tryphena, *see* Sparks

Turner, J. M. W., 115
Two on a Tower, 95, 97–8

Under the Greenwood Tree, 53, 55–7, 168

Valency river, 39, 42, 44, 176
Victoria, Queen, 113, 150, 155

Waight, Mary, 21
Waterloo, 75, 148, 167
Waterston Manor, 69
Webster, John, 29, 52
Well-Beloved, The, 149
Wessex (dog), 184, 192
'Wessex' edition, 149, 174
Wessex Poems, 151–4
Wessex Tales, 114
West Knighton, 137
Weymouth, 24, 38, 85, 119, 166
Whymper, Edward, 139
Wimborne, 72, 93–9
Woodlanders, The, 108, 109–12, 174, 184
Woolf, Virginia, 64, 192–3
Wordsworth, W., 2, 29, 34, 63, 89, 174

Yeovil, 73, 75

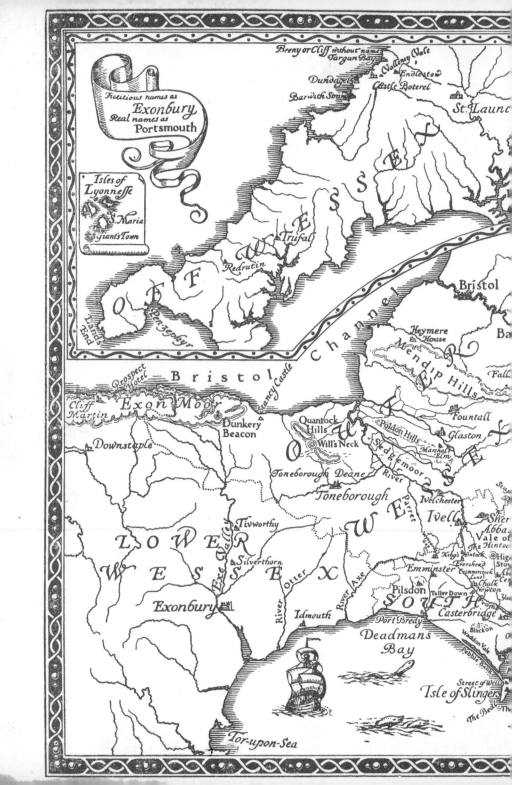

Fictitious names as
Exonbury
Real names as
Portsmouth

Isles of
Lyonnesse
S. Maria
Giant's Town

Beeny or Cliff without name
Targan Bay
Dundagel
Barwith Strand
Valleney Vale
Endelstow
Castle Boterel
St. Launc

OFF WESSEX

Trufal
Redrutin

Lands End
Penzephyr

Bristol Channel
Stancy Castle

Bristol
Ba

Heymere House
Mendip Hills
Fountall
Glaston
Fall

Prospect Hotel
Cliff Martin
Exon Moor
Dunkery Beacon

Downstaple

Quantock Hills
Will's Neck
Poldon Hills
Marshal's Elm
OUTER WESSEX

Toneborough Deane
Toneborough
Sedgemoor River
St. de

Ivelchester
Parret

Ivell
Sher
Abba
Vale of
the Hintoc

LOWER WESSEX

Tivworthy
Silverthorn

Exe Valley

Exonbury

WESSEX

River Otter
River Axe

Idmouth

King's Hintock
Evershead
Emminster
Crimmercock
Lane

Higl
Stoy
Ab
Chalk
Newton
Toller Down

Pilsdon
Port Bredy
Deadmans Bay

SOUTH
Casterbridge
From

Black
Waddon Vale
Pebble

Street of Well
Isle of Slingers

Blackon

Tor-upon-Sea